MAXIMIZING
THE VALUE OF
360-DEGREE FEEDBACK

THE BOOK TEAM

(From left to right): Nur D. Gryskiewicz, Walter W. Tornow, Carol A. Paradise-Tornow, William W. Sternbergh, Jennifer W. Martineau, Cynthia D. McCauley, Jean Brittain Leslie, Maxine A. Dalton, Ellen Van Velsor, John W. Fleenor, Manuel London

Not shown: Stéphane Brutus, Lily Kelly-Radford, and Patricia O'Connor Wilson

MAXIMIZING
THE VALUE OF
360-DEGREE
FEEDBACK

A PROCESS FOR
SUCCESSFUL
INDIVIDUAL AND
ORGANIZATIONAL
DEVELOPMENT

WALTER W. TORNOW
MANUEL LONDON
AND CCL ASSOCIATES

Jossey-Bass Publishers
San Francisco

CENTER FOR CREATIVE LEADERSHIP

Substantial discounts on bulk quantities of Jossey-Bass books are available to corporations, professional associations, and other organizations. For details and discount information, contact the special sales department at Jossey-Bass Inc., Publishers (415) 433-1740; Fax (800) 605-2665.

For sales outside the United States, please contact your local Simon & Schuster International Office.

www.josseybass.com

 Manufactured in the United States of America on Lyons Falls Turin Book. This paper is acid-free and 100 percent totally chlorine-free.

Library of Congress Cataloging-in-Publication Data

Maximizing the value of 360-degree feedback : a process for successful
  individual and organizational development / Walter W. Tornow, Manuel
London, and CCL Associates. — 1st ed.
      p. cm. — (A joint publication of the Jossey-Bass business &
      management series and the Center for Creative Leadership)
  Includes bibliographical references and index.
  ISBN 0-7879-0958-0
  (cloth : acid-free paper)
    1. 360-degree feedback (Rating of employees) 2. Employees–Rating
of. I. Tornow, Walter W., date. II. London, Manuel.
III. Center for Creative Leadership. IV. Title: Maximizing the value
of three hundred sixty degree feedback. V. Series.
HF5549.5.R3M26   1998
658.3'125–dc21   97-45460

FIRST EDITION
HB Printing 10 9 8 7 6 5 4 3 2 1

A joint publication of the Jossey-Bass
Business & Management Series
and the Center for Creative Leadership

CONTENTS

Foreword   xi
    George P. Hollenbeck

Preface   xiii
Acknowledgments   xvii
The Authors   xix
Introduction: 360-Degree Feedback—More Than a Tool!   1
    Manuel London and Walter W. Tornow

**Part One: Maximizing the Value of 360-Degree
Feedback for Individual Development**   **9**

1.   Elements of Effective 360-Degree Feedback   11
      Stéphane Brutus, John W. Fleenor, and Manuel London

2.   360 in Action: Following Catharine's Footsteps
      Through a Leadership Development Program   28
      William W. Sternbergh

**Part Two: Maximizing the Value of 360-Degree
Feedback for Organizational Development**   **57**

3.   Best Practices: Five Rationales for Using
      360-Degree Feedback in Organizations   59
      Maxine A. Dalton

4.   Forces That Affect the 360-Degree
      Feedback Process   78
      Walter W. Tornow

5. The Competitive Advantage of Customer
    Involvement in 360-Degree Feedback   101
    Carol A. Paradise-Tornow

6. 360-Degree Feedback in the Establishment
    of Learning Cultures   120
    Patricia O'Connor Wilson, Cynthia D. McCauley,
    and Lily Kelly-Radford

**Part Three: Maximizing the Value of 360-Degree
Feedback Through Design, Implementation,
and Measurement   147**

7. Designing 360-Degree Feedback to Enhance
    Involvement, Self-Determination,
    and Commitment   149
    Ellen Van Velsor

8. Understanding Cultural Influences
    on the 360-Degree Feedback Process   196
    Jean Brittain Leslie, Nur D. Gryskiewicz,
    and Maxine A. Dalton

9. Using 360-Degree Surveys to Assess Change   217
    Jennifer W. Martineau

Conclusion: Challenges and Implications
    for Maximizing 360-Degree Feedback   249
    Walter W. Tornow and Manuel London

References   259
About the Center for Creative Leadership   271
Index   275

FOREWORD

"It's about time." That's the thought that kept running through my mind as I read *Maximizing the Value of 360-Degree Feedback*. The more I read, the more I knew I was right. On a number of levels, this is indeed a book whose time has come.

First, as a collection of chapters addressing the broad issue of using 360-degree feedback for individual and organizational development, the time is right. Too much has been said and not enough has been written. Every day, brochures arrive describing new "best practice" conferences, new instruments, new product offerings. Few are the organizations that don't use 360-degree feedback of some sort. Yes, it's about time.

Second, it's about time that the Center for Creative Leadership (CCL) opened the tent to a broader audience and shared what it has been doing on 360-degree feedback. It's not that CCL hasn't been generous with its time and talent in presentations and publications, but to my knowledge never before has a book so displayed the thinking behind the feedback-based programs that have made CCL first in class. And never have those thoughts been shared in one place for so many people.

Third, this book has an all-star author line-up. Despite long associations and acquaintances with many of CCL's authors, I read with a touch of awe the extraordinary list of the authors and their qualifications. If it is true that "the people make the place," it is easy to see why CCL is, in the minds of many, a special place. It's about time we saw more of these authors.

Fourth, *Maximizing* provides an example for all of us of values in action. Intentionally or not, the pieces here are written from the heart. So it's no surprise that feedback for development (rather than evaluation) is the theme—no surprise that there is an optimistic, sincere, humanistic bent to the writing—no surprise that the recommended practice is careful and thoughtful and is based on good science and research. The writings and prescriptions follow the care on which CCL is founded.

And last but not least, *Maximizing* is a book for a broad audience. Having been asked to write the Foreword, I cannot but wonder, Why me? Of all the choices available, why was I the one? Perhaps in this case the answer is my protean career, a career that has encompassed many roles, including human resources executive, in-house researcher and practitioner of industrial and organizational psychology, semi-academic (always as an adjunct), sometime author, and now executive performance consultant regularly using 360-degree feedback. Perhaps it's this diverse nature of my career that has provided me with an appreciation for this book from the perspective of all these intended audiences.

But diverse and talented authors do not a book make. That task falls to purposeful, talented editors. Messrs. Tornow and London, chapter authors themselves, have exercised their purpose and talents well to produce a book of wisdom and practice. Now, with its considerable popularity, 360-degree feedback has the potential to advance our efforts at development but also to waste scarce resources at a time when the future of individuals and organizations depends increasingly on continuous improvement. *Maximizing* weighs in on the side of advancing potential. We are lucky, indeed, that the book is out. It's about time.

Livingston, Texas   GEORGE P. HOLLENBECK

PREFACE

The use of 360-degree feedback in organizations has increased dramatically in recent years. Today, most people have heard of it, and many are familiar with its basic elements and procedures: a person's performance is rated by a range of co-workers, including supervisors, peers, subordinates, and occasionally customers; these are fed back to the person and compared with self-ratings; development goals are set, often in connection with a strategy for achieving these goals. Sometimes, the ratings are used by the organization to make administrative decisions about such things as pay raises and promotions.

Despite the growing popularity of 360-degree feedback, only a few people have a detailed understanding of how it can be used to enhance—and indeed maximize—individual and organizational development. With this book, we aim to help people who are responsible for, or interested in, such development gain that understanding and determine whether 360-degree feedback will work in their organization.

More specifically, our primary audience is human resources managers who are involved in designing and implementing systems for human performance and organization development: in-house professionals or consultants, as well as executives and managers who are using 360-degree feedback or who are considering using it for their organizations. A secondary audience is academics who are interested in the interaction of management science and practice. Also, students in human resources management and development, industrial and organizational psychology, organizational development, and instructional design and training should find this book of interest.

A glimpse at the professional affiliations cited in the author biographies that follow this Preface will alert the reader to an important point: what we have to say here draws predominantly on the practical knowledge and experience of the Center for Creative Leadership (CCL). For twenty-eight years, CCL has been offering public and custom-designed executive development programs anchored by 360-degree feedback and has been conducting research on managerial development. The insights offered by each author are of course influenced by his or her independent academic and practitioner activities, but they are primarily the product of a long-term, collective effort to improve the understanding and practice of leadership.

Although this book draws on and cites theoretical and research literature, it is essentially practical. We want to help people who already understand 360-degree feedback to use it to transform their organizations. That is why the reader will find, throughout the book, discussions of important practical questions such as, What are the critical components of constructive feedback? How can individuals use it to improve their performance with various constituencies? How can 360-degree feedback be used to help achieve an organization's performance objectives? How can it help establish a continuous learning culture? How can it be used to track changes in organizational and individual performance?

Overview of Contents

The book begins with an Introduction that makes the point that 360-degree feedback should be thought of as a process, not just a tool. After a brief review of the origins of the process, the Introduction describes the essential themes that run through subsequent chapters: that 360-degree feedback should be a core part of self-development; that it fits the realities of the new workplace; and that it is multifaceted in purpose and value.

The Introduction is followed by three parts (nine chapters). Part One, which contains Chapters One and Two, will help you understand how to maximize the value of the 360-degree feedback process for individual development. Chapter One defines the process and provides detailed information on how its basic elements, individually and together, are related to its benefits. Chapter Two then illustrates how the process can be enhanced by putting it into the context of a development program.

Part Two (Chapters Three through Six) will help you understand how to maximize the value of 360-degree feedback for organizational development. Chapter Three considers the benefits of the 360-degree feedback process for organizations and how current practices affect these benefits. Chapter Four describes the major ways that the process can promote organizational development. Chapter Five examines the advantage of involving customers in the 360-degree feedback process and in the development of organizational strategy. Finally, Chapter Six focuses on how the process can be used to create a continuous learning culture and presents questions that can be used to assess organizational readiness for a 360-degree feedback process that supports a learning culture.

Part Three, containing Chapters Seven, Eight, and Nine, will help you understand the 360-degree feedback process from administrative and technical perspectives. Chapter Seven evaluates alternative designs for feedback instruments with respect to the ways development is affected and to how individual and organizational involvement and commitment can be enhanced. Chapter Eight discusses what is involved in applying the process in different countries in a multinational organization—for instance, the underlying cultural assumptions that influence the ratings and the interpretation of ratings. Chapter Nine then addresses a fundamental question: Given our aim of using the 360-degree feedback process to help individuals and organizations develop, how can we tell if we are successful?

The Conclusion takes an overall view of the challenges of using the 360-degree process, and it reflects on some fieldwide issues and implications in its use.

ACKNOWLEDGMENTS

This book blends the science and practice of 360-degree feedback through the unique knowledge and experience base of the chapter contributors and the Center for Creative Leadership. We are delighted with the collaborative work the book represents. Thanks to the expert expression of our contributors, the book captures the considerable wisdom, insight, and know-how residing in CCL that comes from almost three decades of experience with thousands upon thousands of practicing leaders coming from virtually all walks of life. We are very proud and appreciative of our contributors for the artful job they've done in capturing this wisdom, insight, and know-how.

Also, we are especially indebted and grateful to the many unnamed CCL clients who have participated in our leadership development programs and experienced 360-degree feedback, and with whom we have learned so much. Learning with our participants has been a continuing source of intellectual and creative stimulation that has made CCL an exciting place to work.

In addition to the chapter contributors, many other individuals have played important and helpful roles in the creation of this book. First, many people affiliated with CCL have served as reviewers, providing feedback on early versions of the chapter drafts, including Karen Boylston, Jerry Brightman, Bob Burnside, David Campbell, Richard Campbell, Craig Chappelow, Rob Goldberg, Michael Hoppe, Bill Howland, Karen Kirkland, Daryl Anne Kline, Dana McDonald-Mann, Susan Melton, Bill Morley, Russ Moxley, Dianne Nilsen, Mayra Reyes de Solomon, Philippe Rosinski, Joan Tavares, Michael Wakefield, and Randall White (RPW Executive Development, Inc.).

Second, Martin Wilcox, Marcia Horowitz, and Joanne Ferguson, of CCL's editorial publication function, provided invaluable support for making the book reader-friendly. They worked behind the scenes, but the outcome of their efforts is quite apparent for all to see and appreciate in this book. They nicely complemented the fine editorial work that Byron Schneider provided, along with the important motivational support for this project by Larry Alexander; Byron and Larry are both at Jossey-Bass. And, speaking of support, we also wish to acknowledge the special role that Bob Lee and John Alexander, CCL's past and current presidents, respectively, have played with their welcome encouragement for this book.

Third, a special thanks to the many professionals and leaders in organizations who helped us with examples and case studies for this book project. They include Debbie Brady of Ralston Purina; John Coné of Dell Computers; Ben Dowell of Bristol-Myers Squibb; Brett Lauter of First Union National Bank; Paul Leslie of Greensboro College; and Nancy Wendt of the Winhall Group. Also a collective thank-you goes to all the other unnamed but special people in organizations who helped us with the case studies and examples throughout the book.

Finally, a special note of appreciation to Tom Kealey and Laura Iemma and all the other wonderful support staff at CCL and Jossey-Bass who saw to it that the manuscript metamorphosed into this nicely finished product.

To all of the above individuals, we at CCL are especially grateful for the important and helpful roles you have played.

January 1998

WALTER W. TORNOW
Greensboro, N.C.

MANUEL LONDON
Stony Brook, N.Y.

THE AUTHORS

Stéphane Brutus is an assistant professor of management at Concordia University in Montreal. Previously, he was a research associate at the Center for Creative Leadership. His interests include 360-degree feedback, performance appraisal, developmental assignments, and workplace diversity. He has published articles in *Leadership Quarterly* and *Journal of Business and Psychology*. Stéphane obtained his Ph.D. in industrial and organizational psychology from Bowling Green State University in 1995.

Maxine A. Dalton is a research scientist and program manager at the Center for Creative Leadership. She received her B.S. in nursing from Vanderbilt University, an M.A. in rehabilitation counseling from the University of South Florida, and an M.A. and Ph.D. from the University of South Florida. She was a consultant with Drake Beam Morin for five years before coming to CCL in 1990 as manager of the instrument group. In 1993, she changed her role within CCL to include research, training, and program management. Maxine is the author of several articles on the 360-degree feedback process and has made many presentations on various aspects of the topic. She has trained hundreds of feedback specialists and given feedback to hundreds of individuals and groups since being introduced to the concept in 1989; she has worked with human resources development professionals in a CCL program designed to teach them how to implement developmental processes using CCL research concepts. She has recently been active in managing the process of the translation and adaptation of 360-degree feedback instruments in other countries. Her current research interests include global leadership and learning to learn.

John W. Fleenor is an adjunct researcher at the Center for Creative Leadership and a research scientist at Mediappraise Corporation, a provider of 360-degree feedback services via the Internet. His research focuses on the development, use, and validation of 360-degree feedback instruments. A coauthor of *Feedback to Managers* (3rd ed.) (CCL, 1998) and *Choosing 360: A Guide to Evaluating Multi-rater Feedback Instruments for Management Development* (CCL, 1997), John has also published in journals such as *Leadership Quarterly, Journal of Management Development, Educational and Psychological Measurement,* and *Journal of Business and Psychology.* In addition, he reviews instruments for the *Mental Measurements Yearbook.* His Ph.D. is in industrial and organizational psychology from North Carolina State University (1988), where he is an adjunct member of the psychology faculty. John is a member of the Society for Industrial and Organizational Psychology (SIOP) and the American Psychological Association (APA).

Nur D. Gryskiewicz is an associate professor in the Bryan School of Business and Economics at the University of North Carolina at Greensboro. She received her Ph.D. from the University of London in occupational psychology. Nur has experience as a practitioner and an academician in cross-cultural assessment for management development in numerous countries in Europe, the Middle East, and Scandinavia. She has been affiliated with the Center for Creative Leadership since 1983 as a feedback specialist. She is also licensed as a practicing psychologist in North Carolina. Nur has published in numerous journals including *Human Resources Management Review, Journal of Small Business Management, Educational and Psychological Measurements,* and *Creativity Research Journal.*

Lily Kelly-Radford is the director of the Center for Creative Leadership's Greensboro Branch, which conducts public and contract training programs both domestically and internationally. Prior to joining CCL in 1990, Lily trained in the Leadership Development Program for seven years with various CCL Network Associates. Her professional experiences since joining CCL include training numerous programs, holding the position of director of the Leadership Development Program worldwide (including Network Associates), as well as chief assessor for all branch locations. Lily has trained in several countries and customizes programs to correspond with international business and cultural issues. She holds a Ph.D. in clinical psychology from the University of Georgia and is licensed to practice in four states. Her work experiences include service with Howard University as a tenured associate professor and with Harvard University Medical School as an assistant attending psychologist; she has also been the senior principal with Kelly-Radford and Associates, where she did organizational consulting with public and private sectors and clinical private practice.

Jean Brittain Leslie is a research associate and manager of the production of translations at the Center for Creative Leadership. Her current research focuses on psychometric analyses of CCL instruments and cross-cultural applicability of leadership models. Jean is coauthor of *Feedback to Managers* (3rd ed.) (CCL, 1998), *Choosing 360: A Guide to Evaluating Multi-rater Feedback Instruments for Management Development* (CCL, 1992), *A Look at Derailment Today: North America and Europe* (CCL, 1996), and several articles published in management and sociology-related journals. She has an M.A. in sociology from the University of North Carolina at Greensboro.

Manuel London is an adjunct research fellow at the Center for Creative Leadership. He received his B.A. in psychology and philosophy from Case Western Reserve University and his M.A. and Ph.D. in industrial and organizational psychology from The Ohio State University. Manny taught at the University of Illinois at Champaign-Urbana for three years. He then was a researcher and human resources manager at AT&T for twelve years before assuming his present position as director of the Center for Human Resource Management at the State University of New York at Stony Brook. He is the author of several books, including *Change Agents: New Roles and Innovation Strategies for Human Resource Professionals* published by Jossey-Bass in 1988. He has conducted research on upward feedback, 360-degree feedback, and, more broadly, management development and career motivation. His practice and writing have also focused on human resources contributions to organization change and development. His recent review of 360-degree feedback theory and research (with James Smither in *Personnel Psychology,* 1995) provided a framework for understanding how managers process 360-degree feedback.

Jennifer W. Martineau is a research scientist at the Center for Creative Leadership. Her current research focuses on development systems: the various factors that either help individuals to learn, develop, and make changes in their behaviors or that prevent them from doing so. Part of her research in this area is also useful for demonstrating the impact of CCL's programs on participants and their organizations. Jennifer has coauthored several publications, including "Individual and Situational Influences on the Development of Self-efficacy: Implications for Training Effectiveness" (*Personnel Psychology*, 1993) and "Individual and Situational Influences on Training Motivation," in *Improving Training Effectiveness in Work Organizations* (1996, Ford, Editor). Jennifer earned a Ph.D. in industrial and organizational psychology from The Pennsylvania State University.

Cynthia D. McCauley is a research scientist at the Center for Creative Leadership. She received her B.A. in psychology from King College and her M.A. and Ph.D. in industrial and organizational psychology from the University of Georgia. She has been a part of the research staff since 1984 and has coauthored two of CCL's management feedback instruments, *Benchmarks* and the *Developmental Challenge Profile: Learning from Job Experiences*. She has written several CCL reports and has published articles in *Journal of Management, Academy of Management Journal, Nonprofit Management and Leadership, Journal of Applied Psychology,* and *Leadership Quarterly*. She is also coeditor of *The Center for Creative Leadership Handbook for Leadership Development* (Jossey-Bass, 1998). Cindy has conducted research on 360-degree feedback, the impact of leadership development programs, learning through job assignments, and developmental relationships.

Carol A. Paradise-Tornow is an adjunct staff member of the Center for Creative Leadership and president of Strategic HR Management Systems in Greensboro, North Carolina. She received her B.A. in psychology from Wright State University and her doctorate in industrial and organizational psychology from the University of Minnesota. She taught business strategy at the University of North Carolina at Greensboro for several years and continues to maintain a consulting practice in the areas of strategic management and human resources planning. In addition to her teaching and consulting experience, she has spent over ten years as an internal human resource planning consultant in a variety of large corporations. She is the author of a book chapter and numerous published articles in the areas of performance management, leadership effectiveness, team performance, and customer service.

William W. Sternbergh is a senior fellow at the Center for Creative Leadership. Bill has been deeply involved in the "assessment for development" philosophy and was part of the original design team for the Leadership Development Program. Since coming to CCL in 1970, he has conducted training on five continents, including a four-month staff exchange with the Ashridge Management College in England. Bill holds an A.B. in psychology from Guilford College and has completed graduate work in psychology at the University of North Carolina at Greensboro and the University of West Florida at Pensacola.

Walter W. Tornow is a senior fellow and former vice president for research and publication at the Center for Creative Leadership. He received his Ph.D. in industrial and organizational psychology from the University of Minnesota. Walt is a licensed consulting psychologist, certified as a senior professional in human resources. He has had extensive applied research, consulting, teaching, and management experience, including executive positions at Control Data Corporation. He was a board member of the Human Resource Certification Institute of the Society for Human Resource Management. Walt has published widely on human resources management issues, including executive and management jobs, performance management, service quality, assessment technologies, and the "changing psychological contract." His 1993 edited special issue on 360-degree feedback for the *Human Resource Management Journal* was one of the first publications to bring together extant research and practice on 360-degree feedback.

Ellen Van Velsor is a research scientist at the Center for Creative Leadership. In this position, she is responsible for work in the Tools Research Cluster, which involves the development of leadership assessment instruments and other assessment-for-development products. She is coauthor of *Breaking the Glass Ceiling: Can Women*

Reach the Top of America's Largest Organizations? (Addison-Wesley, 1992), *Choosing 360: A Guide to Evaluating Multi-rater Feedback Instruments for Management Development* (CCL, 1997), and *Feedback to Managers* (CCL, 1991), as well as numerous other chapters and articles. She is also coeditor of *The Center for Creative Leadership Handbook of Leadership Development* (Jossey-Bass, 1998). She received her B.A. degree (1973) in sociology from the State University of New York at Stony Brook and her M.A. (1978) and Ph.D. (1980) degrees in sociology from the University of Florida.

Patricia O'Connor Wilson is a liaison for business development and heads up the New York Client Liaison office of the Center for Creative Leadership. In this role, she works with clients to assess their current and future leadership development needs and identifies those CCL resources that best respond to those needs. She also serves as a training resource for the Leadership and High-Performance Teams program. Patricia has ten years of managerial and staff experience, having served in sales, finance, and human resources development functions prior to joining CCL. She has recently coauthored *The Breakdown of Hierarchy: Communicating in the Evolving Workplace* (Butterworth Heinenmann, 1997) and has research interests in the areas of high-performance teams, large systems strategic change, and development systems. Patricia holds a B.S. in human resources from the University of Illinois (Champaign-Urbana), an M.B.A. in organizational behavior from Bernard M. Baruch College (City University of New York), and has completed doctoral work in the area of organizational behavior.

MAXIMIZING
THE VALUE OF
360-DEGREE FEEDBACK

360-Degree Feedback— More Than a Tool!

Manuel London
Walter W. Tornow

There is an opportunity in organizations today that we can't afford to miss. In a time when it is generally acknowledged that we must transform ourselves and our institutions to meet the challenges of an ever-changing reality, we are witnessing the growth in popularity of a tool—360-degree feedback—that has the potential to play a key role in the creation of cultures that can enable the necessary individual and organizational development.

If this is to occur, though, 360-degree feedback cannot be seen merely as a tool or used as a one-time event. Rather, it must be understood as part of an ongoing process of assessment, performance evaluation, and discussion of performance with supervisors, subordinates, peers, and others. The 360-degree feedback process should include setting goals, creating development experiences, improving performance, and enhancing organizational development. And people must have a clear sense of how the process can affect, for good or ill, the creation of continuous learning cultures. In the following pages we aim to give you this understanding.

After a few words about the origins of 360-degree feedback in organizations, we will introduce some key themes that you will encounter throughout the book.

Origins of 360-Degree Feedback

The use of 360-degree feedback in organizations today—with people receiving ratings on their performance from a range of co-workers (including supervisors, peers, and subordinates) and more and more frequently from customers as well, and using this information for developmental purposes—has its roots in several traditions in industrial and organizational psychology. One is the employee attitude survey and its role in effecting and measuring organizational change (Nadler, 1977). This survey generally asks employees to rate their satisfaction with a number of aspects of the organization, including policies, procedures, the work environment, pay, benefits, the immediate supervisor, and top executives. The data are averaged across employees, and the results are reported for each department or the organization as a whole as a basis for discussing and identifying areas for organizational change. Managers usually don't receive reports from these surveys about how their immediate subordinates rated them.

Another root is in performance appraisal. Traditionally, appraisals have involved a supervisor rating immediate subordinates. This has been extended by research that compared traditional supervisor ratings to subordinate, peer, and self-ratings in order to determine, for instance, the reliability of ratings from these different sources and the relationship between ratings of oneself and ratings made by others.

However, the primary source of the popularity of 360-degree feedback in organizations is, in our view, the need for managers to adjust to ever-changing business environments (London and Smither, 1995). Information from different sources can represent important constituencies inside and outside the organization (Bernardin and Beatty, 1987; London, Wohlers, and Gallagher, 1990; Nonaka, 1994). Such information is key if organizations are to be adaptive.

Use of 360-Degree Feedback Today

For several reasons, 360-degree feedback has become a popular technique in organizations today. The complexity of jobs requires that employees have feedback from a variety of constituencies, not just their supervisor, who has traditionally been the source of feedback and performance review. Also, organizational restructuring and downsizing place the burden of development on the employee. Today's organizations generally do not provide structured career paths with promises of job security and advancement.

Rather, individuals need to be responsible for their continued ability to add value to the organization. The organization enables this by providing a variety of resources, which often include access to training to improve current job performance and prepare for tomorrow; 360-degree feedback may be part of this development process.

Organizations implement 360-degree feedback in a variety of ways. Feedback may be an organizationwide process in which all employees and managers participate by rating others and receiving feedback reports. The performance dimensions on which people are rated communicate the job behaviors that are important for accomplishing the organization's business strategy. Organizations vary in the groups asked to make such judgments. The process may be limited to subordinates, in which case it is more appropriately called upward evaluation. It may include subordinates, peers, and the immediate supervisor, as well as self-ratings (a typical 360-degree process). It may also include customer evaluations, or it may be limited to customer ratings (which is not 360-degree feedback per se). The idea in all these variations is that ratings are made about specific individuals, the individuals receive feedback reports, and the ratings are averaged across raters within each group so that the individual raters remain anonymous.

On occasion, 360-degree feedback may be implemented within a single department. The department manager may hire a consultant to help with the process, or the survey may be designed and administered by employees who determine the performance dimensions to be rated, collect the data, and hire temporary employees to collate the data and generate the reports.

Organizations also vary in the extent to which feedback recipients are offered support to help them interpret and apply the results. Training programs and opportunities for developmental job assignments may be available, supported by supervisors who are trained and expected to work with their subordinates to establish development goals and coach them as they progress.

Also, 360-degree feedback may be part of a development program. As an example, an organization increasing its international business wants managers to learn how to manage in a multicultural environment. The human resources department works with executives to develop performance dimensions reflecting this strategy and design a week-long training program to help managers learn and practice behaviors associated with the dimensions. Prior to attending the training, participants ask their subordinates, peers, supervisors, and customers to complete a rating form and return it to the training program administrators. Receiving and interpreting the feedback report is the first part of the development program. After all managers attend the training, the 360-degree process becomes part of the firm's performance evaluation process.

Similarly, 360-degree feedback is a core part of assessment-for-development at the Center for Creative Leadership (CCL). Participants in a typical CCL leadership development program come from a variety of organizations. Prior to attending the program, they distribute a 360-degree rating form to subordinates, peers, and supervisors. The report is the foundation for each participant's self-analysis at the start of the program. It is used along with other information, including feedback from fellow participants involved in small-group exercises, as the basis for development during the program and planning for further development after the program.

360-Degree Feedback as the Core of Self-Development

One way of picturing work and work relationships is through the concept of *connectivity*. Individuals are connected in that they derive meaning with and through other people about what is expected of them and how well they're doing. The 360-degree process allows individuals to become connected. It can strengthen relationships between supervisors and subordinates, customers and suppliers, and peers. Thus, it contributes to individual, group, and organizational development.

This connectivity is facilitated in a variety of ways. For example, the organization, through its 360-degree instrumentation and language, sensitizes employees to the organization's expectations. Furthermore, individuals' self-awareness is heightened when receiving feedback from others. This insight, combined with a person's own sense of self, can be felt as a gap between self-perceptions and the perceptions of others. Addressing this gap can serve as powerful motivation for change, growth, and development. Insight also can come from areas of agreement between self- and others' ratings. Others' ratings can validate a person's impression about where improvement is needed. Similarly, they can validate a person's impressions about the strengths that should be maintained and leveraged.

Such a process also suggests that self-development is a continuous journey, and 360-degree feedback becomes a compass to guide that journey. This means that we, as individuals and as organizations, need to treat 360-degree feedback not as a one-time event bounded by time and place but as a continuous process (Dalton and Hollenbeck, 1996). Further, we need to look at this process holistically and from a systems perspective. That is, we need to see how it fits into the other kinds of tools and processes that are designed to promote development, so as to ensure that all the different pieces play together in harmony. Finally, if 360-degree feedback is to effectively serve as a self-development process, it must be integrated into the work and development system at both the individual and the organizational level. This way, development activities are not separated from the work that needs to be done but will serve important work needs for the individual and the organization. At the same time, important work assignments will provide the needed opportunities for continued development.

360-Degree Feedback and the New Workplace

Clearly, both work and workplace have been changing significantly. Work is more interdependent because of team structures, matrix management forms, and other changes in organization functioning that have made the traditional command-and-control structure less meaningful. Also, everyone has a customer (sometimes many customers) inside and outside the organization boundaries.

All this means that an employee's manager is no longer the sole source, or even the most important source, of information regarding expectations or feedback. Instead, the employee's multiple customers or constituencies need to be connected so that they can give meaningful, comprehensive feedback. It also means that employees should take responsibility for managing—or co-managing—this process. In a sense, employees need to see themselves as essential to the 360-degree feedback process and orchestrate the seeking of feedback. That way, they can be more in charge of their performance and of managing their careers.

360-Degree Feedback as a Multifaceted Challenge

Giving and receiving feedback seem to be commodities hard to come by, both from the individual and the organizational perspective. And judging by the reactions of those who give and receive it, dealing with feedback constructively is not necessarily a talent we're born with. Rather, we need to learn and practice it.

Given that people are not always good at giving and receiving feedback (London, 1997), it is not surprising that organizations usually work hard at developing communication systems that incorporate this objective—usually as part of their performance appraisal and development systems. However, candid feedback that individuals are not afraid to give, nor afraid to receive and use, takes a lot of effort to achieve. Effective 360-degree feedback processes, when designed and implemented appropriately, will pay particular attention to the administrative conditions that facilitate these goals.

Clearly, change is the name of the game for the individual receiving feedback and for the organization interested in having such change translated into improved organizational functioning. However, change, growth, and development can be difficult to accomplish and assess. For example, at the individual level, important changes may be under way, but they may not be readily visible to others. Or at the organizational level, many factors can influence organizational functioning besides the performance of any one player.

Organizational support systems have to be in place if change is to be obtained and sustained. Clear expectations need to be set about what the organization seeks and why, as a context for development planning. Further, supervisors and others in the organization associated with an employee's development have important roles to play as coaches and supporters to provide follow-up support.

However, all the external development support available to the employee by the organization will be insufficient unless individual employees take ownership of their feedback and development. That is, to own their assessment is to accept the feedback results and to feel committed to using them to guide their development and performance improvement. Then, the organization's 360-degree feedback process is theirs to use as a means of empowerment and self-determination.

The Power of Purpose

A debate is now going on about whether 360-degree feedback should be used for development or for appraisal (Bracken, Dalton, Jako, McCauley, and Pollman, 1997). Some of the authors in this book clearly fall on the side of development. This is not surprising because the Center for Creative Leadership focuses on leadership development. A principal underlying value and belief at CCL is that individuals, in order to be ready to change and develop, need to "own" their assessment. And to own it, they need to feel psychologically safe and to believe that the feedback data are credible and candid. Toward these ends, rater anonymity promotes feedback candor, and keeping a target individual's results confidential enhances the safety that is so important for personal growth.

Conditions for personal growth frequently can be at odds in an organizational environment where there are concerns over issues of trust, candor, and openness of communication. In such a situation, it is not surprising to find that when 360-degree feedback is used as part of performance appraisal, the organization risks losing the value of individual and organizational development because the conditions necessary for such change are taken away. For example, the feedback may not be kept confidential because the person's manager also sees it; and sometimes, unfortunately, neither the process nor the reason why the organization wants to do it is clearly communicated or understood. When 360-degree feedback is used for administrative decisions, such as how much an employee will be paid, recipients may get defensive. As a result, they don't focus on the implications of the feedback for their development.

Obviously, these conditions are not conducive to individual and organizational development. Perhaps what is called for is a reframing of the debate. Instead of posing the issue in terms of whether to use 360-degree feedback for *either* development *or* appraisal, the question should be more like this: Under what conditions can *both* purposes exist, and under what conditions can they not? Then, we can begin designing 360-degree feedback processes and systems that create conditions in our organizations that are conducive to development, while integrating 360-degree feedback with other human resources management processes such as reward systems. Perhaps when first introduced in an organization, 360-degree feedback should be solely for development. When employees and managers get used to using feedback for development—accepting the results, trying to understand them, incorporating them into their development plans, and tracking performance improvement—the ratings can then be used to evaluate and make decisions about the ratees. In organizations where there is already an environment of trust and where employees feel comfortable seeking feedback and discussing performance issues, 360-degree feedback can be used successfully for evaluation and development when it is first introduced.

As will be demonstrated in the following pages, 360-degree feedback can fit with and help create an organizational environment that supports continuous, self-directed development. Our goal is to show how 360-degree feedback works and to build an understanding of the ways organizations and individuals can get the most from the process.

Part One

Maximizing the Value of 360-Degree Feedback for Individual Development

Elements of Effective 360-Degree Feedback

Stéphane Brutus
John W. Fleenor
Manuel London

The effectiveness of 360-degree feedback depends on four inter-connected elements. These elements are depicted in Exhibit 1.1, and they form the outline for this chapter.

The first section of the chapter deals with the standards and dimensions of performance that are rated in a 360-degree survey, how these dimensions are derived, and what their importance is to the process as a whole. The second section—performance information from feedback—focuses on the quality of the ratings and

Exhibit 1.1. Elements of the 360-Degree Feedback Process.

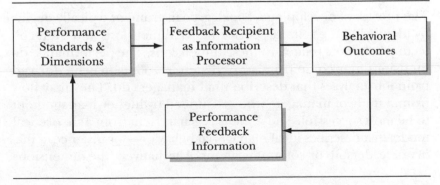

the information they convey to the feedback recipients. The third section considers how recipients process the feedback, that is, how they perceive, integrate, and use the 360-degree feedback results. The fourth section examines the outcomes of the 360-degree feedback for performance improvement and development. Throughout this chapter, we concentrate on managers because they are likely to have feedback from all directions—subordinates, peers, supervisors, and customers. However, the processes we discuss are also applicable to other employees who may receive feedback from two or three sources (for example, salespeople who are rated by their supervisor and customers, and technical personnel who are rated by their supervisor and peers).

Performance Standards and Dimensions for 360-Degree Feedback

The performance dimensions measured by a 360-degree feedback instrument represent the standards used to evaluate members of the organization. Each performance dimension, such as leadership or communications, consists of a group of behaviors. Ratings on behaviors may be averaged to derive a dimension score. Traits or personal characteristics such as judgment and charisma may also be used to define performance dimensions. However, traits are not easily judged by raters and are more general and personally threatening to feedback recipients than behaviors.

Establishing Performance Dimensions

The process of developing a 360-degree instrument typically begins by identifying the relevant performance dimensions and then collecting behaviors related to these dimensions. The performance dimensions may come from several sources. They may be derived from job analyses that describe what managers do. They may flow from a study of managers who are judged by higher management to be most successful. The dimensions may stem from a theoretical model that describes ideal managerial behavior—for instance, a theory of leadership or communications. Alternatively, the dimensions may come from interviews with top executives about the behaviors they want their employees and managers to use in the future to help the organization accomplish its strategies. Strategically oriented managerial behaviors and performance dimensions require input from different constituencies.

London and Mone (1994) provide an example of how a model of managerial dimensions can be coupled with organizational strategy to develop performance dimensions for 360-degree feedback. Recognizing increased competition and the need for managers to be decision makers rather than bureaucrats, an organization conducted a future-oriented job analysis asking top executives what the company expected from managers, given the new corporate environment. Dimensions identified included "setting performance goals," "creating meaningful job and work group structures," "building a cohesive team," "developing networks and alliances," and "meeting departmental performance goals." These became the new managerial standards espoused by this organization. Several years later, the organization revised the set of dimensions in light of the evolving business environment and corporate strategies. New managerial performance dimensions centered on quality enhancement, people management, knowledge of technology, and knowledge of basic business skills; 360-degree instruments were found to be particularly helpful in measuring dimensions related to quality (for example, data on customer satisfaction) and people (for example, subordinate ratings of the manager's support for career development).

Communicating Standards Through Performance Dimensions

As a communication process, 360-degree feedback can provide an effective means of disseminating organizational standards. The items on a 360-degree feedback instrument communicate what is important or what behaviors are expected in the organization. The following three items, for example, were taken from Benchmarks (Lombardo and McCauley, 1994), a 360-degree feedback instrument developed by the Center for Creative Leadership:

This person patiently allows good people to develop.

This person gives his or her direct reports visibility with higher management.

This person sets a challenging climate to encourage individual growth.

Because 360-degree feedback involves multiple constituencies across different levels of the organization, these items can send a clear and powerful message about what is expected from organizational members. A peer evaluating a co-worker on these items would infer that creating a developmental climate for subordinates is valued by the organization—an extremely important piece of information in itself.

The survey process may affect both the recipient of the feedback and the rater. Involving employees and managers in identifying effective performance starts a process of acceptance of the resulting performance standards and the behaviors the organization needs to accomplish its strategies. Also, when co-workers evaluate each other, they internalize the same organizational standards. For example, a manager can rate a peer with items that are related to customer service. By evaluating the peer on these specific dimensions, the manager will perceive that the organization is serious about customer service. Also, when managers receive feedback on the dimensions, they recognize that these are the behaviors that the organization values and wants to see enhanced.

In summary, behaviorally based performance dimensions may come from different sources. They may reflect current, ideal, or future-oriented elements of performance. The process of identifying and using the behaviors as ratings is a way to communicate the importance of the performance dimensions to raters and feedback recipients.

Performance Information from 360-Degree Feedback

The quality of information is vital for any feedback system, including 360-degree feedback. The accurate assessment of job performance is an issue that has perplexed behavioral scientists for years (Austin and Villanova, 1992). This is especially true of managerial effectiveness, an elusive, ever-changing construct that can be very difficult to capture. Even so, steps can be taken to ensure the quality of ratings. These include (1) clearly explaining how the ratings will be used, (2) holding the raters accountable for their ratings, and (3) training the raters on the intricacies of the rating process (Borman, 1991).

The Value of Multiple Perspectives

The use of multiple rating sources or perspectives is clearly a strength of 360-degree feedback, and the contributions of different perspectives are especially interesting. London and Smither (1995) state that "in the socially constructed world in which employees work, others' judgments about them (no matter how biased they may be) constitute an important reality" (p. 809). Traditionally, supervisors have been charged with assessing the effectiveness of managers reporting to them. In 360-degree feedback, other raters, such as peers and subordinates, bring different, and possibly inconsistent, information to the rating process. It is possible, therefore, that a feedback recipient may be seen as effective from one person's perspective but as ineffective from another's perspective. According to contingency theories of leadership, leaders constantly adjust their behaviors to the particular situation (Yukl and Van Fleet, 1992). It follows that managers who behave differently toward their co-workers will be rated differently by these individuals. So each rating source may be valid from its own perspective. This can be true, for example, if a feedback recipient behaves differently toward different raters. For example, the manager may be interpersonally skilled with peers but act cold and aloof with subordinates. This manager, therefore, could accurately be rated as high on interpersonal skills by peers and low on this dimension by subordinates. In this case, the feedback recipient can be thought of as a moving target. However, by using 360-degree feedback, this "movement" can be assessed and fed back to the manager.

The ratings from self and others constitute the core of the 360-degree feedback process. How are the different ratings produced? How does rating a supervisor differ from rating a peer or a subordinate? The question of how these ratings are perceived must be addressed. Does the feedback recipient view peer ratings differently from supervisor ratings? These questions are important because the value of 360-degree feedback lies in these nuances—in the diversity of information it provides to the feedback recipient and how he or she interprets this information.

Downward Ratings

Supervisory, or downward, evaluations are the most common type of ratings. They fit nicely within the top-down control of traditional organizations. As stated by Murphy and Cleveland (1995), "Supervisory evaluations follow the natural flow of power and authority [within organizations]" (p. 135). Evaluating subordinates' performance is generally part of the supervisor's job. Supervisors communicate their expectations about the level of performance they expect from their employees. However, supervisors view only a portion of subordinates' performance (Howard, Byham, and Hauenstein, 1994; London, 1995).

In most cases, supervisor ratings, as opposed to other sources, are not confidential. In other words, the feedback recipient is aware of the ratings given by the supervisor because these ratings are not aggregated with other raters, as is the case with peer, subordinate, or customer ratings. As a result, supervisors must be prepared to defend their ratings to subordinates. This may make the ratings less reliable or more one-sided than ratings derived from a group of raters.

Upward Ratings

Upward ratings are an important part of 360-degree feedback for managers. Typically, the evaluations from four to six subordinates are collected (London and Smither, 1995; Van Velsor and Leslie, 1991). By shifting the traditional roles of the rater and the ratee, a new set of dynamics takes place. From the supervisor perspective, receiving upward ratings is potentially threatening. A few studies, however, have found that reactions to upward feedback are generally positive (Bernardin, Dahmus, and Redmon, 1993; London, Wohlers, and Gallagher, 1990). This represents one of the areas in which 360-degree feedback contributes to a new way of thinking about performance evaluations.

From the perspective of subordinates, upward ratings are a change, or even a disturbance, in the normal flow of power within the organization (Murphy and Cleveland, 1995). This represents a rare instance in which subordinates can directly and anonymously affect their supervisor. In most 360-degree processes, the anonymity of peers and subordinates is protected by the use of averaged ratings. Subordinates are privy to very important information about their manager, and these ratings are often valuable. If the role of the manager is to lead, then the subordinates' perceptions are a critical aspect of leadership. For example, subordinates may have the best perspective on the extent to which a supervisor gives feedback or helps with career planning.

A potentially negative aspect of an employee rating a supervisor is the possibility of retaliation. Supervisors who are aware that subordinates have given them negative ratings may punish them by assigning undesirable tasks, withholding salary increases, or generally making the employees' jobs more difficult. The fear of retaliation, real or imagined, may work to positively bias the ratings.

Peer Ratings

Peer evaluations refer to situations in which rater and ratee are from the same organizational level. Peer evaluations have been found to be valid and reliable (Landy and Farr, 1983; Reilly and Chao, 1982). However, this does not mean that they are free from biases. For example, research has shown that most people have a tendency to rate peers who are similar to themselves higher than peers who are dissimilar (Fox, Ben-Nahum, and Yinon, 1989). Another finding is that high performers seem to be more discriminating than low performers toward peers (Saavedra and Kwun, 1993). Additionally, peers may be reluctant to evaluate each other because such ratings may disturb a positive group climate (Liden and Mitchell, 1983). Peers often compete for promotions and may feel that they are evaluated against one another. The perceived competition among members of a peer group may affect their ratings of one another.

Customer Ratings

The 360-degree feedback process often incorporates customer ratings. In their survey of industry practices, London and Smither (1995) report that about 60 percent of 360-degree feedback users collect ratings from internal or external customers. Customers are essentially concerned with results—whether they receive the desired products or services in a timely manner and generally whether their needs, as customers, are met (Howard and others, 1994). Because external customers belong to different organizational cultures, their ratings have a high level of credibility to feedback recipients. Moreover, this information is important because of its close proximity to the organization's bottom line.

Making Use of Multiple Rating Perspectives

Different rating sources provide unique information about managers' performance and, as a result, the ratings that managers receive from subordinates, peers, and supervisors often differ (Harris and Schaubroeck, 1988; Mabe and West, 1982). These differences are likely the result of raters at different organizational levels observing different facets of the manager's job performance (Borman, 1974). For example, Murphy and Cleveland (1995) indicate that subordinates and peers have more opportunity than supervisors to observe interpersonal behavior. To illustrate this, some generic performance dimensions and the rating source(s) that can best capture these behaviors are presented in Exhibit 1.2.

Given the differences among the rating perspectives, combining all raters together into one category is not an appropriate strategy (London and Smither, 1995). Usually, 360-degree feedback instruments have a common set of dimensions for which it is useful to have different rating perspectives. In addition to the common dimensions, each rater group also may rate a different set of dimensions specifically designed for that group. For example, subordinates might evaluate elements of supervisor-subordinate relationships such as leadership and empowerment dimensions, whereas peers might rate interpersonal skills in dealing with colleagues. As discussed by Paradise-Tornow in Chapter Five of this volume, customers are a valuable source of information pertaining

**Exhibit 1.2. Performance Dimensions
Likely to Be Observed by Different Rating Sources.**

Performance Dimensions	Subordinates	Peers	Supervisors	Customers
Administrative			✓	
Leadership	✓			
Communication	✓	✓		
Interpersonal	✓	✓		✓
Decision making		✓	✓	
Technical		✓	✓	✓
Personal motivation		✓	✓	✓
Customer orientation				✓

to both the quality of the service or product being provided and the quality of the process behind the delivery.

As we stated, managerial effectiveness is an elusive concept. For this reason, the use of multiple sources allows for the most complete picture available of managerial effectiveness. Together, the unique perspectives from each rating source provide a fuller picture of managerial effectiveness—one that can be used to initiate individual development by comparing it against the standards set by the organization.

Self-Ratings

Self-ratings are often a very important part of the 360-degree feedback process, even though ratings by others may be more accurate than self-ratings (Harris and Schaubroeck, 1988). Self-ratings require introspection—the process of looking inward and evaluating where one stands in relation to some effectiveness standard. Self-ratings, within the context of 360-degree feedback, are the first step to development for the feedback recipient. As managers sit down and take time to fill out a questionnaire about their own effectiveness, they begin to think about and reevaluate their situation.

The Feedback Recipient as Information Processor

This section addresses how feedback recipients react to, integrate, interpret, and use the results. The extent to which 360-degree feedback information is accepted and internalized by the recipient is crucial for individual development. Consider the hypothetical situation of a manager whose effectiveness has been assessed by her co-workers with great precision; all of the manager's strengths and weaknesses have been identified. Before development can take place, this information has to be clearly presented to the manager. With 360-degree feedback, the difficulty is that there is an enormous amount of information to be absorbed. The feedback usually covers multiple performance dimensions, each being rated by multiple sources. For example, one 360-degree feedback survey we know of contains twenty-two performance ratings from self, supervisors, peers, and subordinates. This generates eighty-eight separate data points for the feedback recipient to digest.

This abundance of information has led researchers and practitioners to explore possible improvements in reporting 360-degree feedback information. Issues related to attention mechanisms such as selective perception and information distortion are relevant (London and Beatty, 1993). London and Smither's (1995) survey reported that 80 percent of 360-degree feedback reports explicitly contrast ratings from the different sources, 90 percent contrast these ratings with self-ratings, and 70 percent report an indicator of within-source agreement (for example, standard deviation). The clarity of the feedback report is an important factor affecting receptivity to the feedback (London and Smither, 1995).

The communication of feedback must be designed to capture the feedback recipient's attention. The mere presentation of information does not guarantee that it will be received appropriately. This is a critical moment in the feedback process. At this juncture, feedback recipients are confronted with two essential pieces of information: (1) others' perceptions of their effectiveness in relation to organizational standards and (2) their own perceptions of their effectiveness. Much of the impact of 360-degree feedback lies in the first element. Discovering what others think of them is often very difficult for feedback recipients to accept. The knowledge that others think positively (or negatively) about their abilities is very powerful. This impact is increased when the perception of others is different from self-perception.

Self-reflection is a rare activity for managers. Mintzberg (1989) observes that managerial activities are characterized by brevity, variety, and discontinuity. The relentless pace at which most managers operate leaves little room for reflection. Daudelin (1996) argues that the process of reflection "allows one to momentarily suspend the intense flow of new information to the brain. This enhances the processing of existing information, thereby better preparing the person to handle the demands of the rapidly changing environment" (p. 39).

As we suggested earlier, the rating process may create personal change even before feedback is given to the recipient. For example, raters learn about the performance standards of the organization as they rate themselves and each other, which makes these standards more conspicuous in the organization (Reilly, Smither, and Vasilopoulous, 1996). Additionally, the observational skills of the raters may improve as they participate in the rating process, and raters therefore may pay more attention to their own behavior as well as to that of others.

Openness to Feedback

Some people develop self-insight by observing how people react to them or by asking for feedback. These individuals are open to new ideas about themselves. Other people have a crystallized view of themselves and interpret others' behaviors and reactions as consistent with that self-view. As a result, they fail to learn much from their observations or from feedback.

Psychological mechanisms related to how we operate in social environments may become impediments to accurate self-assessment; this may be especially true for individuals in organizational settings. Mechanisms exist that make honest self-assessment more difficult. Some of these mechanisms are related to filters through which we tend to view ourselves; others are related to the kind of information about ourselves that is available.

Employees need to develop their ability to observe and evaluate their behavior in more objective fashion. We all possess self-schemas—mental representations of ourselves. These schemas have been built over time through the selective accumulation of information about ourselves. As we reach adulthood, these schemas become very stable. This stability arises when we develop a tendency to seek confirming information about ourselves and to avoid disconfirming information. Information that challenges our self-view is not easily accepted. The first step in changing our self-perception is the reception of disconfirming information. Managers who see themselves as great communicators will not necessarily alter their self-view at the first hint of their inability to conduct a productive meeting; only selected information will make its way through.

London (1995) outlined several elements that contribute to feedback acceptance. Favorability of the feedback is an obvious one; positive evaluations tend to be received more favorably than negative ones. Other factors, such as agreement among the different rating sources, extreme ratings, and consistency of ratings across the different dimensions, also contribute to feedback acceptance.

Comparing self-perception to others' views is a complex task involving social information processing and interpersonal insight (London, 1994). *Interpersonal insight* refers to the degree to which people recognize their strengths and weaknesses. The acquisition of this insight (or lack thereof) is the result of a process that includes (1) receiving information about oneself and others, (2) integrating the information, (3) interpreting the information, and (4) incorporating the information into a preexisting set of perceptions.

When a person first receives feedback, the tendency is to try to categorize it automatically into impressions that have already been formed. So, for example, a piece of positive feedback that conforms to a person's existing self-image will be processed automatically as supporting that self-image. Some accompanying negative information may be conveniently ignored or possibly categorized as fitting a preexisting conception of the source of the information—for instance, that the source always says something negative to appear tough but doesn't really mean it. When the information does not automatically fit the preexisting self-impressions because it is unexpected or unusual, the individual must process the information carefully (mindfully) to determine if it fits another category of how the individual views him- or herself or others. If not, a new category may be needed. This mindful processing includes making an attribution that explains the information. An external attribution leads to new judgments about others, whereas an internal attribution leads to self-insight. Individuals alter their self-image when they determine that the information tells them something new about themselves. In the process, the individual compares the information to a standard (for example, how he or she was rated previously, information about how others were rated, or information about organizational standards and expectations). This analysis suggests how the revised self-image can be used to establish goals for behavior change.

As stated earlier, the world of managers who deal with multiple constituencies with varying points of view allows for discrepancies between how managers view themselves and how others view them. Some managers tend to overestimate their performance; some underestimate their performance; others tend to be right on target about how others perceive them (Fleenor, McCauley, and Brutus, 1996). Interestingly, these rating tendencies have been found to be stable over time, in that managers who overestimate their effectiveness, for example, will tend to do so repeatedly (Nilsen and Campbell, 1993).

Individual Characteristics and 360-Degree Feedback

This section focuses on discrepancies between self- and others' ratings and attempts to shed some light on why some managers rate themselves higher than others rate them, whereas other managers do not. Some of the factors involved in these tendencies are personality characteristics, gender, ethnicity, age, and organizational level.

A great deal of research has been directed at the relationship between individual characteristics and rating tendencies; the research has focused on characteristics of the raters, the ratee, or both. Although a complete review of this literature is beyond the scope of this chapter, an overview of the research will shed light on the complexity of rating tendencies in 360-degree feedback.

First, various factors have been found to influence self-perceptions. For example, characteristics of feedback recipients such as gender, race, age, self-esteem, introversion, sensitivity, and dominance are related to self-evaluation (Brutus, Fleenor, and

McCauley, 1996; Peterson, 1992). Also, characteristics of feedback recipients are related to the evaluation of others. The gender, race, age, and personality of managers affect how others evaluate them. For example, there is some evidence that raters tend to evaluate women lower than men for occupations that are stereotypically male (Heilman, Block, Martell, and Simon, 1989). Recent meta-analytic evidence supports the notion that women are evaluated more positively when placed in more feminine roles (Eagly, Karau, and Makhijani, 1995). Unfortunately, managerial occupations still appear to be evaluated largely against masculine standards. Heilman and others (1989) found that descriptions of successful managers were more similar to descriptions of men than descriptions of women.

Recent investigations have focused on factors related to the discrepancy between self- and others' ratings. For example, if age is positively related to self-ratings but not to others' ratings, the relationship of self-ratings to others' ratings would change with age. Age, gender, organizational level, dominance, introversion, and achievement motivation have been found to be related to self-other rating discrepancies (London and Wohlers, 1991; Mabe and West, 1982). For example, Brutus and others (1996) found a relationship between age and self-other rating discrepancy. In this study, older managers exhibited a tendency to overestimate their effectiveness in relation to supervisor ratings.

Self-supervisor, self-peer, self-subordinate, and self-customer relationships possess distinctive features that may affect differences in performance perceptions (Brutus and others, 1996; Peterson, 1992). Each has unique parameters, defined by its organizational role, within which both actors interact and evaluate each other. For example, the relationship between an individual and his or her supervisor may involve certain personality characteristics that will, in turn, influence the supervisor's ratings. These same characteristics may be irrelevant and inconsequential when this individual interacts with subordinates or peers. Exposure to different raters also may vary on certain individual characteristics. Raters often rely on fragmentary information about their subordinates, peers, or supervisors when evaluating their effectiveness (Murphy and Cleveland, 1995). An introverted manager, for example, may be less visible to peers than an extroverted manager.

In summary, this section focused on the integration of 360-degree feedback information by the feedback recipient. Unfortunately, what we know about the integration of the large amount of data generated by 360-degree feedback is limited. People possess many mechanisms that distort, block, and amplify social information. One of the primary reasons 360-degree feedback is effective for individual development is that it minimizes the effect of these mechanisms and sends a clear message to the feedback recipient: "This is where you stand in relation to our [the organization's] standards."

Outcomes of 360-Degree Feedback

This section deals with the impact and the changes in behavior that result from 360-degree feedback. The process of 360-degree feedback is aimed at improving managerial effectiveness. At this stage of the feedback process, information has been gathered and fed back, and adjustments are made. This is where the feedback process completes its cycle. This is the end of the process for managers if they have had the opportunity to identify areas for development and have taken steps to adjust their behavior accordingly. In another sense, the process is starting over because the manager's "new" self needs to be recalibrated in relation to the standards. At this point, managers can participate in another round of formal feedback, or they can collect information more informally by actively seeking feedback from their co-workers.

A common misperception among researchers and practitioners is that feedback will automatically lead to an improvement in performance (London and Smither, 1995). All too often, managers act as if feedback is all that is required for performance improvement (Kaplan, Drath, and Kofodimos, 1987). Kluger and DeNisi (1996) present a strong case for wide variations in the effects of feedback on performance. In a review of over six hundred feedback studies, these researchers found that one-third of feedback interventions led to negative changes in performance; only one-third actually yielded improvements in performance; the remaining interventions had no impact. In light of these results, it seems appropriate to take a critical look at the impact of feedback interventions, specifically 360-degree feedback, on performance.

Only a few studies have systematically investigated the impact of 360-degree feedback on managerial effectiveness (London and Smither, 1995). One such study by Hazucha, Hezlett, and Schneider

(1993) found an increase in effectiveness and in self-other agreement two years after the provision of 360-degree feedback. The absence of a comparison group in this study, however, makes it difficult to determine the actual role of 360-degree feedback in the increase of effectiveness. Reilly and others (1996) followed ninety-two managers over a two-year period, during which time up to four upward feedback sessions were administered. Results indicated that managers whose initial levels of effectiveness were low were able to improve after the first feedback session. This improvement was sustained over the two-year observation period. Hazucha and others (1993) also found that skills increased two years after the administration of 360-degree feedback. Interestingly, Reilly and others (1996) found that the degree of improvement was not related to how many times the process was administered. Most managers improved after the first feedback intervention and remained stable afterward.

Using 360-degree feedback to establish a development plan is a critical part of the 360-degree feedback process. Individuals constantly adjust and match their behaviors to a goal or standard; this self-regulation process drives us (Carver and Scheier, 1982; Nelson, 1993). Discrepancies between behaviors and goals activate responses aimed at reducing the discrepancies. When managers realize that their interpersonal skills are much lower than they had originally thought (that is, the ratings of others are lower than self-ratings), they are likely to attempt some sort of behavioral adjustment, assuming that they care about their interpersonal skills.

Goal-setting theory addresses the relationship between goals, motivation, and performance. Locke (1968) stated that goals are a source of motivation and that they serve to direct behavior. To positively influence performance, however, two conditions must be met: individuals must have a clear understanding of what the goal entails, and they must accept the goal as something that is worth accomplishing. Kluger and DeNisi (1996) found that feedback with goal-setting results in larger gains than feedback administered alone. According to goal-setting theory, the best goals (that is, those that best motivate and direct behaviors) are specific, difficult, and attainable. Certainly, most 360-degree feedback contains enough information for managers to choose goals that meet these criteria.

Unfortunately, little is known about how managers receiving 360-degree feedback set goals to change their behavior and improve their performance. Managers can set goals based on discrepancies between self and supervisor ratings, for example, disregarding peers and subordinates. They also can set developmental goals based on discrepancies between the ratings of others and an ideal performance level (for example, "I need to get all 5s next time"). One thing is certain, 360-degree feedback provides much information that can be used for goal setting.

Most evidence supporting the impact of 360-degree feedback points to the importance of the time period after the feedback is received. Of the many factors that seem to influence the impact of 360-degree feedback, support following the feedback process is essential. Without systematic planning and some sort of support system, performance improvement efforts will be lost in the crunch of daily activities. The provision of a well-designed feedback report alone, without appropriate support, will decrease the impact of 360-degree feedback. Needed support can come from supervisors, coaches, trainers, or trusted colleagues. Their support can surface in a variety of ways, from helping managers to set goals, to linking the process to developmental activities and enabling the review of development plans. In their review of twenty organizations responsible for the delivery of 360-degree feedback, London and Smither (1995) found that only 40 percent always linked 360-degree feedback to a specific developmental activity. Of those that did not use developmental activities to support their programs, 50 percent did not have a process to ensure that participants set goals based on the feedback.

Conclusion

The basic idea underlying 360-degree feedback is relatively simple: performance information from multiple sources can help people develop and improve their performance. This requires that the feedback be linked to developmental planning, goal setting, and organizational support. The next chapter looks at an example of how one manager felt about and reacted to 360-degree feedback, and how a development program helped her understand and use the feedback.

Chapter Two

360 in Action

Following Catharine's Footsteps Through a Leadership Development Program

William W. Sternbergh

The 360-degree feedback process is often carried out within the context of a development program. In some cases the feedback is integral to the program, that is, it supports the purpose of the program, and the program increases the value of 360-degree feedback. In other cases it is virtually an add-on: the feedback report is given to participants, but the program barely makes mention of it.

This chapter will describe the kind of program that can enhance the 360-degree process by presenting a case study of a participant.[1] The case is not that of one particular person; rather, it represents a composite based on the typical experience of participants in CCL's Leadership Development Program (LDP).[2] The narrative form will provide the reader with rich insight and understanding of how 360-degree feedback works from the perspective of a participant-observer.

Introduction to the Case

LDP is a six-day program for middle-to-upper-level managers and executives. It combines lectures, group exercises, assessment questionnaires (both 360 and non-360 types), and individual feedback to help participants develop their capacity for leadership. LDP aims to help participants acquire a better understanding of their strengths and weaknesses, improve their ability to give constructive feedback to direct reports and team members, and develop their leadership style and effectiveness.

Catharine is a division manager of a large manufacturing firm, and she has been sent to the program as part of her company's commitment to developing managers at her level. Her world is changing. Catharine's company has flattened out and downsized within the last three years. She is neither a high-flyer nor a problem manager.

The 360-degree feedback questionnaire used in the program will provide Catharine with a number of perspectives on her effectiveness. In preparation for the program, she gave one copy of the instrument questionnaire to her boss, four to her subordinates, and four to her peers—and, of course, she filled one out on herself. Normally, it is the disparity between the way the participant rates him- or herself and the ratings of others that provides the most eye-opening experiences.

Initial Reactions to Feedback

On the second day of the program, the data combined from these individuals are presented to the participants. Let's follow Catharine's reactions to her 360-degree feedback data:

> Later in the morning we start talking about the feedback instrument we gave to the people back home, and suddenly the room is very quiet. Rachel, the trainer, is being casual about it, but I can see the other people in the room sitting up a little bit straighter in their seats and paying a little more attention. She starts talking through the research that went into the instrument. She emphasizes the importance of the data being research-based and tells us the items that this instrument measures are the factors that make the difference between managers who are successful and those who derail. "The issues measured by this instrument make a difference in the real world," she says.

> Finally, the books presenting each person's data are handed out, and Rachel says, "Don't look at it yet. Wait until we can walk through it together."

> As she describes this instrument and these data, I start trying to remember who I gave this to, why exactly I gave it to them, and what the issues involved were. Well, we walk through the data. The first page—I'm glad to see I got all my data, because not everybody did. A few people are raising their hands and

saying, "Wait a minute. Why don't I have mine? They said they filled this out; they said they sent it in." Rachel talks about how the mail isn't always perfect, and how, unfortunately, sometimes people will lie to you. That's why issues of confidentiality are so important. Without confidentiality, people won't always be honest with you. The respondents were promised anonymity, but sometimes people don't believe it, and if they don't believe their response will be anonymous, they won't send it in, or if they do send it in, it won't be valid—which is why the self-management model of feedback is so important. What is the self-management model of feedback? I guess we get into that later.

The first thing we do is look at a simple chart. Here are the sixteen skills and perspectives that are measured by this instrument—divided into three parts, apparently. The first has to do with job challenges, the second with leading subordinates, and the third with balancing work and self. The question is, Which eight of the sixteen are the most important? I've chosen eight, and my boss has chosen eight.

I never would have thought he'd check that one, and that one too. Well, on five of the eight we agree. That feels good. We agree on the ones that I thought were absolutely the most important.

The ones we didn't agree on are interesting, though. On two of those, my subordinates agreed with me, but on this other one—"hiring talented staff"—I didn't think was as important, but my boss did, and all of the other respondents, my peers, and subordinates thought it was important, too. I wonder why. It sounds like people are saying that I don't do a good job of selecting good folks. Heck, I selected half of them.

Second section. OK, on this graph I'm looking at self and others. "S" means self; "O" is others, and I can see where I rated myself on each of these perspectives, and I can see where everybody else, on average, rated me on these perspectives. I notice my data on "decisiveness." Now that just blows me away. I mean, I would have thought that the people I work with would see me as decisive. I certainly rated myself high on that, but they don't see me that way at all.

The trainer is talking about the "rule of thumb" that if the ratings are more than a thumb width apart on the graph, then that's probably a significant difference. I can get my whole hand between those two! Over here, on "leading people" though, we're pretty much the same, up toward the high end. That feels good. I like that. A few other things here, but that decisiveness . . . I'll come back and look at that again.

We turn the page. The second graph looks just like the first one, except now it's got boss, direct reports, and peers. It's got "S" for subordinates and "P" for peers. OK, now there's a significant amount of difference here. Because on this decisiveness issue, my subordinates are in the middle area, my peers are down farther, and my boss is real low. Interesting. My boss doesn't see me as being decisive. Boy, that's a surprise. Even though we've worked together for years, I never remember that coming up in our conversations before. That's definitely interesting. On "resourcefulness" he thinks I'm pretty good. Peers are sort of in the middle, and my subordinates rate me high. As I look, I notice my subordinates tend to rate me higher on most things. Well, I've got a good group of folks, and we work hard together. But what was this thing, "hiring talented staff"? It's down here in "leading people." Once again, my subordinates rated me reasonably high, but my peers and boss rate me low.

We draw lines from one dot to another with our colored pencils, and as the trainers briefly walk around behind us, Rachel points at something in my book and says, "Well, you should feel pretty good about that."

"Feel good about that?" I say, "Look at this!"

She points out that I seem to be hung up on what's going wrong and not on what's going right. There seem to be a lot of things that are going pretty well. I say, "Thank you very much," but I still don't feel that great about it.

We're now looking at each perspective and at each item that makes up that perspective, and I'm going to have to look at how I rated myself, how on average everyone else rated me, and finally how each group—my boss, my peers, and my subordinates—rated me. This is going to take a while. So I grab my colored pens, and I mark in green where they are among the highest and in red where they are among the lowest of the scores. I look through to see if there are any patterns. The two I see are the same as the concerns I had earlier, and as I get to the items on "decisiveness," sure enough, my boss and my peers tend to rate me down on "displays a real bias for action," "is action-oriented," and "is quick and approximate rather than slow and precise in making decisions." They rate me pretty low on that, and I've always prided myself on being thoughtful on decision making—on not jumping to conclusions or going off half-cocked. It looks as though they don't think that's such a good thing. I wonder if that's what Rachel was talking about when she said, "Strengths can become weaknesses."

My subordinates don't seem to mind that I take some time to decide on an issue; I get to spend more time with them, and they get to hear all the things we're thinking about. Well, I'm going to dog-ear that page. I'll probably have to come back to that one as well.

The other thing I note here is that I'm "below average" on some of these items, and yet my rating is a 4 out of 5. So I raise my hand and the other trainer comes over. He reminds me about the absolute rating and the normative rating. The absolute rating is the number that my respondents actually gave me on a particular item, and the normative data show how that number compares with other managers at my level. Even though on this item I was rated a 4, most other managers were rated a 5. So, the questions that I have to struggle with are, How high is high enough, and How low is too low? The normative information gives me a chance to look at myself within a larger group of managers. OK, that helps me figure where I am on a lot of these items.

The other one is hiring talented staff: "recruits good people," "hires people who are not afraid of responsibility or risks," "surrounds herself with the best people." Well, I've got to talk to my boss about that. Apparently he doesn't think that's what I do. I'll have to dog-ear that page too. I am aware that at times the trainer is saying something, and I'm only getting half of it because it's awful hard not to read through this thing and to still keep turning pages. I think they're trying to get me to organize the data to make more sense of them, but they're really kind of overwhelming. Every now and then an item will jump out at me such as "is widely counted on by peers." Well, my subordinates seem to think that's true; my boss thinks I do a good job at that; and my peers give me a 2.5 out of 5 on that. I am stunned. I mean, I've worked with some of these people for ten years, and to think that this is the way they perceive me. . . .

When we finally stop, I notice I've been looking at these data for an hour and a half. It's been the quickest hour and a half of my life.

Catharine's response to her feedback is primarily focused on the data that she feels show weaknesses, and this is the response of most participants. People tend to focus on the problems and not on the things that are going right. This is understandable. Catharine needs to pay attention to those negative items if she wants to make changes back home that are truly going to make a difference. But it is vital that she spend an equal amount of time on the effective aspects of her behavior that the data highlighted. She needs to continually develop and capitalize on her strengths—those things she appears to be doing right. By making changes in the negative behavior and building on the positive behavior, Catharine can become a better manager. But how is she to digest the feedback and use the data most effectively? This program promotes the "self-management model of feedback" as a way in which participants can systematically make sense of the 360-degree feedback data they receive.

Digesting the Feedback

After lunch, we all sit back around the table, and Rachel says to us, "I want to talk for a little while about a process we can use called the self-management model of feedback. You've already received an incredible amount of information about yourself," she says, "from a number of different sources, and in order for you to use it effectively, you have to remember that you're the one in charge of that information.

"As we look at all these data again, you should pay attention to three crucial variables. The first and foremost of those is the accuracy of the data. Does the information make sense to you? You know yourself better than any battery of tests could possibly show, so if you see something on there that you don't think is right, don't come to me wanting to pick a fight. You'll be disappointed. You'll find out that I'm on your side.

"If you tell me this really isn't the way you are, then the question is, How are you then? What really makes the most sense to you? Accuracy is first and foremost.

"Let me be clear," she continues. "The instruments we're using were not chosen at random. All the test-retest data and all the reliability data indicate that these are good solid instruments, so I'm very comfortable looking at the group and saying 'These data are accurate,' but when I look at Catharine, I know only Catharine can truly tell me whether or not her data are correct.

"The second crucial variable is the evaluative meaning of the data. Do I like this information or not? Is this good for me, or is this bad for me? We can talk about options, we can talk about alternatives, we can talk about consequences, and we can talk about outcomes, but in the final analysis only you can say, 'Yeah, I like that about me,' or 'Hmm, I'm not too sure.'

"The third crucial variable is the importance of the data. You may see something on one of these instruments, and you may say, 'Oh yeah, that's me all right. That's accurate,' and you can also say, 'I'm not really happy about that . . . but the heck with it. It's not important enough for me to invest the time, energy, motivation to do anything about it.' Only you can decide if you want to put forth the effort to do anything about the data.

"So those are the three elements to the self-management model. First, is it accurate? Second, what is its value to me? Third, what is its importance?

"Now," she says very seriously, "when I speak about the self-management model, I'm talking about how you can apply that to any kind of feedback, but there's one of those three elements that you cannot argue with when the feedback is from a 360-degree instrument. You don't get to assess the accuracy of it.

"You may ask, 'Why not?' Well, I'm going to tell you—because that's what your people said. It is accurate about what they said. You may not know exactly what they meant yet, but you don't get to think, 'Well, they didn't really mean to say . . .' because they did say that. It's accurate. You still need to assess whether it's good or bad for you, and you still have to weigh how important it is to you, but you've got to understand that the data in your 360-degree books are accurate to the extent that they are based exactly on the responses your own people gave about you.

"Any questions?" she asks.

I look around the room, and there aren't any questions. People are nodding their heads. That does make sense.

The Self-Management Model

The self-management model of feedback is an important tool for understanding and framing 360-degree feedback. It is important to apply the data to this three-step process. As Rachel pointed out, participants do not get to decide about the accuracy of the data because "that's what your people said," but it is critical that individuals make a judgment about the data's value and importance. It is common for a participant to be more concerned about a rating of 4 (with 5 being the highest) on one item than a 2 on another item. It is possible that a rating of 2 on, say, "building effective teams," would not upset someone because that person doesn't place a high value on that particular element. Conversely, a rating of 4 on, say, "completes assignments on time" may be very upsetting to the individual because he or she may know that this element is a critical component of the job. It's up to the individual to make this choice.

The third element, and the second choice, has to do with importance. The question is, What am I going to do about it? If the item is important, then a commitment should be made to improve in this area. It's possible, however, that a rating of 3 on "decisiveness" may be very upsetting to an individual like Catharine, but the person may say to him- or herself, "That's just not important enough to me to do anything about it. I mean, if that's the way they see me, then so be it. I think I do an effective job in that area, and the heck with them if they don't think so." Again, this is entirely up to the individuals. Only they can make a judgment about what the data mean to them and what they're going to do in response.

Recognizing the Need for Change

In Catharine's case, however, the issues of decisiveness and hiring talented staff are important—important enough for her to do something about them. This is a primary way in which a 360-degree instrument in a program can be enhanced. Relating 360-degree data to several kinds of activities and making it possible for the participant to actively consider the data will increase the likelihood that the data will become a catalyst for change. Catharine is just beginning to see the need for change:

> My boss seems to think I'm not decisive enough, and I'm not sure why that is. I'm also not quite sure what he sees as the problem in how I deal with my subordinates. My subordinates seem to think I'm doing a good job, and if I think over the past few months, we certainly have turned out the work. I mean, it's not that the performance is down; we're doing well. Well, my boss and I need to have a serious chat when I get home. This may be a good chance for him and me to sit down and hammer this stuff out. He's a smart man, and I've worked with him a long time, but in the last few years, the way the business has been growing, it suddenly occurs to me, I don't think he and I have ever had lunch, and I think he and his wife have only been out for dinner once with my husband and me in the past two years. That used to be a fairly frequent kind of thing. It looks like it's time to sit down and have a good heart-to-heart with him. I get the sense that he doesn't see what's really going on in my shop.

The job of the program is to provide Catharine with a systematic set of activities that will help her make the changes that she believes are necessary. These will be discussed later in this chapter, but it is through the partnership between Catharine and the program that she has seen the problems, and the partnership will help her find solutions to those problems.

The combination of expertise on the part of the individual about himself or herself and the expertise of the program about the data is critical in a 360-degree development program.

Let's look in on more of Rachel's thoughts about the self-management model of feedback:

> The way I see this session is that we're going to put together two sets of expertise. I've been working with these kinds of data for about fifteen years, and if I do say so, I believe I've got a good deal of expertise on what all these numbers mean and how they all fit together. So, let's think about this as a combination of knowledge, because each of you has been living with yourself for anywhere from thirty-five to fifty-some years, and I know for a fact that you are an expert on yourself. Let's make sure we combine my expertise with your expertise to help you decide what you're going to do with these data. Remember, this is not something that I'm doing to you or for you. This is something we're doing together.

Already, Rachel has combined two of the three partners in the 360-degree development process: (1) the individual and the program with (2) the trainers representing the program. The third partner is, of course, the individual's organization, and this partner has already contributed by sending the individual to the program and by providing much of the data in the 360-degree instrument. There are further steps that all three partners must take, and these steps will be discussed throughout this chapter.

In the meantime, Catharine can help herself focus on her strengths and weaknesses by learning about other forms of feedback. This is a key element of any effective development program.

Peer Feedback

Another form of feedback to consider is peer feedback; Catharine and her fellow participants are introduced to this concept and activity early in the program.

The trainers talk to us about peer feedback. They hand out some cards, and the one I get has my name at the top and the names of two other people who are going to be my primary partners. It also lists seven other people, who are my "secondaries."

Catharine is about to learn how to receive feedback. Many of the exercises in a development program are a combination of tools: half skill-building exercises and half opportunities for additional feedback. It may also be said that seeking feedback is a skill. Catharine explains one of these exercises called Building Effective Teams.

We're given this problem to solve, and I've seen this type before, where first we come up with a solution on our own, and then we do a solution as a group. This particular exercise has to do with a blizzard. My group and I are stranded in a snowstorm, but we've managed to salvage fifteen items from our Jeep. These range from a knife, to a hubcap, to a cigarette lighter, to a map. So, we sit down individually and rank those items in terms of their importance to our survival. We work on it for about twenty minutes, and then we join up in groups of six and sit down to see if we can come up with a better rank order as a group. Here are some folks I haven't had a chance to work with yet this week. We're told we're being videotaped, so as we start to dig in as a group, we're all being prim and proper and raise our hands to talk; that lasts for all of three minutes.

We're suddenly very involved. This very simple and artificial exercise has certainly grabbed our interest. People are standing up and making lots of gestures, and they're pushing at each other, verbally, a little bit. They're not being ugly, but they are definitely pushing at one another. I think to myself, "You thought you knew how to run a meeting, but look here, this is a mess." Everybody's talking; nobody's listening, and so I try to get things organized and calmed down, and I seem to get them to slow down for a little while. I think I'll have to see what our staff meetings back home look like. I mean, are we like this there—doing this thing that I think we do so well?

We finally end up agreeing, although it seems like chaos to me. Yet, looking at the final results, we seem to have rearranged some items, and the list is now different from my original results, but it does make more sense to me now. We go back into the big group, and as we're scoring it, my fellow discussants and I start getting kind of excited because we see that our team is doing really, really well. By the time we get finished, I am aware that the team score has beaten my score by about fifteen points, and as we end up getting all our scores put up, lo and behold, I had the lowest score in the group, but we still beat everyone's individual score. So, let me rethink this chaos I saw. We ended up doing some really good things.

I guess we can say our team won. We're high-fiving one another. We sure are competitive, even when we're trying to be cooperative.

So, the next thing we do is watch the videotape of our group. I see people not paying attention, and yet as I really watch, there are some good things going on. Small things. Maybe it isn't the classic version of how a meeting should be run, and yet things really did start pulling together. Why did it really begin to work? One woman in our group observes that even though people are loud and pushy and all that, we aren't arguing for our own perspective necessarily. Everybody seems to be looking for the best answer rather than getting the group to accept their personal answer. That's different than back home sometimes. The trouble is, how do I get people to be honest about that? Rachel kept talking about how to get people to practice working together in a group. That's probably what she's talking about—organizations don't get a chance to practice. They're always in the game. Basketball teams practice, orchestras practice, choirs practice, all other teams practice, but not organizations.

I open up my learning journal and write, "How can I get my team to practice?" We work as a team really well, but maybe with a little practice, with a chance to push away from the game for a moment, we can do it even better.

When we break up into a group of about six we begin an exercise called Questions for Feedback, and I've got a chance to ask the group for some of their opinions of me. I reach down and pull out my report from the feedback instrument. I say to them, "Do you see me as one who is decisive?"

They sort of sit up at the table, and then look at me, and almost to a person they say, "No, we don't." They continue, "What we do see you doing is working with the group to come up with a decision. We don't see you coming up with the decision just by yourself, so we think that's a good thing."

"Thank you," I say.

We go around the table, and everyone gets a chance to get some feedback and answer some questions, and we get into doing that. Pretty soon, though, we're not following the rules of social etiquette, and people are beginning to be really honest about their perceptions. Not everything was positive. I mean a couple of times they said to me that they were bothered when I leaned back from the table and crossed my arms and sort of pulled away. I can remember doing that. I saw it on the videotape. When I was doing that I was being really thoughtful. I was just trying to think through something, and yet they perceived me as kind of turning off—as not helping the group.

So that made me think about what I do as a manager and as a team member. People can't read my mind; they can't see what I'm doing if I don't tell them or if we don't get a chance to talk about what our personal preferences are. This morning, Rachel was talking about the importance of communication as a two-way street: sending out an e-mail or a memo isn't really communicating, and now that's really been highlighted by this group. There has to be that two-way communication or people may misinterpret what I'm doing.

Once again, I pull out my learning journal and make a note of that. I'm not much into keeping a journal, but I sure have been using it a lot this week. These are things I'll need to think about when I get home.

Well, one of the trainers has to come down and knock on the door and get us out of that room. We were really into this feedback thing. It's exciting to be in an environment where people will be that straight with us. We were all straight with each other without having an ax to grind—no one's trying to get our jobs or make us look bad. Here we all are, a group of talented, bright folks truly communicating with each other.

It's becoming very clear to us that we don't get enough real feedback in our organizations, and when we're in an environment like this one, where we're receiving it and giving it on a regular basis, it makes us stop and think, "Yeah, feedback is essential."

Practicing New Behaviors

A good portion of a development program that enhances 360-degree feedback is the element that Catharine yearns for at home: practice. In particular, receiving feedback needs to be practiced, and a program should systematically provide several opportunities for participants to improve their performance in this area.

Many development programs use outdoor activities to teach the importance of team building and trust, much like Outward Bound programs do. Another component of these experiences, however, is the opportunity for participants to observe one another; after all, good feedback (and practice for this feedback) comes from good observations:

> Just before lunch the outdoor trainers come in, and we're all going to do some outdoor exercises. Well, this is perfect weather to go outside. A number of folks have done this kind of thing before, and they talk about Outward Bound, but these new outdoor trainers tell us the level of physical activity is going to be nothing more than light gardening. Who cares anyway? We're going to be outside.
>
> So we begin by thinking that this is going to be fun and games. It is fun, and it is games, but I am amazed at how we keep playing out the same characteristics. How the things we're good at, and the things we're not so good at, even when we think we're constantly trying to do something about them, keep coming up. The people who've received feedback that they interrupt, and who are bound and determined that they're not going to interrupt, are still interrupting. Those of us who talk too much are still talking too much, and those of us who don't talk enough are still not talking enough. I guess what they've been saying all along is, "Change is difficult," and they're right. So, how are we going to change these things about ourselves that we seem to want to change? I'll have to ask that a little later.
>
> What was it the trainers kept telling us about peer feedback? We're supposed to go back and re-read our notes on our partners. Well, I don't feel real strong about that. I mean, I've tried to keep real good notes on all my learning partners, but it's been a problem. I haven't always been in the same room with them, and sometimes at least one of them hasn't done much at all, so I haven't felt like I had much to write down. A couple of them I've got some good stuff on, but these outdoor activities, in particular, helped. It gave me a chance to confirm a lot of the things I'd been seeing, and yet I still feel a little uneasy about giving feedback.

The exercises in the program help Catharine practice many different types of skills, and these experiences and this practice culminate near the end of the program—in the peer feedback sessions:

> As we start off the morning, we're going to do peer feedback. When it's my turn to receive feedback, one of the participants says, "Do you remember that blizzard exercise we did? You asked us if we thought you were decisive. Well, when I was thinking about that, I decided there are two kinds of decision mak-

ing with a group—the foot-stomping fashion and the let's-work-this-out-to-gether fashion, and I think you prefer the latter type. And I'd have to say you're really good at that. I really liked the way you helped the group work together. The problem, though, was that we didn't really know how you felt about the subject. I mean, it seemed to me that you were holding back on us, and I really needed you to speak out clearly. I was hoping you were going to be more direct about your opinion, and even though I think the group, as a whole, worked well, I felt like we could've done a better job if you'd been more direct in the beginning."

When she finishes, I look over at the other people and almost all of them are nodding their heads, and so finally I nod my head too, and I say, "Thanks, Susan, now tell me more."

It is amazing how from simple stuff, good thoughts come. We talked for a while about how I appear to people, especially on the issue of decisiveness, and by the time we were done, I had a better grasp on the changes I needed to make when I went home. We filled a lot of pages in our learning journals in that session, and one of the things I wrote was, "It's good to tell people what you think," a statement that sounds obvious, but it meant a lot to me about decisiveness.

One-On-One Session

Another important feedback event is the one-on-one session.

Thursday morning it's a quiet ride because I think most everybody is feeling the same uneasiness that I'm feeling: today we have a one-on-one session with a feedback specialist. Even though the week has gone well, there's just something about today that feels different, and the trainers told us it would.

At the start of the morning, as one of the trainers is talking about the logistics and all that, twelve people walk into the room. They introduce themselves; some of them we'd met on Sunday, but there are a few new faces today. One of them, Linda, introduces herself and says she's going to be giving me and Roger feedback. As it turns out Roger is going first, which means I won't get my one-on-one session until this afternoon. So I'm going to do peer feedback now. . . .

At one o'clock Linda comes to get me, and we go to an office and sit down. She turns on the tape recorder. Tape recorder? She explains that the tape will be mine, that I don't have to take notes if I don't want to. Good idea.

She kind of gets into explaining what's going to happen. I joke a little about how this is my therapy session and ask whether I should lie down or not. Linda smiles and says that this is going to be a different kind of opportunity. It's not therapy. It's more like co-inquiry. She tells me she's been working with these kinds of data for about fifteen years, and she thinks she's got a good deal of expertise in what all the numbers from the instruments mean and how they all fit together. Her confidence and warmth make me feel better.

She tells me I've been living with me for forty-six years now. She got my birthday right. She says that I'm an expert on the subject of me. I appreciate her saying that, although at this point in the week I'm not so sure how true that is. She tells me this session is not something that she's doing for me or to me; it's something she's doing with me.

So what we're going to try to do is put together those two sets of expertise—hers and mine. As we're getting started she refers to the self-management model of feedback, and she reminds me of its three basic aspects: accuracy (Do I think the data are right?), value (How do I feel about the data?), and importance (How significant are the data to me?).

Then it's time to go to work. She has a lot of material that I want to see because I haven't been given all the instrument feedback yet. We certainly cover more ground than I ever thought was possible. I never remember three and one-half hours going so fast. I thought we would talk about the organization, and we do spend a fair amount of time on issues relating to that, but we end up spending a lot more time on personal things, such as the problems I'm having with my teenager.

She does a lot of talking, and I do a lot of talking, and I have to admit that although much of it was difficult, I really have a sense of comfort when it's over—the kind of ease that comes from not having to hide. It feels good knowing that I just spent time with somebody who accepts me the way I am and who still wants to help me figure out what to do to make the world more like the place I want it to be. We have come up with a list of seven things I want to invest serious energy in. This session is probably worth the whole price of admission.

The peer feedback sessions and the one-on-one session made a deep impression on Catharine, encouraging her to reevaluate her work as a manager and the way in which her co-workers view her work.

Essential Program Components

For a development program to enhance the benefits of the 360-degree feedback process, it should be relevant, generate commitment, allow for goal setting, be safe, be challenging, have a distraction-free environment, and be able to provide follow-up.

Relevance

The exercises, instruments, and trainers should all be focused on the most important elements of the participant's job. Through the exercises and feedback of the program, the participant should begin to see the contrast between what he or she is doing differently in the program and what he or she is doing back home. The experience of a participant thus acts as a catalyst for change, and this can be seen many ways in Catharine's case.

Probably one of Catharine's most important insights was the recognition of the problems between her and her boss. This first became evident in the 360-degree feedback session, but it was illustrated again and again as the week went on. As we'll come to see, by the end of the program Catharine will decide that working on this relationship is the most important thing she can do to make her work performance more effective.

Another experience of great relevance to Catharine is an exercise called The Hollow Square:

> I'm suddenly a volunteer. We're going to do another exercise, and this time I'm going to be the observer. About four of us are watching from the back of the room as the rest of the participants are split into two groups: the "planners" and the "implementers." The planners are doing something called The Hollow Square. In this exercise, the planners are given a problem to solve, and they've also got to come up with a list of instructions for the implementers to make it happen. As I'm watching them go through this I think, "Here they are making up all this stuff about what they presume is going to work, and meanwhile, the implementers are left in the dark. Why don't they include them in the discussion? I mean, all they've got to do is walk over there and knock on the door, and here they are making all this stuff up. That doesn't make any sense."
>
> Then I think, "That's just like when Sally and I were doing Roger's project back at work—we sat there and made all those decisions on our own, without

asking the people involved." I don't really want to admit it, but I'm doing this puzzle thing back at home all the time.

The four of us who observed the exercise got to debrief the others on what we saw. We sat at the end of the table, and I began by saying, "You people made a botch of the whole thing." They were taken aback by that, but instead of talking about what they did, I instead told them about how I'd botched almost the exact same thing at work. I said, "I didn't know it until I was watching you going through the exercise, but it's so apparent that we need to include other people, especially when they're the ones who are going to have to make the project happen." Everyone agreed with that, and a number of other people had similar stories about what they do at home. One of the other observers said, "It was so apparent to us that you needed to go get those other folks, but I think if I'd been in the middle of it, instead of observing, I'd have done the same thing. It's like, when we have a task in front of us, we completely ignore the other people involved."

That seems simple to all of us, but as one of the planners said later, "It's so profound about how we treat people in organizations."

Relevance in many ways can be measured by how the program relates to what the participants do at home. One question would be, Are these exercises meaningful to me? Another would be, Am I learning anything that I can use in my organization? Catharine's group certainly did—in this exercise and throughout the program.

Ultimately, the relevance of a program is measured by what the individual does when he or she goes home. This is why it is imperative that a development program emphasizes the importance of setting goals, and not only setting them but also following through on them. Participants in LDP are told on their arrival, "Friday [the last day] is the most important." Friday is all about taking the information from the rest of the program and placing it into a concrete form so that the individual can make needed changes when he or she returns home.

Making a Commitment

So far, Catharine has concentrated on her experiences at work, through the data in the 360-degree instrument and other forms of feedback, but commitment to change and goal setting, as with the rest of any effective development program, must be about the complete person. Here is Catharine's Friday experience:

Rachel is standing up and saying, "Remember, I told you that Friday will be the most important day of this program? Well, here it is, and the reason it's important is because today you're going to make some commitments about what you're going to change when you go home."

She tells us about a longitudinal study at Harvard, where those who left the school with some specific goals in mind, ten years later were making three times as much money as those who left without specific goals, and that those who had them written down were doing five times better.

Some of us want to argue about money being the measure of success, and Rachel nods her head in agreement, but says, "Do you get my point?"

We say, "Yes."

She heads off into giving us her philosophy on goal setting, and it has to do with that funny red button that she's been wearing all week on her name tag. She presents one to each of us, and we in turn put it on our name tags. There are four white dots on the button, and she starts describing what each one stands for, the first one being personal: we have to think about things we want to do for ourselves.

Personally, I want to lose fifteen pounds, but more important, I want to spend more time at home.

The second area is family. She defines family as those with whom we are connected by a bond of love. She asks us to make a list of those people in our lives, and so I do. When I'm finished, I realize it's bigger than I thought it would be. It's not just family, either. It's good friends. I like that.

I'd say, though, the goal for family that really sticks in my mind has to do with my seventeen-year-old son, whom I seem to feel more distant from every day. I have absolutely without a doubt got to do something about that. I want to spend more time with him. Maybe if I did that, he and I can figure out why we're always fighting.

The third area is our careers. Yeah, that's why we're all here, and that's what pays the bills. I guess one of the things I learned here is that my career is going pretty well. There are some things I need to do, and I think there are some things that will really make a difference. I mean, this decisiveness thing kept floating to the surface. My goal there is to talk to my boss about what we need to do to start seeing more eye-to-eye. We used to have a great working relationship, and I feel like it's been pulled apart and strained. Certainly, there were pieces on the back-home feedback showing that he and I don't seem to be seeing things the same anymore. I guess I'll say, "I'll go talk to my boss about this feedback." That's a goal.

The last area is our community, and this area I feel pretty good about, because last year I started getting involved with Habitat for Humanity, and I really get a sense of doing something important through my work with that organization.

So, we take about a half-hour to think about these four areas, and I could've taken a lot longer, because these things are really important to me. Rachel turns to the guy who's sitting to her left, near the head of the class, and says, "Well, why don't we just share one of the goals that we're working on? We don't have to share them all, just pick one of the things that you want to do."

So people start off, picking out one of the things they want to talk about. The first guy says he wants to work more efficiently in the office. By the time it gets to me, I've heard about six people say, "I want to spend more time at home." Or is that spend less time in the office? Is that the same thing? No, I guess not.

When it comes to me, I talk about how I resonate to that issue. For the last month my husband and I have been talking about how we haven't been doing the kinds of things that we used to do together as a family. I'm not sure if we've begun to do anything about it yet, but I think we're on the track to doing so, and during this week I've been thinking how I really need to get started.

I think, though, the one that's the toughest for me is the one with my boss. This is a man whom I've worked with for close to fifteen years. We have always had a good relationship, but I guess some time in the last four to seven years, I'm not sure when, things started to change. As I'm looking at the feedback from him, it's clear that he and I are looking at things very differently, and that came as a huge surprise to me this week. So, my goal is to talk to him about those issues.

We go around the room, and everyone shares one or two of their goals, and Rachel stands up and says, "The rainbow over this day reads, 'A goal without a plan is but a daydream.'"

She walks over to one of the early people who talked about spending some more time at home, and I'm glad it wasn't me, because she got right down in this guy's face and said, "You want to spend more time at home, eh? And how are you going to measure that? Who's going to help you do that? Who's not going to help you do that? Who's going to not want you to spend more time at home? When are you going to have it done? What resources are you going to use?"

She went around to about four or five people and asked very, very difficult questions around planning, and I suppose that's what goal setting is about—not just about setting them, it's doing something about them. I remember Rachel saying that she'd like us to leave with a list of specific behaviors so when we get home the first day we'll have some real steps to work on. She tells us, "When you pull open that desk drawer and see your goal report, I want you to have enough concreteness so you remember what's important, why it was so important, and how you're going to go about making those important things happen."

She asks us to divide up into small goal groups so that we can be, in her words, "good, hard, tough, and loving consultants" to one another. We need to ask the tough questions: the how, the who, the time, the resources, and particularly, who might not want us to do these things, so we can understand that not everybody at home is eagerly waiting for us to come home changed. One of the lines that I've heard over the past week is, "Any change in your behavior in a relationship requires a change in the behavior of the other person." That does make sense, because if I don't ask the same questions, the other person can't give me the same answers. So when I'm working on a change in a relationship, I really have to be inclusive in that change—everybody has to be involved. That's worthy of a note.

Well, four of us ended up eating lunch a lot together, and we found that we had some things in common around hobbies and work styles, so we get together now and go off and sit down. People are, not surprisingly, a little shy about saying, "Well, here's what I want to accomplish." I don't know if it's shyness or if there's something about not really wanting to make a commitment, because once you start talking about something in public, it makes it a little harder not to do it. The public statement of a goal is kind of like driving a stake into the ground.

So, one of the guys says, "I have a couple of goals that are important to me, but for one of them I just don't have the foggiest notion about what to do." He continues, "Yet I accept the value of it, and that is doing something in the community. I guess I feel so isolated out in my little suburbia that I don't feel much connected to my community."

Because this is the one area that I feel pretty good about, I speak up and tell him about my experience in doing volunteer work for Habitat for Humanity. I tell him, "Yeah, they need lots of different kinds of help—carpentry, obviously, but others things, too. I've got some fair writing skills, and I enjoy planning for renovation work around our house, so it just sort of made sense that this organization was a place where I could make a difference."

And he says, "Wow, my grandfather was a carpenter, and I learned a lot about the craft from him." So, he opens up his goal report and writes, "Volunteer for Habitat."

He's pretty happy about it, and he's just about to put it aside when I remember what Rachel said about being good, tough consultants, so I turn to him and I say, "Roger, when are you going to do this?"

He frowns and says, "What?" I say again, "When are you going to do this?"

He replies, "Well, when I get back I'll put some time aside . . ."

But I cut him off and say, "Roger, when?" He looks over at me, and in good humor hurls a curse at me, and then he pauses to think, and then he opens up his goal report again and writes, "Wednesday morning at 9 A.M.—Call Habitat for Humanity House." And I feel pretty good about that, and I think he does too.

Well, we go on and we are similarly brutal with one another around goals. It's almost with a gleeful brutality because we know this is really important. We are building some concrete steps for home. We feel pleasure in doing this—in each of us being unbridled consultants.

The problem that I'm really struggling with is with my boss. I say, "Let me show you all the problem." I take out my report from the feedback instrument, and I show them the graph where we've plotted the different perspectives, where I'd added my "self" scores to the list so they can see where I rated me as opposed to where my boss rated me. They say, "Ouch, that must be painful."

I say, "Yes, but you've also got to understand that this man is a good friend of mine." All their eyes roll to the ceiling. We start talking about what it's like to work for, and work with, friends. Probably the most important aspect of that relationship is communication. If in fact your boss used to be a peer, and you used to be real close, and she or he becomes your boss, then there's an extra problem to that. As they kind of talk and meander, it becomes clear to me that their concerns were right on, because when this person was promoted to being my boss, something else happened too: we got caught in a merger and he moved away, so the amount of time he and I spent together got less and less and less. Initially, I remember he and I said that was OK, because we had such a strong working relationship and understanding with one another, and so there wouldn't be a problem. It looks like I was wrong about that.

The group and I decide I need to call him immediately when I get back and schedule an informal meeting. How do I schedule an informal meeting? That's a good thought. He and I need to talk in general about my concerns, and probably move into a more formal meeting where we talk specifically about the feedback. And I've got to be prepared to go with the conversation as it comes up.

As we get a little closure on that, I wish I had more information on how to guarantee success, but it's very clear that there is no guarantee of success. The only thing I can guarantee is that he and I will have that conversation, and we will clarify the issues.

Finally, as we all start talking about spending more time at home, the thing that rushes out of my mouth before I even have the time to think is, "I've got to spend more time with my seventeen-year-old. As we've been going through the week and from time to time we've talked about our families and our children and all those sorts of things, I've thought how I really am concerned about Brian. As I'm sitting here, I'm almost afraid I'm going to lose him. He and I spend so little time together that we hardly talk, and I'm almost at a loss about what to do—so much at a loss that I don't think I've ever said this out loud before."

The others nod their heads at me, and then Roger leans over and he says, "Listen, you can't change history, but the thing you can do is reach out and start talking. It's in many ways a similar situation between you and your boss—you've got to start communicating," he says. "And, if you're really that concerned, as my wife and I were concerned about my daughter, Angela, you should think about using professional help. I know for a fact, in our situation, that was money and time well spent."

It was interesting when I brought that up, all the usual impersonality disappeared. Whenever someone shared something personal, the rest of us really circled the wagons, and we all had something to say, because it turned out that they all had stories like mine.

We did as requested and marked our calendars to make a telephone conference call. One of the others said, "You know, folks, that's why I work for the telephone company. I can make that happen; it's not a problem." We all nodded very appreciatively at his willingness to take on that task, and we all agreed that at 8 A.M. Eastern Standard Time on that date the phone would ring, and we will have blocked out at least an hour so that we can talk about how we are doing on our goals.

Goal Setting

The trainer is right: a goal without a plan is but a daydream, and one of the most important experiences for a participant in a good program is the goal-setting conclusion. The learning journal that Catharine refers to is a key element of this. During the course of the week, Catharine's notes have been crucial to what she will decide to do on the last day.

Catharine's most important goals are (1) to concentrate her energies at work to improving the relationship with her boss and (2) to reach out to her seventeen-year-old son.

Hold on a minute. That last one doesn't have anything to do with Catharine's performance at work. Wrong. This program is about a person's effectiveness in a number of important areas, and one of the most important is the career, but overall the program is about who the person is in any organization—business, family, and community. His or her effectiveness cannot be separated out among those elements of his or her life. If Catharine's relationship with her own son suffers because of a lack of communication and commitment, what can then be said of her relationships at work? As a manager, her job is all about relationships—with her boss, with her customers, with her subordinates, and with her peers. An effective development program allows participants to discover the ways in which they can improve their relationships, wherever those take place.

The learning exercises, the discussions, and the 360-degree feedback all contribute to the relevance of the program. In particular, the 360-degree instrument provides the data so that individuals can decide which aspects of their life are relevant for change and which are not. The goal setting and its follow-through are ultimately how the program should be measured in terms of effectiveness and relevance.

Four additional elements of an effective development program have been touched on in this chapter but have not yet been thoroughly discussed: safety, challenge, environment, and follow-up.

Safety

A key element in a development program that enhances the use of 360-degree feedback is a sense of safety—not only for the participant but also for the respondents to the instruments.

A 360-degree instrument can only be effective if the data are accurate, and in order for this to happen the program must provide for the anonymity of respondents. The accuracy of the "letters from home" is crucial, because it is based *entirely* on what the respondents said, and they will only be honest if the anonymity of their answers is carefully protected.

Another important aspect of safety is the confidentiality of the participant's data. The program, and the feedback that comes with it, is not about job assessment or salary considerations. It is about the development of the individual as a manager and as a person. The information shared during the week of a program is not, in any way, shape, or form, to be shared with the organization *except* by that individual, if he or she chooses to do so. This sharing of information by the manager, however, should be encouraged. It is a way for them to begin receiving new feedback in their workplace.

Another aspect of safety has to do with the impact of the 360-degree instrument. Participants are frequently blindsided by what they learn. That is, they get data that come as a complete surprise to them—the areas where they rated themselves high are rated low by their subordinates, peers, or boss. In a few areas, Catharine did get slam-dunked. Overall, on her "letters from home" she got very high marks, but she was totally unprepared for the data on decisiveness and hiring good staff. Some people take their data more personally than others, but overall, 360-degree feedback is potent information.

Trainers should be well aware of who is likely to be blindsided before it ever happens. The trainers have seen all the data on each participant beforehand, and they should know enough about the person to gauge his or her emotional reaction.

One way to lessen the impact of getting surprised, while not lessening the importance of the data, is for trainers in a program to go through the data with the participants. It is important not to leave participants alone with this powerful feedback. At least two trainers should be in the room for a group such as Catharine's (approximately twenty-four people): one to go through the data and one to keep an eye on reactions and answer questions. This is one of the safety releases for a 360-degree program. Another is created by the shared experience of the group. It is rare that any participant wouldn't feel slam-dunked on at least one item of his or her feedback. It's important for participants to discuss their data with one another, just as Catharine's group did at the lunch table. This is one of the added advantages of going through the data as a group—individuals can share stories, complaints, and emotions with one another.

Any effective program must be ready to deal honestly, professionally, and sometimes subtly with participant reactions to this incredibly potent feedback.

Challenge

One of the key statements made to participants on the first day of an LDP program is, "This is the kind of experience where the more you put into it, the more you're going to get out of it." This absolutely must be true for any development program.

Each of the modules of the LDP program—including assessment, 360-degree feedback, decision making, team building, and the outdoor activities—is designed to use both the individual skills of participants and the knowledge they are gaining during the course of the program.

Another statement made to participants on the first day is, "With your active involvement, you will leave here better prepared to build the kind of world you want to live in."

In order to build this kind of world, a participant like Catharine needs three important pieces. Initially, she must know what that world would look like; next, she must have the knowledge and skills to build it; and finally, she must have the motivation to carry on when there is little-to-no reinforcement.

Each activity in a development program should be a challenge to participants, both in competitive and cooperative ways, and the entire program should support and engage the vision of improvement in their career and personal life.

Distraction-Free Environment

Another ingredient of a development program that enhances 360-degree feedback is the environment, which provides for the resources and comfort of the participants.

Elements of the environment include the hotel room, transportation to and from the program, meals, and even the furniture, particularly the chairs in the classroom. These may seem to be of secondary importance to the rest of the program. They are not.

The participants are there to develop, not deal with inconveniences and discomforts. A good program has good feedback, it provides for safety, it is challenging, it has relevance, and it provides follow-up. These ingredients will all become secondary if participants are distracted by shoddy services and equipment. It does no good to have the best development program in the world if the participants are each thinking, "I'm still hungry, and what I ate wasn't very good anyway. And hey, I think my behind has fallen asleep in this darn chair."

Good food, transportation, hospitality, and equipment begin with a commitment on the part of the program to invest in comfortable and quality goods and services. Hospitality continues with a solid support staff who provide for minimum hassle with airplane tickets, hotel reservations, telephone and computer access, and other needs of today's business people.

If a development program does not prove to be either relevant or enjoyable for participants, it should be because the designers of the instruments, modules, or exercises were not successful and not because the participants didn't like the tuna salad, or the hotel beds, or the folding metal chairs.

Able to Provide Follow-Up

The final, and perhaps most crucial, element of a program that enhances 360-degree feedback is follow-up, both by the individual and the organization. In Catharine's case, she has begun this process herself by scheduling a meeting with her boss. This meeting to make the company aware of Catharine's goals and expectations should be matched with the boss's expectations and some shared goals that they and others can work on together. The insights into the organization that Catharine noted during the program week should also be discussed. An honest, concrete discussion about what resources are available for Catharine should take place soon after her return.

Other long-term developmental commitments are executive mentoring programs, developmental assignments, and especially the scheduling of additional 360-degree instrument testing. A 360-degree instrument acts as a snapshot—as a view of individuals where they are at a given time. Another 360-degree instrument given in twelve to eighteen months can give individuals a clear picture of where they are going with their goals and, additionally, more data on how their relationships within the company are improving.

That, after all, is the goal of a 360-degree instrument: knowledge that leads to improvement. Through feedback, individuals receive data that can help them recognize areas in their behavior that need improvement, and this recognition can be focused through the self-management model of feedback. A manager such as Catharine has to (1) accept that the feedback is accurate, (2) decide if the feedback is good or bad for him or her, and (3) conclude that these things are important—important enough to make a change over the long term. When the individual decides what changes need to be made, the next step is to decide *how* these changes will be made. The follow-up to the program must include concrete goals and a solid commitment to achieve them.

Chapter Nine in this book deals specifically with follow-up to 360-degree feedback as part of the process of assessing change.

Conclusion

It is important here to restate something that Rachel, the trainer, explained about the self-management model of feedback. "This is not something we're doing to you or for you. This is something we're doing together." A good program allows, and in fact encourages, participants to have a very active role in their own development.

Catharine's active involvement began when she reviewed her data from the 360-degree instrument, and the specific data that jumped out at her had to do with decisiveness. She rated herself high, whereas others rated her low. It was important for her to note as she went through the data that the majority of discrepancies between herself and her boss were much greater than the discrepancies between herself and her peers and subordinates. This information allows her to focus on problem areas and problem relationships.

Beginning with the feedback instrument and continuing throughout the week, it became clear to Catharine that the working and personal relationship between her and her boss had deteriorated over the course of many years. There are always differences between how two individuals see a particular situation or goal, but by providing Catharine with these data, the program allows her a tool and a perspective on the relationship with her boss. Clearly, only Catharine can assess the magnitude of the problem. She should have a good grasp on what works best for her, and by matching this knowledge with an effective, research-based, 360-degree instrument and program, a process for improvement can be created.

Also, by including normative information, a chance for comparison with how other managers at her level have scored, Catharine can better understand exactly how relevant her own scores are.

In many ways, Catharine is a typical participant in a development program. She does a lot of things well and has a few blind spots. The 360-degree instrument can act as a mirror for the participant to see how others see him or her. The job of the program is to provide the tools for people like Catharine to make improvements where they feel they should.

Another important aspect of feedback in programs is the giving of feedback. Catharine did this for most of the week, but it was most clearly revealed in the peer feedback session. It is important to return to the classroom scene where the trainer asked, "How many of you are concerned about what you're going to hear?"

No one was.

However, she also asked, "How many of you are concerned about what you're going to say?"

At this point almost everyone raised their hand.

We all seek feedback from the people around us, and yet most people don't give enough. This makes for an unequal equation: demand far outstrips supply, and yet the supply is really there. A goal of a development program should be to show individuals the absolute necessity in giving good feedback to their subordinates, their peers, and their boss. When a program gives participants the chance to practice giving feedback, as Catharine did in The Hollow Square exercise and the peer feedback sessions, their relationships with their co-workers back home will be more effective.

A development program that enhances 360-degree feedback should itself be a 360 process. It should provide many and varied forms of feedback, and it should help participants discover where they can find additional feedback from their peers, their subordinates, their boss, as well as in other relationships. Finally, one of the most vital outcomes of such a development program is the value that individuals place on giving feedback when they return home. This is one of their most important responsibilities as managers and as human beings.

The most dynamic combination for the continued improvement and development of an individual encompasses three elements: (1) an effective 360-degree feedback instrument, (2) a well-designed 360-degree development program, and (3) an active participation on the part of the individual and the organization. If all three of these elements are present, then managers—or any individuals for that matter—will be able to use their new tools to achieve their personal goals of improving their world, their organization, and their relationships.

This chapter has shown you how a development program increases the value of 360-degree feedback through a set of systematic, programmatic experiences. The next four chapters will switch the focus from the value of 360-degree feedback for individual development to its value for organizational development. This will include looking at some of the more innovative and better practices, the forces that affect these practices, what happens when customers are involved, and ways organizations can systematically become learning cultures.

Notes

1. I wish to express my deep thanks to Tom Kealey, without whose patient and expert help this chapter would never have made it from my head to this paper.
2. Of course, LDP is not the only program that supports 360-degree feedback. There are such programs in nonprofit organizations, universities, and even internal development departments. These may be open-enrollment or customized for people in the same organization or intact work group. They use a variety of development techniques. I am using LDP because it is the program I know best.

Part Two

Maximizing the Value of 360-Degree Feedback for Organizational Development

Best Practices

Five Rationales for Using 360-Degree Feedback in Organizations

Maxine A. Dalton

The organizational value of 360-degree feedback has two closely related but distinct dimensions. One is a by-product of individual value, that is, when the performance of individual managers is improved, it is generally assumed that the organization will be better off. The first section of this book focuses on individual value.

The second section will focus more explicitly on the other dimension—the value that 360-degree feedback provides directly to organizations and their development. As readers know by now, the use of 360-degree feedback instruments in organizations has exploded during the past ten to fifteen years. In fact, it is difficult to find a Fortune 1000 company in the United States that has not tried a 360-degree assessment somewhere in the organization at least once. There are a variety of reasons for initiating this practice, and the reasons—couched as a statement of purpose or a set of expectations—suggest whether the practice will succeed or fail. If the reason for using 360-degree feedback is clear, business-driven, and tied to conditions under which an individual is likely to be able to accept and use the feedback, then the activity will probably be successful. If the reasons are vague and event-driven, or if the feedback is threatening or thoughtless, then the 360-feedback practice will probably be unsuccessful. In the latter case the outcomes are likely to be worse than wasted time and money. The real loss may be the credibility of human resources development

(HRD), which may be coupled with cynicism toward future human resources initiatives.

What reasons do organizations have for launching a 360-degree feedback process? Are they good reasons? This chapter will present a discussion, with examples, of five commonly offered rationales for the use of 360-degree feedback. It will end with a summary of the lessons that can be drawn from the examples about what leads to a successful organizational intervention and what leads to an unsuccessful one.

Rationale 1: Addressing the Needs of Strategically Important Populations

In spite of the background noise about individuals taking charge of their own careers and their own development, most major organizations still believe it is important to do succession planning—to identify and prepare individuals who will be ready to lead the business at some future time (see Eastman, 1995, for an overview of the topic of succession planning). Core to most succession-planning programs is the identification and development of high-potential employees who will provide continuity and bench strength to the organization. Organizations then take an active role in designing programs of feedback and development for these strategically important employees.

To most such high-potential programs, 360-degree feedback is integral. After an individual is designated as high-potential, 360-degree feedback is often the first step in a process of intentional development planning. The feedback provides the individual with baseline information about his or her perceived impact from a variety of organizational perspectives.

The multiple perspectives are important, as the immediate boss may be assumed to be pleased with the high-potential person's past performance or that person would not have received such a designation in the first place. The person may already know what the boss thinks. But it is possible for a young manager who has received glowing reviews from a boss to be shocked to find that subordinates think she is a bully and peers consider her to be uncooperative and overly ambitious.

Managers early in their careers may be able to respond to this kind of feedback and change others' perceptions, whereas they may not be able to do that after years of building a reputation for being a certain way. Additionally, 360-degree feedback for the high-potential person can provide the perspective of the boss's boss, which often represents the reality of the organization at a different level of scope and complexity than the high-potential candidate is accustomed to.

In high-potential development programs, the 360-degree feedback results are used to form the basis for a development plan. Typically included in the plan are opportunities to engage in specific kinds of challenging assignments; to be exposed to experts, coaches, and role models; to experience a feedback-rich environment; and to do course work (Dalton and Hollenbeck, 1996; McCauley, Ruderman, Ohlott, and Morrow, 1994; Seibert, Hall, and Kram, 1995).

This development plan is shared with the organization; typically, the immediate boss sees it, and it is often seen by others—for instance, peers and members of the executive development committee. The organization uses such plans to make assignments and allocate development dollars.

An individual plan can also be employed as a monitoring tool to establish accountability for the high-potential and the high-potential's boss. For example, consider a person who, in order to become a better speaker, commits to attending Toastmasters, taping all of his or her speeches in the next fiscal year and soliciting feedback on the tapes from his or her boss and others. The high-potential is then accountable for doing these things, and the boss is accountable for providing the time and money for the person to attend, for giving the person the time to review the taped speeches, and for critiquing them. Though neither can guarantee that the high-potential will become a better speaker, both he or she and the boss are held accountable for the learning efforts and the activities described in the plan.

The plan becomes a road map by which to measure progress. It becomes a tool to show individuals how management and leadership skills are learned from the work itself. When these programs are done well, the skills measured by the 360-degree feedback baseline survey are driven by anticipated business needs and conditions. Furthermore, the managers of high-potential people are equipped to support the process, and the process is continuously evaluated so that program designers can see whether individuals are changing as a result of the intervention. They can also find out whether those on the high-potential list are ultimately being chosen for senior-level positions because of their participation in the organizationally sponsored program.

In successful high-potential programs, very senior management will be active in the high-potential selection process and in supporting the steps recommended in the development plan. The 360-degree feedback is usually confidential (it is seen only by the individual receiving the feedback and the individual giving the feedback), but the plan is developed jointly by the high-potential employee, the boss, and the HRD specialist. A review of progress against plan may become an integral part of the succession-planning process, and 360-degree feedback may be readministered to the high-potential person over time as one of the ongoing feedback mechanisms (Eastman, 1995).

One of the best examples of such a focused process for high-potential employees is an intensive coaching program designed by a major U.S. food producer. Each year, fifty high-potential people in this company of forty thousand are nominated by their managers to take part in the program. At the same time, fifty internal people, primarily but not exclusively HR professionals, are chosen to be coaches. These coaches are trained in the use of a 360-degree feedback tool; they are also trained in how to give feedback, how to coach, and how to help an individual design an assignment-based development plan. Coaches are assigned to high-potential employees, who can veto the choice if they feel that this particular coach might provide a threat to their privacy. Coaches have the candidate complete the feedback instrument; they also conduct extensive interviews with the candidate and the person's boss to add flesh to the bones of the hard data provided by the 360-degree instrument. Interview results and test results are fed back to the high-potential candidate in a series of meetings; the coach and the candidate work together to write a development plan. This plan is designed to capitalize on the developmental opportunities and business needs current in the business. The coach and the employee then hold a three-way meeting with the employee's boss to refine the plan and to seek commitment from the boss to the plan. When agreement has been reached on the plan, implementation is passed off to the new partnership: the high-potential employee and his or her boss. Evaluation data of this program over a three-year period show a high level of participant satisfaction. Seventy-four percent of the participants reported that the program was either very high or high in usefulness, and 50 percent cited the 360-degree feedback process itself as the most useful element of the program. Of course, the real test is whether individuals develop the skills that have been identified as important and whether the organization draws from this pool of prepared, high-potential employees to fill senior positions as they come open.

Clearly, this is an example of a 360-degree feedback program that is thoughtful, intense, and tied to the business. It also distributes the responsibility and accountability for the success of the program between the human resources department, the coach, the individual, and his or her boss. Parenthetically, it illustrates an exemplary effort and is not representative of many high-potential programs, which seem to conclude when the list of high-potentials is complete and safely hidden away in a three-ring binder until it is time to begin the exercise again the next year. It is an example of an organization choosing to cast a small net with a concentration of resources to serve a strategic purpose. The hole in the program may be the line manager who—in this program—does not receive training in how to be a coach once the process is turned over to him or her. One of the factors in determining whether an individual will follow up with a development plan is the response of the boss to the plan and to the proposed effort. The boss's understanding of his or her role, the boss's skill in carrying out the role, and the organizational reward system for the boss's participation or lack thereof are key to the success of any developmental process that is built around a 360-degree feedback survey (Dalton and Hollenbeck, 1996).

Rationale 2: Take Charge of Your Own Career

The popular press continues to tell us that a new employment contract is changing the nature of careers in organizations. Individuals are being advised to look to themselves, not the organization, to plan, shepherd, and nurture their own career growth. Individuals must develop, maintain, and constantly upgrade a portfolio of skills to remain employable. (See Chapter Four for additional discussion of the new employment contract.)

However, organizations are realizing that, changing employment contracts notwithstanding, the organization still has a role to play in employee career development. To recruit and retain good people, organizations must at a minimum provide employees with the opportunity to engage in experiences that support development. If organizations can no longer solicit long-term loyalty, they at least must try to engender commitment to the work.

Some organizations have responded by providing do-it-yourself development programs. Individuals are given access to 360-degree feedback tools—either PC-based or paper-and-pencil—that they may use to gather information about themselves. The package of tools may include information about how to use the instruments, exercises to analyze the results, and guides to help individuals determine how certain skills are best developed (for example, people with a low score on X should try Y). Individuals decide for themselves whether they wish to use these tools and whether they want to act on the 360-degree feedback results. The feedback is not facilitated by an internal or external professional but is carried out by the individual.

This type of process challenges many of the assumptions held by HRD professionals and social scientists. Those in the field of HRD have typically been trained in one of the social sciences and influenced to some extent by the knowledge base and practices of the counseling field. We include *facilitator* and *counselor* as part of our role definition. We think individuals can usually accept negative feedback better and make better use of it when a skilled, objective facilitator is available to help them make sense of it. Additionally, assessment feedback was traditionally the domain of psychology, and psychology has couched the assessment-and-feedback process in a strongly held tradition of standards and practices. Emanating from the influence of counseling and psychology, many organizations and many feedback givers believe they have some responsibility for helping a person who receives a particularly negative and unexpected feedback report. There is concern about the one or two out of a thousand who may become overly insecure or inappropriately hostile or may turn their anger inward and harm themselves. Some HRD professionals feel responsible for knowing what the data look like in advance, helping the individual cope with it, and being able to refer the individual to a professional psychologist or the company employee assistance program if necessary.

And finally, most HRD professionals like facilitating the 360-degree feedback process because it allows them to play a significant value-added role in the development of both individuals and the organization.

Given this context, feedback going directly to the individual without the presence of a trained facilitator is a practice that goes against the grain of many practitioners (including this author). For that reason, this practice should be investigated as intentionally and objectively as possible.

I will illustrate with an example. In one very successful high-tech organization, the 360-degree feedback process is made available as a do-it-yourself and company-hands-off activity because a senior HRD professional believes that to *require* the process to be part of a facilitated intervention or workshop is to treat highly competent adults like children—that doing so fosters dependency. The argument is that if individuals can read a financial report or write a complicated computer program, they can certainly make sense of their own feedback reports.

In this company, employees who want to receive 360-degree feedback can call a vendor previously selected by the company and have the 360 materials sent; these can be distributed to whomever the employees choose. The materials are returned to the vendor for scoring, and within a few days the feedback reports are in the mail. If employees want to purchase further services from the vendor—for example, to receive help in understanding the report, writing a development plan, facilitating a follow-up discussion with their boss, or setting up a long-term coaching relationship—they can contract for that service with the vendor. The employees may do as much or as little with the 360-degree feedback report as they wish. The employees pay for this service themselves—the feedback survey as well as any follow-up that they wish to purchase.

The HRD specialist who created this system reports high use levels and employee satisfaction with the system. Employees are not reporting any difficulty understanding what the data mean, and the system is tied into the company's confidential employee assistance program in case anyone feels emotionally overwhelmed by the data. The designer of this system does not believe that it precludes strategically driven organizational interventions as described in the first example. This employee-initiated process is simply part of the cultural context of the organization—a service that is available for anyone who wants it.

I am providing a second example of a hands-off intervention because the motivation for its design is quite different; the organization described next has added some steps to the process. In this organizational culture, the value is on egalitarian processes and access. Their philosophy of development is to provide 360-degree feedback and support for development to the greatest possible number of people. However, the organization is constrained by the amount of money it can spend on this very inclusive feedback-and-development process. Because it chooses to cast a wide net, the organization is offering self-directed workbooks and PC-based access to 360 tools rather than a more intense one-on-one intervention that is only available to a small, targeted group of people. The initiation, interpretation, and implementation of the 360-degree feedback process is completely in the hands of the employee, but the organization provides managers with training on how to coach and assist individuals who come to them with development plans.

The experienced HRD professional in this organization—a large company with a small HRD group—also recruited a training advisory board made up of senior people who report directly to the president. The existence of this board is symbolic of the value that the organization places on the feedback-and-development process. Also, the board was instrumental in designing the confidential, self-initiated 360-degree feedback process by building it on a Lotus Notebook platform. The program was designed for easy access and processing—a problem with some paper-and-pencil administrations.

Having senior management involved in the design of the process helped ensure that it would be tied to the needs of the business. Having senior management support allowed the HRD specialist to fend off some demands within the organization to make this process mandatory and use it for appraisal purposes. She felt that using the system in this way would destroy the intent—to create a broad-based and accessible developmental environment—and the training advisory board supported her. Also unique to this company is a full day of training for all employees on how to use the system and how to give day-to-day performance and developmental feedback. This training ensures equal access across the organization and probably increases interest in the process.

Because all employees understand that 10 percent to 20 percent of their pay is based on developmental effort, there has been wide use of the system; employees are voluntarily bringing the results of their feedback reports into performance management discussions.

The key here is that the system is supported by senior management. Development is incorporated into the incentive system, but it is still a process within the individual's control. To quote the program designer, "Nothing is required. The learning options are the employees. If the employees choose not to improve, that is their choice and the consequences are theirs as well." The organization has provided a broad-based opportunity for all individuals who want to use it.

It is too soon to know if these hands-off programs will produce the desired results. Evaluation of more conventional 360-degree feedback programs highlights the role of the boss in responding to an individual's developmental effort and the shared accountability for learning as key factors in predicting whether individuals will benefit from the process (Hazucha, Hezlett, and Schneider, 1993). The utility of a hands-off, do-it-yourself process may be low if there is no organizational expectation that the 360-degree feedback will lead to the writing of a development plan that will be shared with the boss.

However, individual readiness is important to the success of a 360-degree feedback intervention (McCauley and Hughes-James, 1994). This suggests that a do-it-yourself process requires motivation and readiness to respond to the feedback with a plan for personal change.

Finally, a few organizations have added radical and powerful incentives to these hands-off processes by dismantling the training department and making the former training budget available to individuals on a case-by-case basis. Those who approach their management with a worthwhile development plan built around their 360-degree feedback experience may apply for a portion of this money to fund a special developmental activity.

To summarize the differences between these two ways 360-degree feedback is used in organizations: in the do-it-yourself program the company chose to make 360-degree feedback available to every employee, not just a select few; the company relies heavily on the motivation of the individual employee to follow through. Organizational incentives and support may or may not be part of the process. Impact is hard to measure, but one organization with such a system reports that only 12 percent of those eligible to use an online system of 360-degree feedback and development planning had even called the materials up on their screens. In contrast, the smaller, more focused high-potential program reaches fewer people and requires more resources but has the opportunity to gather better evaluation data and to ensure greater certainty of outcome.

The trade-off seems to be the numbers reached versus the certainty and focus of the outcomes. Either strategy seems appropriate if it is thought out and purposeful and if there is a process in place to evaluate outcomes.

Although the philosophy of recognizing employees as adults, providing them with access to the tools, and leaving them alone has some appeal, the notion that individuals will be moved to seek feedback and change in a fast-paced, overloaded work environment that either does not support or is at best neutral to such behavior may be somewhat unrealistic. Those most in need of feedback would probably be least likely to seek it, and those already evidencing such inclinations to learn from experience (McCall and Spreitzer, 1993) will be doing it anyway. Conversely, the examples of hands-off interventions are creative, innovative, and thoughtful and need to be monitored for results.

Rationale 3: Bring Everyone up to the Standard

In some organizations all individuals who reach a certain level are given a basic supervisory or management-skills program. These programs are meant to ensure that every supervisor and manager has the basic skills to do his or her job and knows what is expected. Some of these programs are minimalist in their offering—a one-day group activity that includes feedback from a 360-degree feedback instrument. Others are more elaborate and include assistance in the design and implementation of a development plan and an intentional connection to the ongoing work of the organization. In some organizations, the skill set that is measured by the 360 process is embedded in the performance appraisal process. The practice of using 360-degree feedback for appraisal remains very controversial (Bracken, Dalton, Jako, McCauley, and Pollman, 1997).

The argument for making the 360-degree feedback process part of the performance appraisal process is that, unlike the high-potential program in which individuals receive feedback about skills they need to learn for the future, in the appraisal process supervisors and managers receive evaluative feedback about the performance of skills that are part of their current job. Using 360-degree feedback for appraisal has two implications for the process: (1) the immediate boss will see the results; they will not be confidential, and (2) the individual will be rewarded or punished (salary increases, promotions, and so on) based on the results.

The arguments for using 360-degree feedback for evaluation are that (1) the appraisal process should be just as comprehensive as the development process and that (2) individuals should be rewarded for having skills that the organization values, as seen from multiple perspectives. Proponents for using 360-degree feedback for appraisal believe that the data are only useful if they are shared with the supervisor and if they end in a development plan that is tied to results, as well as to subsequent organizational rewards and punishments. Some proponents of using 360-degree feedback for appraisal believe that bosses cannot make people change if they don't know what the individual's feedback report looks like and that without the boss's input into the process the individual may choose the "wrong" thing to work on. Proponents of using 360-degree feedback for appraisal argue that continuing to allow only the voice of the boss to be heard in the appraisal process perpetuates a rigid and autocratic culture (C. D. McCauley, personal communication, 1997). This is viewed as particularly inappropriate in the flatter, team-based organization that is emerging as the structure of choice in many organizations. Work is transitioning to team-based, flatter structures, increased numbers of peers, and reliance on shared understandings; communication is virtually a product today. Insulating the feedback process from the operational currency of the organization and keeping results secret from the manager symbolizes a contradictory philosophy. Team members and leaders need to know each other's strengths as well as weaknesses in order to capitalize on the group's collective talent and knowledge. Isolating 360-degree feedback as an anonymous measurement, devoid of any visible link to operations, denies team members the opportunity to fully leverage their team's potential (Bracken and others, 1997). Further, the argument is made that the appraisal process is improved when data are provided by colleagues and subordinates, not just the boss.

Conversely, using 360-degree feedback as part of the appraisal process represents naiveté to issues of hierarchy, status, and retribution and violates the condition of psychological safety that is necessary for a person to receive dissonant information about the self (Bracken and others, 1997; Dalton, 1996). It is extremely stressful for individuals to receive information about themselves that is discrepant from their self-image. The greater the level of discrepancy, the greater the stress and the more likely the individual will be to defend against the information; and so the defense mechanisms of denial, projection, and so on may kick in. To have feedback shared with the supervisor, who may or may not be skillful at processing the feedback with the subordinate, and to tie the results to pay and promotion, increases the stress and the likelihood of triggering the defenses that interfere with the individual receiving benefit from the feedback.

As to the other arguments offered by proponents of using 360-degree feedback for appraisal, individuals only attempt to change what they are ready to change, and it is possible to tie desired development goals to real and accountable outcomes without having feedback be part of an appraisal process.

Finally, using 360 surveys for appraisal ignores the fact that subordinates and peers may be unwilling to give accurate feedback when they believe it will be used for administrative purposes (pay, promotion, and so forth). Raters say they would change the scores they gave if they thought the feedback results were to be used for administrative purposes (London and Smither, 1995). There is additional empirical support for this argument in the literature (Farh, Cannella, and Bedeian, 1991; Hazucha, Szymanski, and Birkeland, 1992), but this issue is far from resolved, and the defining studies have not been done.

An example of this—using 360-degree feedback as part of the appraisal process—is provided by a small consulting firm that regularly asks employees to solicit feedback from bosses, peers, and subordinates as part of the annual appraisal process. In this case the

360-degree feedback process is not a paper-and-pencil or stylized format; instead, individuals solicit feedback from the appropriate stakeholders by e-mail, and respondents may send their comments to the individual or, in confidence, to the individual's boss.

In this organization the appraisal process is separated from the annual salary review, which is tied (in theory) only to the achievement of yearly goals. Although no formal evaluation of this system exists, the results appear to be mixed. Direct reports are less likely to respond to the request for feedback data than colleagues. In some cases, collaborative work relationships have been disrupted because of information shared with a boss by a work colleague. In other cases, individuals have reported receiving dissonant but helpful feedback from colleagues. Because this process is a relatively voluntary activity, it seems to be benign.

In other organizations, the 360-degree feedback appraisal process has violated the basic condition necessary for an individual to be able to accept dissonant information about self—the condition of psychological safety discussed at the beginning of this chapter—and the process has been abandoned as destructive and unproductive.

Organizations known to this author that have successfully integrated 360-degree feedback processes into their appraisal systems have done it as part of a larger initiative in which team formation and team building occurred before the process was introduced. The integration of 360 appraisal for one small team occurred as a step in the maturing of the organization; in that culture, learning had become a valued norm. The HRD professional worked for a year with senior managers to help them become a cohesive team; 360-degree feedback gave individuals in the team a way to help them understand the impact of their own behaviors on the team. At the end of the year, the members of the team asked to have the feedback data made public within the team and asked to have it rolled into measures of their effectiveness as a team and as individuals within the team.

Timmreck and Bracken (1997) have reported on a survey of twenty-three organizations who are members of the Upward Feedback Forum and their use of 360-degree feedback for appraisal. They found that of fifteen organizations that had previously reported their intention to use 360 for appraisal purposes, seven had ceased to do so. The reasons for stopping the practice included re-design of the process, negative employee reaction, and inflated ratings that did not discriminate among employees. Six organizations that had reported earlier that they were moving toward using 360 for appraisal had changed their minds for a variety of reasons, including legal concerns, budget cuts, and the removal of merit pay from the system. The main conclusion reached by Timmreck and Bracken is that there is not much systematic comparison of the 360 process as it is used for appraisal and as it is used for development, so it is hard to know the conditions under which either works best.

HRD professionals who are considering using 360 assessment as an appraisal tool should take the opportunity to do some experimentation on the credibility of the process. For example, the instrument could be introduced simultaneously at several geographically dispersed locations. In some locations the process could be confidential; in others it could be used for appraisal purposes. A look at the variances and mean score differences in these locations by rater group should give some indication as to the veridicality of the data when they are used for appraisal purposes.

The Upward Feedback Forum, a consortium of organizations using 360 for upward feedback, have joined together to share and discuss their experiences and to learn from the process (Timmreck and Bracken, 1997). Timmreck and Bracken, Forum founders, offer the following guidelines for instituting 360-degree feedback as an appraisal strategy:

1. Ensure that sponsors have clear expectations for the process.
2. Ensure that sponsors have a clear understanding of the implications of their process design decisions.
3. Use pilot groups.
4. Train raters and ratees.
5. Train managers who will use the data for decisions.
6. Hold raters accountable for their input.
7. Involve raters in feedback and action planning.
8. Hold ratees accountable for feedback and action planning.
9. Implement follow-up processes to ensure compliance.
10. Provide adequate resources for coaching, counseling, and skill development.

It is hoped that the continuing experience and learning of those in the Upward Feedback Forum using 360-degree feedback for appraisal will, in time, inform the field and influence practice.

At the very least, if 360-degree feedback is to be used for appraisal, it should be done at the end of a careful series of interventions designed to build trust in the organization, not as a punitive mandate. Individuals need to see that they will not be punished for giving honest ratings, and they need to see that individuals who receive low scores will have time to correct them. They also need to see a payoff for high scores.

Rationale 4: 360-Degree Feedback as a Tool to Change the Culture

As will be discussed at the conceptual level in Chapter Four, 360-degree feedback is used in some organizations as a strategy to communicate to employees that new skills will be needed to effectively implement a new business strategy or direction. A company may be moving into new markets as, for example, they become international. It may be attempting to instill more collaborative and interdependent work-flow processes in order to become more responsive to internal and external information, that is, to become a continuous learning organization. It may be attempting to reposition itself in the market, for example, recognizing that it is not really in the business of developing hardware but rather in the business of helping its customers solve their information-processing problems—convincing its hard-core engineers that they must become customer-oriented problem solvers. The feedback process may be used to call out for the employees the new direction, the behaviors that will be needed to implement the strategy and provide a common language for the culture change across groups.

For example, a major manufacturing organization had been successful for years as the sole provider of a particular product. Successful employees were highly technical individual contributors who eschewed what they called the soft stuff as silly and trivial. When they were finally faced with competition in the marketplace, this organization started to lose business to competitors who had the interpersonal skills and consulting skills to listen to their customers and differentiate their products in the marketplace. A 360-degree feedback survey that encompassed the skills deemed necessary to respond to the competitive pressures was introduced with great fanfare, and an entire level of management received feedback on the tool—but nothing happened. On a day-to-day basis, individuals continued to evidence the skills of the highly technical engineer and eschew the skills of the interpersonally adept, customer-oriented consultant.

The second year, the HRD professional determined that no culture change had occurred because there was no developmental planning following the 360 event. The intervention was offered again, and all of the participants were required to complete an individual development plan and to share the plan with their bosses. Again, there was no real behavioral change in the majority of the employees.

The third year, the intervention was repeated, and the managers were provided with coaches to help them achieve their individual goals. It was during the evaluation of the third-year process that the "aha" experience occurred. One of the program designers recognized that the behaviors being measured and written about in the individual development plans were not required by the work itself and were not rewarded by the organization. After extensive consultation with senior management, a smaller group of senior managers was provided with the opportunity to receive 360-degree feedback on the requisite skills, but this time the development planning was done in the context of the work itself. Individuals were required to integrate their personal development goals into a critical work task that could not be accomplished without the cooperation of the whole group and the recognition of the needs of the customer. The president personally assigned the project, and the entire team was provided with access to a coach when the process issues started to overwhelm the desired group outcomes. The 360 process was integrated with a business-driven plan that reflected the new direction the organization needed to take. The culture change started to take hold.

The lesson in using 360-degree feedback as a cultural change intervention comes from architecture. Form follows function; 360-degree feedback may be announced as a vehicle to effect a change in the skill set needed by the organization. But unless the environment presses for the use of these new skills, the announcement will be ignored or quickly forgotten.

Rationale 5: The Norms Around the Giving and Receiving of Feedback Should Be Changed

Organizations resort to the use of 360-degree feedback because people in organizations do not talk to each other enough about the impact of their behavior on getting the work done in a more or less integrated and collaborative fashion; 360-degree feedback surveys substitute for what individuals cannot or will not tell each other. People don't tell for a variety of reasons—differences based on power and status, fear of retribution, hierarchical organizational structures, lack of skill, unwillingness to be accountable, and fear of hurting someone's feelings.

Ultimately, the goal behind the introduction of a 360-degree feedback process into the organization is to do away with the need for feedback surveys. When the process becomes part of a strategy demonstrating that 360-degree feedback is simply information and that information is essential to learning and growth, individuals will learn that they can talk to each other and give up the scannable bubble forms.

For example, one organization introduced access to 360-degree feedback on demand and also included questions about the feedback process in the annual climate survey. Within one year, climate scores increased on each of the following climate measures: (the feedback system) "encourages managers to give timely feedback," "encourages employees to ask for constructive feedback," "encourages managers to provide coaching to employees," "encourages managers to develop action plans for development." These findings suggest that, at least in one organization, the introduction of feedback surveys is starting to change the organizational norms around the giving and receiving of feedback in general.

Conclusion

Based on the reasons that organizations cite for adopting 360-degree feedback, the following summary of the practices that will maximize the value of the process can be offered.

1. *The intervention is business-driven.* The development process itself, of which the 360-degree feedback survey is a part, has a rationale that can be quickly explained and understood by anyone walking up to the 360-degree feedback sponsor in the hall and saying, "Why do I have to do this?" Drawing from the discussion in the body of the chapter, possible answers include, "We have no bench strength," "We are losing some of our best people," "We are changing our production processes," "We are losing our creative edge and our market share."

2. *The organization needs the behaviors that are being measured.* It is important to keep in mind that change is very difficult and that individuals receiving feedback need to be able to make a connection between the skill set embedded in the feedback tool and the work that needs to be done. Everyone loves a team, but there is no value in receiving feedback on team behaviors if the work does not lend itself to collaboration.

3. *The 360-degree survey instrument chosen to measure a set of behaviors must be reliable and valid* (see Chapters Seven and Eight). If the survey is not reliable, there is no consistency of measurement from time to time, and the survey is just words on paper. Scores are the result of ambiguous and poorly worded questions, not real descriptions of real behaviors. If an instrument is not valid, there is no evidence that it measures what it purports to measure. People ought not to be asked to change their behavior based on a measure of management or leadership effectiveness if there is no evidence that the behaviors measured are critical to management or leadership effectiveness.

4. *Conditions for learning the new skill set exist—that is, managers support development.* Effort toward learning is rewarded. Individuals are prepared to share their development goals, and others are prepared to give them ongoing and constructive feedback about their efforts toward goal achievement. The process of feedback is embedded in a system designed to leverage the feedback event; 360-degree feedback in an organization that is suspicious and punitive is a catalyst for further cynicism.

The practices that don't maximize, and in fact diminish, value should also be mentioned because a lot of money has been spent on 360-degree feedback programs that accomplished nothing.

When 360 interventions don't work, the primary reason is that they aren't tied to anything. They are not tied to business-driven developmental strategies. Proper conditions for accepting feedback and acting on it do not exist. Feedback givers are not credible or well trained. Feedback is provided under punitive, threatening, or embarrassing conditions. The organizational climate does not support learning—that is, providing opportunities for feedback and ongoing practice of new skills and behaviors within an environment where it is acceptable to say, "I don't know how."

The other gap in the practice of HRD is the systematic evaluation of the programs and processes that are built around 360-degree feedback. This is discussed more fully in Chapter Nine. HRD professionals using 360 instruments as a part of their practice should be looking for ways to anticipate and measure the desired outcomes, to inform their own work, and to share with one another. The 360-degree feedback process is a powerful tool that is in danger of being trivialized through thoughtless use.

The next chapter takes a closer look at the forces—both internal and external—that affect these practices, and it considers the ways these forces combine with the process of 360-degree feedback to promote successful organizational development.

Chapter Four

Forces That Affect the 360-Degree Feedback Process

Walter W. Tornow

The process of 360-degree feedback is profoundly affected by the forces of environmental trends—internal and external—that organizations are subject to. In this chapter, I will describe the primary forces that are at work, and I will take a close look at the ways, given these forces, that 360-degree feedback provides value to the organization. Throughout, I will use a case study to point out how this value can be maximized. I will begin by introducing the case.

Case Example

Let's call our case organization Bravo Data Corporation—BDC for short. The story starts with BDC, a large provider of electronic products and services, finding itself in need of major culture change and reinvention. Bravo Data Corporation grew successful on the basis of superior product technology in a market with little competition and a value system that promoted advanced engineering features above defect-free customer applications and user-friendliness. Later, the company began to experience an increasingly competitive market, and customers' interests shifted from engineering features to ease of use, and to quality and maintenance features. The corporation's top management recognized the need for strategic reorientation of the business and decided that a major organizational culture change was needed—one that embraced customer orientation and quality processes as core values.

78

Exhibit 4.1. Example Items and Format from BDC Managerial Behavior Inventory: A 360-Degree Feedback Instrument.

Instructions

As you complete this questionnaire, please note that each item is preceded by the question, "How satisfied are you with the way this manager . . ." Your response choices are HS=HIGHLY SATISFIED, S=SATISFIED, N=NEITHER SATISFIED nor DISSATISFIED, HD=HIGHLY DISSATISFIED, or NI=NO INFORMATION. Please indicate your response by circling your choice at the right of each item.

Consider this manager's effectiveness in the following items.

How satisfied are you with the way this manager . . .

	Highly Dissatisfied	Dissatisfied	Neither Satisfied nor Dissatisfied	Satisfied	Highly Satisfied	No Information
Serving Customers						
1. Creatively responds to customer needs	HD	D	N	S	HS	NI
2. Responds to customer needs in a timely manner	HD	D	N	S	HS	NI
3. Works to meet commitments that have been made to customers	HD	D	N	S	HS	NI
Processes Are the Problem, Not People						
4. Involves employees in decisions that affect their work	HD	D	N	S	HS	NI
5. Asks people what they need to do their work better	HD	D	N	S	HS	NI
6. Strives for continuous improvement in work processes	HD	D	N	S	HS	NI
Reward for Performance						
7. Gives consistently fair and objective performance feedback	HD	D	N	S	HS	NI
8. Effectively deals with performance problems	HD	D	N	S	HS	NI
9. Is willing to exit non-performers in a timely manner	HD	D	N	S	HS	NI

A 360-degree feedback system soon became a central design element in the culture change plan and a critical success factor for making it work. More specifically, the use of a 360-degree feedback system was seen as a key implementation vehicle for translating the desired core values into needed behavioral change. The implementation of the culture change started with the development of a reliable and valid 360-degree feedback instrument. Exhibit 4.1 shows selected parts of this instrument for illustration purposes. Here, we see three core values that the organization had identified—commitment to marketing, to quality, and to people. These were translated on the instrument into several more concrete categories of performance and specific illustrative behaviors. The categories in our example are (1) serving customers, (2) processes are the problem, not people, and (3) reward for performance. Each category shows three behavior statements for more specific definitional purposes. The 360-degree feedback instrument allowed the organization to operationalize the new core values. This was achieved through a series of focus groups that helped to define more specifically what behavioral expectations would exemplify the desired core values.

The resulting instrument was administered to all the managers in Bravo Data Corporation. Each of the managers received feedback anonymously from colleagues and employees on how well they were perceived to be adhering to the values and modeling the desired behaviors. This feedback process was confidential, meaning only the target manager saw the results. Further, the 360-degree feedback became part of a new leadership development program, designed to cascade the organizational culture change from the top of the organization throughout the various levels of management. Through this process, each manager was confronted with a "mirror," showing the gap between "walking the talk" vis-à-vis the espoused new core values.

Feedback generated from this 360-degree feedback process then served as a basis for both organizational and individual development planning and behavior change. Over a period of several years, the organization institutionalized this process. It integrated the 360-degree feedback system with the performance management and reward systems. This was done to further promote the realignment of management behaviors with the new core business values, along with supportive and integrated human resources systems. Also, every year, employee climate surveys were administered to monitor key indicators of employee and management satisfaction. This was done to determine whether the organization was making progress toward the organizational culture change goals, that is, whether management practices were indeed perceived to come more in line with stated organizational goals.

Forces Affecting 360-Degree Feedback

Important trends and transformations are taking place in our organizational landscape, and they have profound implications for the way we work and manage our work. In this context, we can better understand and, indeed, appreciate why 360-degree feedback systems have become so popular. Relevant to the focus of this chapter, 360-degree feedback adds value to organizations and their development because of the unique, facilitative role these systems can play vis-à-vis the following significant trends in organizations: moving from an inside-out to an outside-in orientation, the changing nature of work, and the changing role of management and leadership.

Moving from an Inside-Out to an Outside-In Orientation

Everyone has a customer. This well-known mantra serves to guide attitudes and behaviors of organizations, functions, and individual employees alike. It ensures an awareness that (1) we cannot act independently because, usually, multiple constituencies or parties have a relationship with the product or service provided, and (2) these multiple constituencies need to have a voice about the standards and expectations regarding what satisfactory performance is.

This means that either as organizations, as functions, or as individuals, we can no longer afford the luxury of having an inside-out orientation, driven solely by our own ideas of what needs to be done and what is satisfactory. Instead, we—organizations, functions, and individuals alike—need to become more outside-in or other-oriented by better understanding the needs of those around us. In short, we need to be connected. Organizational priorities need to be driven by their market and the competitive environment; departments must realize the need to integrate across functions to avoid "stovepipe" mind-sets; and individuals need to understand their impact on others with whom they have a working relationship.

Systems of 360-degree feedback can create an environment for connectivity that promotes access to feedback from key constituencies. Such connectivity through 360-degree feedback becomes an important competitive advantage for organizations in adapting to an outside-in trend. Therefore, 360-degree feedback becomes a strategic organizational development tool because of the vital role it plays as a dynamic management and communication process for employees and the groups in which they work. It allows employees, as individuals and as groups, to connect with others who are directly affected by their work and whose opinions therefore should count. Obtaining feedback from their multiple constituencies provides needed insight for individuals and groups regarding the different perspectives and expectations that others have of them.

In our Bravo Data Corporation, a sales manager may get feedback from client relations personnel that customers are very satisfied with the field service representatives because of their quick fixes on the spot, whereas quality engineering may provide the sales manager with less positive feedback. This is because these quick fixes are never documented; they represent only temporary solutions rather than systemic improvements that can be incorporated across all customer sites. Given this conflicting feedback, the sales manager becomes directly aware of an organizational performance issue and a potential conflict between sales and engineering. This can be addressed both at the individual field representative level—through corrective performance feedback, communication, and training—and at the systemic level to ensure that the organizational systems and procedures work in harmony.

Managers, as well as other employees, usually have multiple constituencies, as the authors of Chapter One pointed out. These constituencies may be a manager's direct reports, peers, supervisor, team members, customers, support personnel, or other "suppliers" or "consumers" of the manager's work. Frequently, these different constituencies have multiple and competing agendas, needs, and priorities. Thus, an important and defining part of the manager's job—and one of the things that makes the job complex—is to take full note of this observation. That is, not only are there multiple constituencies, but it is important to understand their needs and perceptions and to keep them in balance. For example, in BDC the marketing management chain may have communicated one thing to the managers, say, urging them to increase customer call ratios. The engineering department, however, may have produced a product that marketing can't sell easily. And, finally, customers may have complained about not getting good and timely service. For the individual marketing managers, these forces shape their work reality. Their challenge becomes one of balancing the forces. In this context, a 360-degree feedback system that can connect these different constituencies becomes a key organizational development tool. It, in effect, decentralizes this multiple constituency management by letting more of the organization's members participate in the feedback process and by sharing responsibility for monitoring perceptions and taking corrective actions when appropriate. Instead of waiting for a centrally located individual in the organization to call the shots, each member becomes responsible for monitoring and quickly adjusting performance in relation to the immediate work environment.

Going from an inside-out to an outside-in orientation also makes for a shift in mind-set about the inevitable connectivity of our working relationships. The mind-set shifts from an independent "me" to an interdependent "we." This other-orientation mind-set recognizes the increasing interdependencies of our work and the need to relate what we do as individuals and groups to what others do and expect. These "others," in a sense, then become customers of the work, whether they are internal or external customers. Chapter Five describes in detail how customer feedback can become an integral part of a 360-degree feedback process for an organization.

Further, this outside-in or other-orientation mind-set causes us to realize that organizations need to promote communication systems that allow for the ongoing monitoring and timely correction of such work interdependencies. Such ongoing monitoring through a 360-degree feedback process ensures mutual satisfaction by the parties directly involved without the intervention of some central authority external to the process. This becomes especially important for organizations that want to be more customer-focused and responsive, organizations that use teams for getting important work done, or organizations that use more decentralized and boundary-spanning forms. Thus, 360-degree feedback systems become strategic vehicles for implementing these newer organizational forms and purposes in a timely, flexible, and organic manner.

The Changing Nature of Work: Context and Content

It comes as no surprise that over the last twenty or so years the context of work has been profoundly changing. The emergence of a *new psychological contract* between employees and their employers is one of the catch phrases used to describe this transformation in their employment relationship (De Meuse and Tornow, 1990; Levinson, Price, Munden, and Solley, 1962). Stability and predictability are out; change and flexibility are in. Job security and employee loyalty are out, yet commitment continues to be an important ingredient that employees and employers alike are looking for. The big question has become, Commitment to what? It is no longer blind commitment to an employer in an undifferentiated way—the company loyalty that was often found in the past. Rather, it is commitment to doing good work in service of customers (Noer, 1993, 1996). A 360-degree feedback system allows an organization to promote this latter kind of commitment. It does so by being clear about who the customers or constituencies are and, through direct feedback from customers, how well this commitment is paying off in customer satisfaction. By being connected directly to their customers, employees can experience a more meaningful job and feel more in control of their performance (Brockner, 1995). These also become critical ingredients for employees' sense of esteem and psychological well-being.

The changing psychological contract also has implications for the roles and responsibilities that employees and managers have relative to performance management and to development. In the past, organizations could be described as paternalistic, that is, they took care of employees. There were structured HR systems for performance and development planning. Predictable career ladders were mapped out, including stable systems for upward mobility. And employees' managers were seen as the guiding agents to make these things happen. In contrast, the present organizational realities demand that employees take greater responsibility for managing their own performance and careers. In this changing work context, 360-degree feedback serves as an important vehicle that organizations can provide to promote employee development through greater self-management and self-reliance. As such, 360-degree feedback becomes more of a learning and preparing tool.

Thus, it is in service of creating an environment that values continuous learning and improvement—for the individual employees and the organization as a whole. For example, in our BDC case, employees understood what the company valued for the future and what behaviors needed to be seen as effective. The 360-degree feedback system then provided a guide or map for the employees on how to go about their development planning and for the organization on what to do to support such plans. Indeed, this is an example of the new psychological contract, where the 360-degree feedback process is a learning and preparing tool in support of individual and organizational development.

Just as the context of work has been changing in significant ways, so has the content. Work for many is far more complex and dynamic than it was twenty or so years ago. As a result, job descriptions are no longer adequate and stable enough to provide the needed guidance as to what the realistic performance expectations and feedback are. Jobs change too frequently for that. In fact, some argue that "de-jobbing" is occurring in our organizations. That is, "jobs" and "positions" are giving way to "assignments" as the basic unit of work (Bridges, 1996; Tornow and De Meuse, 1994). Assignments can be seen as more responsive to the organization's varying needs for the work to be done. Different assignments will, of course, have different constituencies, whose performance expectations and feedback will define success according to their particular needs. Consequently, organizations need more flexible and dynamic systems for communicating performance expectations and feedback. By design, 360-degree feedback systems, with their multiple assignments, roles, and constituencies, are better in tune with the new realities of work.

Finally, as previously noted, work in today's workplace is less frequently done solely as an independent activity. More frequently, it requires cooperation, coordination, and communication among several parties. As a result, more and more organizations use teams and boundary-spanning work units as part of their organizational design. Such interdependencies point out what may be obvious: work depends on relationships among people, so there is a need for relationship-building processes and activities. In this environment, 360-degree feedback serves as a key relationship-building tool that organizations can use to enhance team processes and work interrelationships. As an example of such a tool, the Campbell-Hallam Team Development Survey (TDS) focuses on teams (Hallam and Campbell, 1994). This instrument provides a form of 360-degree feedback by involving team members, leaders, and outside observers regarding team functioning, strengths, and areas to be improved. Exhibit 4.2 shows excerpts from this instrument.

The Changing Role of Management and Leadership

Along with changes in the nature of work context and content, the workplace also is witnessing profound changes in the role of management and leadership. One such change deals with a shift from an emphasis on management control to one of employee commitment (Lawler, 1986). Instead of managing through centralized command-and-control structures, management and commitment are sought through multiple channels. Thus, 360-degree feedback from these multiple sources becomes an important monitoring and regulatory device for employees. This effectively serves to complement supervisory feedback as the sole source of hierarchical command and control. In fact, the employee's supervisor no longer is treated as a sole, or reliable enough, source for performance standards and feedback; 360-degree feedback then becomes an important additional resource to supplement top-down appraisal. Through such multisource feedback, employees are empowered to get a richer assessment of their strengths and weaknesses and enabled to take responsibility for managing more of their performance, development, and careers.

As organizations are undergoing fundamental changes in forms, processes, and relationships, so must our view of leadership change. Here, the trend is toward more distributed forms of leadership. More and more employees need to participate in the "call for leadership" as organizations de-layer, work in teams, and become customer-driven. That is, more employees need to take more initiative and responsibility in the management and leadership of their work. This is in contrast to leaving the task of management and leadership to what traditionally has been associated with the work of a select few in organizations, formally designated by title as supervisors. In a sense, then, every employee becomes a leader, at different times and in different situations. Thus, 360-degree

Exhibit 4.2. TDS Results for ABC Team.

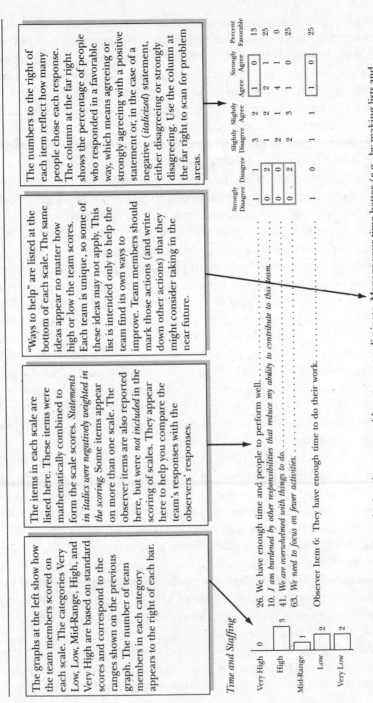

The graphs at the left show how the team members scored on each scale. The categories Very Low, Low, Mid-Range, High, and Very High are based on standard scores and correspond to the ranges shown on the previous graph. The number of team members in each category appears to the right of each bar.

The items in each scale are listed here. These items were mathematically combined to form the scale scores. *Statements in italics were negatively weighted in the scoring.* Some items appear on more than one scale. The observer items are also reported here, but were *not included in the scoring of scales.* They appear here to help you compare the team's responses with the observers' responses.

"Ways to help" are listed at the bottom of each scale. The same ideas appear no matter how high or low the team scores. Each team is unique, so some of these ideas may not apply. This list is intended only to help the team find its own ways to improve. Team members should mark those actions (and write down other actions) that they might consider taking in the near future.

The numbers to the right of each item reflect how many people chose each response. The column at the far right shows the percentage of people who responded in a favorable way, which means agreeing or strongly agreeing with a positive statement or, in the case of a negative (*italicized*) statement, either disagreeing or strongly disagreeing. Use the column at the far right to scan for problem areas.

Time and Staffing

Category	Count
Very High	0
High	3
Mid-Range	1
Low	2
Very Low	2

Item	Strongly Disagree	Disagree	Slightly Disagree	Slightly Agree	Agree	Strongly Agree	Percent Favorable
26. We have enough time and people to perform well.	1		3	2	1	0	13
10. *I am burdened by other responsibilities that reduce my ability to contribute to this team.*	0	2	1	2	2	1	25
41. *We are overwhelmed with things to do.*	0	0	2	1	4	0	0
63. *We need to focus on fewer activities.*	0	2	2	3	1	0	25
Observer Item 6: They have enough time to do their work.	1	0	1	1	1	0	25

Ways to Help: Identify low-priority tasks that the team could postpone or eliminate. Manage your time better (e.g., by making lists and prioritizing what you have to do). Avoid rushed times by planning realistically. Write a job description for selecting a new team member.

Source: Copyright ©1992, 1994, David Campbell, Ph.D. Reproduced by permission of National Computer Systems.

feedback becomes an important leadership development tool that enables employees to enact their new leadership roles as required.

Further, leadership can be seen as a process that takes place within a group or social context, not just as a set of traits or competencies inherent in certain individuals who occupy positions of authority. For example, several staff members at the Center for Creative Leadership define leadership as a process of meaning-making within communities of practice (Drath and Palus, 1994). Meaning-making in the context of other people's work perspectives and expectations then becomes an important leadership activity. It allows people whose work is interdependent to make sense of the work they do—to see how the work each does affects what others do and to see the context in which the work is done. They can see the relevance of their work to the organization and its mission.

Allowing employees to find meaning in their work is also an important psychological job-design and job-enrichment principle (Hackman and Oldham, 1980). This meaning-making is greatly facilitated when employees obtain multisource feedback from those who have a significant stake in their work. For example, 360-degree feedback allows employees to understand the impact of their work on others and to see how others perceive their strengths and weaknesses. Finding meaning in one's work and through others at work has always been an important leadership challenge. Through the use of 360-degree feedback systems, organizations can directly address and institutionalize this challenge.

In our Bravo Data Corporation case, managers received feedback on how satisfied others were about the managers' effectiveness relative to such items as serving customers, asking people what they need to do their work better, and willingness to deal with nonperformers. This turned out to be very meaningful feedback, on a personal level, given that it came from a variety of sources whose perspectives were valued by the BDC managers. Not surprisingly, they took that feedback to heart and did something about it by incorporating it into their development plans. The organization, in turn, had a process in place that allowed important culture change issues to be addressed systemwide.

In sum, the trends discussed all add up to one major fact: the management of performance is more complex than it used to be. Instead of receiving single-source guidance and priority setting from a supervisor, the employee is faced with multiple demands from multiple constituencies. It thus becomes necessary for the employee to take a more active part through greater self-management. This includes recognizing any inherent tensions and trade-offs that need to be made among different constituencies and balancing them appropriately. What is considered to be appropriate, of course, can be a complex judgment—a judgment that the new workplace dynamics may require more frequently of the employee rather than of the employee's supervisor, as was traditionally the case. How 360-degree feedback serves performance management, thereby adding value to organizational development, is discussed next.

How 360-Degree Feedback Adds Value

There are many ways 360-degree feedback can add value to organizations and their development. Examples include facilitating organizational transformations, helping with strategic integration and alignment, making performance management more relevant to new organizational complexities, creating mechanisms for integrating multiple constituencies' inputs, establishing cultures for continuous learning, undergirding the organization's leadership assessment and development programs, and aggregating data across individuals as part of an organizational needs assessment process and ongoing monitoring. Many of these ways are discussed in greater detail in other chapters of this book. The present chapter will highlight only a few for purposes of stage setting. Among the more important ways by which 360-degree feedback systems add value to organizational development are the following: performance management and continuous learning, tracking change, integration and alignment, and contributing to organizational success through effective implementation.

Performance Management and Continuous Learning

A major way in which 360-degree feedback adds value to organizational development is by institutionalizing performance management. It does so through focusing on key communication processes that promote clarity of performance expectations, feedback, and continuous learning. Focusing attention on what the organization considers important is a key strategy for accomplishing this goal. This becomes particularly critical when organizations want to transform themselves. For example, the elements on which managers are rated on a 360-degree feedback instrument communicate aspects of managerial behavior that are considered important to the organization. The ratings direct employees' attention to the key values and the performance factors of success that define these values behaviorally. The example items shown in Exhibit 4.1 illustrate this point.

In our BDC case the organization wanted all to focus on three core values or commitments: (1) commitment to marketing (We will respond creatively to customers' current and future needs); (2) commitment to quality (We will meet customers' expectations for value and service); and (3) commitment to people (We will practice a management philosophy that empowers the people of BDC to reach their full potential). After explicitly calling out what it considered important, the organization next created a behavioral inventory for 360-degree feedback that assessed how well these values were being manifest. This served to ensure a basic, common understanding across BDC and its many members as to the core values and desired behaviors. Thus, 360-degree feedback ratings focused everyone's attention on similar performance standards and expectations—essentially, the dimensions of managerial excellence as defined by the organization. The outcome of such a 360-degree feedback rating process was that the organization was able to raise and then maintain a uniform quality in regard to its stated standards of excellence.

Another way of understanding how the 360-degree feedback process facilitates performance management is as a tool for constructive work relationship building. That is, we can picture "organizations" and "work" as essentially processes that involve relationships. And relationships—to be effective—require mutual understandings and opportunities to influence. Performance management then gets defined as a process of managing effective work relationships that promote mutual understanding and opportunity to influence. Pictured this way, 360-degree feedback can be understood as an important organizational development tool that helps create this kind of connectivity and focus on the building and maintaining of quality working relationships. This is done, for example, by making employees more sensitive to the relationship they have with their supervisor and vice versa. Through 360-degree feedback, both the supervisor and employee realize what they need to contribute to the relationship in order for it to be productive and satisfying to both parties. Another important step is for the employee to be clear about who, in addition to the supervisor, the critical constituencies are. In turn, for these relationships to be effective, the constituencies consisting of other 360-degree feedback raters also should have an important voice, that is, a voice in defining successful job performance and an important source from whom feedback should be sought. The employee's manager becomes a valuable coaching resource in this rater-picking process. This will ensure that the other raters who are picked for input indeed represent significant work interdependencies rather than popularity contests that may have little to do with the employee's work. (Chapter Seven provides additional guidelines on how to pick raters.)

Once other raters have been identified, understanding what each constituency's standards, expectations, and feedback are relative to any target employee represents the next building block for an effective performance management system. Such a system becomes more of a continuous learning system if feedback against expectations is continuously sought and forthcoming and if performance adjustments are possible and then rewarded by the organization. This built-in action orientation around the self-monitoring of gaps in performance between others' expectations and a person's perceived performance is what gives 360-degree feedback processes their motivational power. This power is channeled into self-regulatory behavior for the individuals involved, as well as for setting up a climate for continuous improvement in the organization as a whole. At the same time, participation as a rater in the 360-degree feedback process also promotes organizational development. That is, asking multiple parties to provide 360-degree feedback ratings and then feeding back the results to managers is a visible way to enhance employees' direct communication about, and involvement in, performance assessment and management development. In our case example, employees who provided target managers with their rating input learned as much about organizational expectations as did the target managers. This facilitated "co-management" toward the organization's core values. Helping the target manager refine the action planning and providing ongoing feedback are additional and important means for rater involvement in the performance management process.

Seen through the lens of performance management and continuous learning, 360-degree feedback clearly is not a one-time event. Instead, it should be treated as an ongoing process that the organization promotes; the organizational mind-set and culture needs to value continuous learning and improvement. This means that, instead of 360-degree feedback being implemented as a one-shot program to fix certain problems, it needs to be institutionalized as a vital management and communication process. This way, it becomes part of the organization's fabric for operational excellence. This process then needs to permeate across the organization via the many different parties and times that performance feedback is desirable for purposes of performance management and continuous learning. Finally, it should be integrated with other HR systems. (This idea will be developed more fully in a later section. Also, Chapter Six deals in greater detail with how to establish a continuous learning culture.)

Tracking Change

What else drives 360-degree feedback as a performance management system? In addition to the built-in action orientation to close performance gaps, other forces can promote accountability for such change and be in line with filling these identified performance gaps. One important mechanism resides with repeated 360-degree feedback seeking over a period of time and then tracking the targeted changes in line with performance management and development plans. Changes in results over time can be used to hold managers accountable for performance improvement. Organizations can promote accountability by ensuring that the tracking of changes occurs both at the individual level and at the aggregate organization level. (Chapter Nine has more to say on the topic of assessing change.)

Tracking change at the individual level allows the individual employee to assess how well other people's perceptions are being brought into line with expectations over time. Creating development plans and sharing the results with raters, then making this an explicit part of organizational expectations, can further reinforce accountability (London, Smither, and Adsit, 1997). This promotes self-management and continuous learning by making the individual responsible for seeking the feedback, monitoring changes, and determining whether additional adjustments are called for. The feedback results become a resource for employees to use as they take responsibility for their own development. Low performers, for example, receive feedback that puts them on notice that corrective action is called for. High-performers get reinforced on what their strengths are in the eyes of others. This can help with continued utilization of their strengths, while also working on developmental needs. Top-level managers who are in charge of the organization are thus assured that a process is in place that can identify both high- and low-level performers in a timely and constructive way— and at the level where the work gets done.

When the tracking of change is done at the aggregate organization level across its individual employees, behavioral patterns and trends can be discerned. These aggregate-level data can provide both substantive insight and directional guidance for organizational development needs analysis at the organizationwide or systemic level. For example, if particular performance dimensions consistently show up on individual feedback reports as areas of weakness, this may suggest that corrective action is taken more appropriately at the organization system level rather than only at the individual performance level. This may mean instituting a new training program, or a realignment among different human resources policies, or some other systemic change that addresses this pattern.

Let's go back to our BDC case. Here, we find the company using aggregate 360-degree feedback data to analyze progress and ensure that BDC meets standards of excellence. For example, some of the initial results pointed to issues of customer satisfaction and the need for more immediate and direct feedback from customers—in this case, internal customers. To be specific, aggregate results from analyzing the 360-degree feedback ratings across the organization showed a disproportionately large number of employees expressing dissatisfaction because managers were not "creating an environment where people felt responsible for their work." Further, doubts were expressed that managers "understood that quality means meeting customer expectations" and "treating any recipient of the work product as a customer." (Phrases in quotes were items in the 360-degree feedback instrument that BDC used to assess progress in its organizational culture change effort.) This aggregate organizational needs analysis led to the conclusion that additional changes in work flow and measurement processes needed to be made that involved different internal customers. For that purpose, a work process flow analysis was instituted to identify the critical activities, constituencies, and dependencies associated with the major business processes deemed critical to the organization's success. This helped to sharpen understanding of who the internal customers were for the different component parts of each process. Also, it led to more visibility and appreciation for the interdependencies of work along each step of the process. In turn, that brought about process improvement recommendations for work simplification and appropriate performance measurement and success indicators. This example serves to demonstrate the value of 360-degree feedback as a diagnostic process at the organizational level and its application for subsequent tracking and evaluation.

Integration and Alignment

A third major way 360-degree feedback adds value to organizational development is through the integration of its multiple parts and the alignment of their goals. This integration and alignment can take place in different forms. For one, 360-degree feedback allows the involvement and linking of important multiple constituencies in the management of the target individual's performance. This was described in detail earlier in this chapter. In another form, 360-degree feedback systems can be effective organizational tools for linking and aligning individual, team, and organizational goals. For example, organizations may use 360-degree feedback as part of an organization intervention strategy for transforming an organization's culture around some core values. This was the case with our Bravo Data Corporation. Here, feedback was made available to the individual managers (confidentially) on how well they were seen to exemplify the organization's core values and commitments to marketing, quality, and people. In addition, these results were aggregated and analyzed (keeping individual feedback results anonymous) from an organizational unit perspective. This allowed for the identification of those departments, for example, that had the highest number of managers believed to exemplify the organization's core commitments. Here was an opportunity to learn what these departments had done that produced these successful change results. At the same time, those departments with the lowest number of managers demonstrating commitment to the core values were identified. The latter became targets for more leadership development, as well as additional communication about the critical role they needed to play in helping the organization's culture change effort. This example demonstrates, among other things, the importance of aligning leadership behaviors with work unit results and bringing work unit expectations into line with the organization's strategy and core values. According to London and Beatty (1993), managerial performance measurement needs to include not only the manager's contribution to organizational performance through measures of business success but also the leadership behaviors that are aligned with the business strategy.

A third form of looking at 360-degree feedback systems as tools for integration and alignment is through the lenses of an organization's HR system. Specifically, organizations need to take a broader look at their HR systems and see how well integrated they are in service of the organization's business strategy and goals (Ulrich, 1997). This is to ensure that the different HR systems are in tune and reinforcing one another, particularly the reward system vis-à-vis the performance-management and the management-development systems. Otherwise, the organization runs the risk of engaging in the infamous folly of espousing the value of one type of behavior but paying for a different one (Kerr, 1995). For example, this is frequently the case with organizations wishing to become more team-oriented. With great fanfare, they may promote teamwork and team structures but fail to bring their reward and performance appraisal policies in line so as to actually become team-oriented. Clearly, these HR systems need to be driven by the organization's business strategies so that they are supportive of and reinforce its business goals (Hall, 1995).

Let's go back to our case. Bravo Data Corporation realized early in its organizational culture change effort that HR had a critical role to play. Not only was HR seen as a strategic partner in helping to design and implement the culture change but it was seen as critical that HR practices be aligned with this change effort. Toward that end, therefore, each HR policy, procedure, and tool was critically reviewed in terms of how well it exemplified and served to reinforce the desired core values and commitments. If it didn't, it was brought in line or eliminated. This included the organization's performance appraisal system to make sure it incorporated the relevant performance expectations. It included the pay system to ensure that pay became contingent on demonstrating desired performance results in line with expected commitments. Finally, it also included the organization's promotion system along similar values.

In short, organizations need to look at their management processes from a systems perspective and to ensure that they are integrated within the context of business goals and strategies. This integrated perspective needs to be brought to bear when looking at 360-degree feedback systems as a strategic management vehicle. Doing so will ensure that management processes are aligned and capable of fulfilling their promise for effective performance management and continuous learning.

Effective Implementation for Organizational Success

To add significant value to organizational development—indeed, to create competitive advantage—360-degree feedback systems need to be effectively implemented (Antonioni, 1996; London and Beatty, 1993). Effective implementation involves many factors, including clarity of purpose, involvement and ownership of significant stakeholders, an organizational climate of open communication and trust, and a consistent application of integrated HR systems.

Clarity of purpose is perhaps the most important factor that can influence effective implementation of a 360-degree feedback system. Considerations about clarity of purpose break down into at least two issues: (1) how clear the organization is in communicating intended use and (2) how visible to employees the alignment between message of intent and actual practice is. At its core, the question becomes, How clear is the organization about the driving purpose for using the 360-degree feedback process? Is the feedback primarily for development purposes, or is the feedback to be used for administrative decision-making purposes such as performance appraisal evaluation and salary action?

Although 360-degree feedback systems are often used solely for development purposes, they can also be used to make administrative decisions about employees. When applied for performance appraisal purposes, they frequently are used as an extension of an organization's attempt at culture change around some core values, and to evaluate the progress and impact of such change by determining whether "managers walk their talk." Performance appraisal under these circumstances, then, is used in order to put teeth into the change process and force accountability for the expected behaviors. This was the case with BDC. We recognize that there is a controversy about whether to use 360-degree feedback for development only or also for performance-appraisal and management purposes. (Chapter Three addressed some of this controversy.) This book stresses the value of using it for development purposes. BDC was able to successfully achieve both outcomes because it clearly communicated the program's intents, used a phased-in approach via "development only" to get people used to the process and then evolved to the next phase to include performance appraisal and management. All this was done with great care in terms of employee communication, rater training, and ongoing monitoring for feedback and corrective action.

However, whether to use 360-degree feedback for development purposes versus for administrative decision-making purposes has some important pros and cons (Bracken, Dalton, Jako, McCauley, and Pollman, 1997). Feedback for development assumes openness to feedback and change and a commitment to creating psychologically safe conditions, that is, to keeping ratings anonymous and feedback confidential. In contrast, feedback for appraisal, some fear, may create the opposite kind of environment—one in which these conditions are not maintained. This may lead to inflated scores, defensive feedback recipients, and perhaps little behavior change. In this regard it is prudent to remember a classic dilemma that managers face about performance appraisal, whether it is with 360-degree feedback features or not. And that is, managers inevitably experience role conflict when put in the role of "coach" versus "judge"—performance appraisal for development purposes versus for, say, salary-action purposes (McGregor, 1957; Meyer, Kay, and French, 1965). Not surprisingly then, many management gurus advocate that coaching about performance for the purpose of improving performance is best separated in place and time from any performance appraisal discussions tied to salary decisions (where the manager has to play judge). Otherwise, the risk is defensive reactions on the part of the employee receiving negative feedback and a less-than-expected salary action. This, of course, is in conflict with the desired outcome of employee commitment to improve performance that comes with a performance coaching discussion.

Ultimately, the questions become (1) whether the same process can serve these two apparently conflicting purposes and (2) if 360-degree feedback is used for appraisal and decision making, what it may do to jeopardize its value for enhancing individual and organizational development outcomes. The immediate concern of many practitioners is that the value of the feedback for learning and development is compromised if conditions of psychological safety such as feedback confidentiality and rater anonymity are removed.

Some light is being shed on this controversy from a practitioner's perspective by Carol Timmreck and David Bracken, who co-founded the Upward Feedback Forum (Timmreck and Bracken, 1997). This is an informal consortium that was founded in 1993 and is made up of approximately twenty-five major organizations that meet regularly to discuss their experiences in using 360 for upward feedback purposes. By following up member companies through a practices survey, they are finding that 360-degree feedback for decision making can work in some organizations and not in others. They conclude from their survey research that more in-depth understanding is needed of the factors that lead to success or failure of both decision-making and development-only approaches. Their advice is well taken. Whatever the pluses and minuses are for using 360-degree feedback for both development and appraisal-evaluation purposes, there must be clarity of understanding in the organization regarding the system's purpose, appropriate training and other organizational support, and a realistic set of expectations around the up- and downsides of their respective uses.

Additional important factors in implementing successful 360-degree feedback systems are involvement and psychological ownership in the feedback system with regard to its goals, the process, and the intended results. When the target constituencies have had a stake in the design and implementation of the 360-degree feedback, and when they see it as part of a larger climate that encourages open communication, continuous learning, and valuing feedback as an important means toward those ends, then the chances are signifi-cantly better for the practice to be seen as useful and helpful to the success of the organization. However, an organization without a his-tory of trust and openness in communication may find it more dif-ficult to use 360-degree feedback without suspicion and resistance. In that case, a careful, phased-in implementation plan should be considered. This would include piloting the program in selected pockets of the organization that appear most ready, training raters and ratees, carefully communicating the purpose and setting ex-pectations, and ongoing monitoring for corrective action when needed.

In the example of BDC, psychological ownership in the 360-degree feedback system came about in several ways. One, managers from the top down had a hand in the design and development of the 360-degree feedback instrument. The organization held multiple focus-group sessions with managers representing different businesses, levels, and locations. Discussion focused on the need for the partic-ular core values, what they meant to different individuals and their importance in different contexts, and how one would be able to tell behaviorally whether a value was being practiced. Two, there was clar-ity of purpose in terms of the need for change. The 360-degree feed-back system was seen as a very useful tool that enabled managers to understand what needed changing and to know whether such changes were indeed happening. Three, by using a downward cas-cading implementation approach, managers could model for others the need for and willingness to change, as well as exemplify the de-sired behaviors.

In sum, 360-degree feedback systems allow organizations to institutionalize a continuous learning culture through a more self-monitoring, performance-management process. The process promotes greater alignment in goal setting between what the organization needs relative to its business strategy and the many individuals' goals that need to support such business strategy. Another desir-able and important effect of 360-degree feedback systems on or-ganizational development is that it can result in a culture that begins to value more the giving and receiving of feedback and openness in communication. However, for such a system to be ef-fective, implementation becomes itself an important organizational development issue.

Conclusion

The discussion in this chapter of the forces that affect 360-degree feedback and the ways the process benefits the organization has focused primarily on its effect on internal aspects of organizational development. The next chapter will focus on external aspects—in particular, involving customers in the process of 360-degree feedback within the context of organizational strategy.

Chapter Five

The Competitive Advantage of Customer Involvement in 360-Degree Feedback

Carol A. Paradise-Tornow

In Chapter One, it was briefly mentioned that external raters can be made a part of the 360-degree feedback process. There are several good reasons for doing this. For instance, by adding an outside perspective from which data are provided, organizationally ingrained ways of thinking can be challenged. Also, it is a way of connecting the outside world of the customer to the inside world of the organization. And perhaps most important, involving customers (including internal customers) in the 360-degree feedback process can be a key link between individual performance management and the strategic management of the organization—a link that can maximize the value of the process for both the individual and the organization.

In this chapter, I will take a close look at this link and will provide a case study of one leading organization that is using a comprehensive, customer-focused, 360-degree feedback process.

Focus on the Customer

In the past fifteen to twenty years, organizations have come to see "the customer" as the focal point for defining a winning business strategy. Along with this focus has come a fundamental redefinition and realignment of organizational systems and processes around those activities that add value for the customer (Porter, 1980, 1996). If adding value for customers is the key to competitive success, then customer involvement in shaping performance expectations and providing performance feedback is crucial to keeping the organization and its workers focused on strategy-critical activities (Ulrich and Lake, 1990). The strategic focus on the customer leads to some interesting implications for the role that customers can play in the design, development, and implementation of a successful 360-degree feedback program.

Who Is the Customer?

Although organizations may sometimes be uncertain about how to best define their target markets, they are generally clear that the customer is the one who is buying their products or services. As part of the total quality management (TQM) movement, many managers have also found it useful to apply the customer-supplier model within their organizations. The basic tenet of this model is that every worker has internal customers—those who receive the product of their work—and suppliers who provide them with the information or other raw materials that allow them to do their work. Thus, there are two populations of potential customers—*internal* and *external*—who may be asked to participate in a 360-degree feedback process. Although this chapter focuses on the external customer, many of the issues involving the use of customer input and feedback are the same for internal customers.

The choice of whether to involve internal or external customers should be made based on the nature of the job and the utility of the internal customer-supplier model for the organization. The closer the manager or employee is to directly serving external customers, the more valuable external customer feedback will be. Some experts feel that application of the customer-supplier model inside the organization may detract from a focus on the external customer and interfere with the dynamics of a cross-functional team approach to accomplishing work. However, others have found the customer-supplier model, along with the addition of internal customer feedback, critical to the assessment of staff functions such as human resources and consistent with a TQM philosophy.

The Value of Customer Involvement

Before looking more closely at the competitive advantages of customer involvement in the 360-degree feedback process, let's first consider the value of customer input in the ongoing strategic management of organizations. Exhibit 5.1 offers a simple model showing how customer input begins and ends the process of linking the organization to its market environment. This link to the customer provides a critical mechanism for ensuring the strategic alignment of organizational activities with the needs of the customer.

Exhibit 5.1. Closing the Loop with Customers.

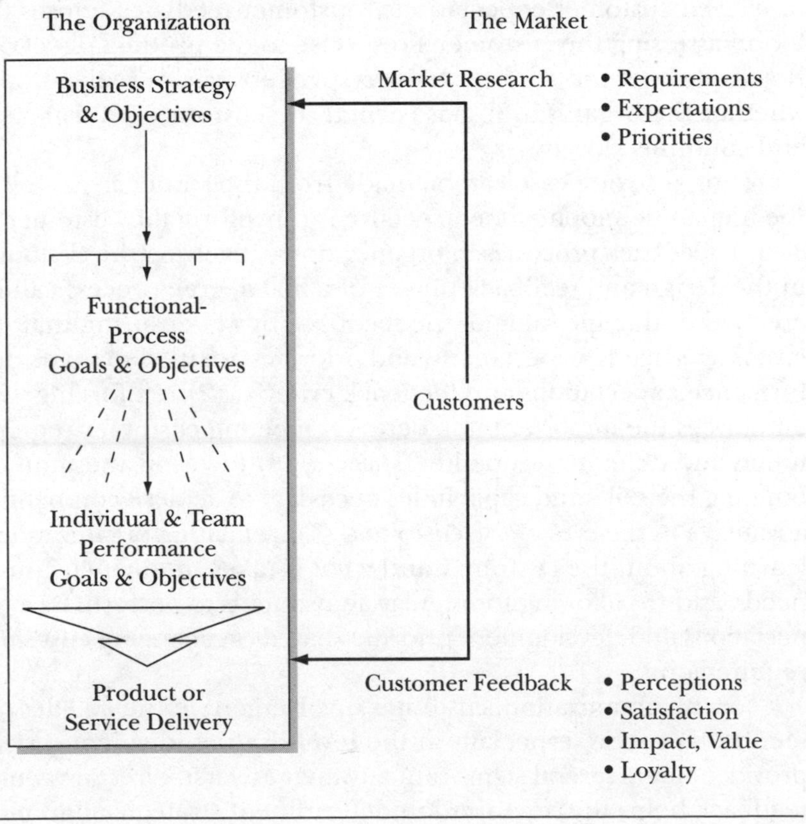

The Organization   The Market

Business Strategy   Market Research   • Requirements
& Objectives   • Expectations
                                                • Priorities

Functional-
Process
Goals & Objectives
                           Customers

Individual & Team
Performance
Goals & Objectives

Product or   Customer Feedback   • Perceptions
Service Delivery   • Satisfaction
                                                 • Impact, Value
                                                 • Loyalty

In most organizations, market research begins the process of strategic alignment by providing the foundation for understanding who the customer is, what the needs and priorities of the customer are, and how the customer hopes and expects to be served. This understanding of the market, combined with an assessment of other industry and competitive factors, shapes a business strategy aligned with the needs of the target market(s) and with the realities of the competitive marketplace (Thompson and Strickland, 1995). Functional-departmental, individual, or team performance goals are established and brought into alignment with the business strategy through good organizational design, process engineering, TQM, and other management mechanisms. With the necessary guidance, resources, and midcourse corrections, these goals are carried out and, ideally, the products and services that result meet or exceed customer expectations. Customer feedback "closes the loop," assessing the customer's response to the product or service received, how the service delivery process was perceived, and whether the organization has earned the customer's satisfaction and continued loyalty.

Thus, a strong case can be made from the strategic, as well as the human development, perspective for involving the customer in critical feedback processes in organizations. Involving the customer in the design and feedback phases of a 360-degree process can increase the strategic value of the feedback by (1) ensuring that the customer's needs, expectations, and priorities are used to shape performance expectations and feedback criteria, (2) reinforcing with employees the important link between meeting customer requirements and ultimate competitive success, (3) focusing attention on building the skills and capabilities necessary to achieve competitive advantage in the eyes of the customer, (4) facilitating organizational learning about the customer and what it takes to meet customer needs, and (5) allowing for regular adjustments to performance expectations and development priorities based on changing customer requirements.

For the organization, customer involvement in the 360-degree feedback process, especially at the level of the individual service provider, offers several significant advantages. First, direct customer feedback helps the organization determine if strategic alignment of performance has been achieved throughout all levels of the organization. Second, customer input and feedback help to ensure that the organization continues to target its efforts at processes the customer finds value-added. Third, customer feedback allows the organization to assess individual and organizational performance outcomes and their impact from the point of view of customers. Further, behavioral feedback from (and about) customers allows the organization to identify and focus on achieving outcomes that lead to desired longer-term behaviors such as customer loyalty and retention, increased referrals, and so on. Finally, there is at least anecdotal evidence that including customers in a 360-degree feedback process can have a positive impact on subsequent customer satisfaction (Edwards and Ewen, 1996), especially when service-related process variables (for example, customer communications, responsiveness) are significant contributors to overall customer satisfaction. (See Chapters Three and Four for further discussion of the organizational benefits of 360-degree feedback programs.)

At the individual or team level, customer input and feedback provide direction for goal setting and for performance and development planning. Such involvement reinforces the focus on the customer and on building those skills and achieving those outcomes that lead to competitive advantage and satisfy customer requirements. Including the customer in the 360-degree feedback process also ensures that employees know whether the desired outcomes have been achieved and how the customers perceived the product or service that has been provided. In other words, customer feedback provides the ultimate reality check on whether performance goals are on target and are being met, in the opinion of the people who pay the bills. Indeed, input from external customers can refocus attention on performance in a way that peer, subordinate, or boss feedback may not (London and Beatty, 1993). (See Chapter One for further discussion of the benefits of 360-degree feedback for individuals.)

Many organizations do not get the most value possible from their 360-degree feedback programs because they fail to design the program with these potential advantages in mind. Many rely on off-the-shelf feedback instruments that primarily focus on leadership behaviors that may or may not be linked to the unique strategic challenges of the firm. Although the challenge of designing more integrated, tailored, and strategically relevant feedback programs may initially appear a bit daunting, it is an investment that will pay dividends.

How to Involve Customers

There are a number of ways to reach out to customers and involve them in a 360-degree feedback process. In the design phase of a program, input from key customers can be helpful. Input might include customers' ideas about the criteria that they feel ought to be part of the process, the expectations they have of employees or managers with whom they come in contact, and the areas in which they would like to provide feedback. They may also want to help shape the process that will be used to gather the feedback and the mechanisms that will be used to solicit their involvement. This input can be obtained through customer focus groups, contact cards, or direct customer calls; soliciting the involvement of a small group of customers to be on the design team is a possibility. This latter option may work well when targeting an internal customer group who might more readily find the opportunity to participate.

If a 360-degree process is already in place, the benefit of customer involvement can be added by identifying customers who would be willing to complete existing feedback instruments. Alternatively, an abbreviated version of the 360 instrument might be designed that is tailored (and therefore shorter) to focus on areas of customer contact. Depending on the nature of the business, involvement in the 360 process can become an integral part of building longstanding customer relationships.

What Feedback Can Customers Provide?

Customers offer a unique opportunity to provide feedback to individuals, teams, and organizations about outcomes, as well as process or behavioral feedback. Process or behavioral feedback includes the customer's perceptions of how the product or service was delivered, what the quality of the product or service was, and what the behaviors or characteristics of the product or service providers were. The majority of organizations focus primarily on gathering this type of customer feedback. However, outcome feedback focuses on the actual or perceived value, usefulness, or impact of the service or product received. Outcome feedback captures the bottom line for customers. The ability to get direct outcome feedback from customers can be an exceptional complement to process or behavioral feedback, and it may provide the feedback recipient with useful insights into the customer's service delivery priorities.

Many traditional 360-degree feedback instruments used for management and leadership assessment and development focus primarily on management and leadership behaviors and characteristics. Customers may be in a position to provide feedback on these instruments if they have had the opportunity to observe the target manager in his or her interactions with peers or direct reports. One challenge with this type of customer feedback is that the behavior of managers in the presence of customers may not be generalizable to their behavior when customers are not around. Thus, the appropriateness of using customers in a feedback process focused on such behavior and characteristics needs to be determined on a case-by-case basis, considering the content of the feedback instrument and the nature of the customer's opportunity to observe the behaviors being assessed.

An extensive literature on service quality has identified several common process-related factors that seem to drive customer satisfaction with direct service providers across a variety of service industries (for example, Tornow, 1991). These include such factors as friendliness, response time, problem recovery, product knowledge, and proactive problem solving. These may be useful in a 360-degree feedback program for nonmanagerial employees or, on an aggregate basis, for managers of service workers.

Although research shows a relationship between service quality characteristics and overall customer satisfaction, research on the relationship between short-term customer service measures and longer-term customer outcomes such as loyalty, retention, and repeat business is just emerging. One recent study found a clear relationship between customer perceptions of service quality and customer intentions to continue to do business with the firm (Zeithaml, Berry, and Parasuraman, 1996). In practice, many organizations have chosen to translate these, or similar, service quality measures into performance dimensions and criteria for use in their appraisal or development processes for service workers, including 360-degree feedback programs.

The challenge of determining what areas of feedback to ask for from customers is one that deserves careful consideration. The necessity of minimizing the demand on customer time, attention, and interest calls for selecting areas for feedback that will appear timely, relevant, and value-added. One obvious place to begin is with an organization's existing market research data on customer requirements and expectations. These data, along with a careful analysis of the human skill and capability requirements implicit in the organization's business strategy, should facilitate the development of relevant performance requirements and feedback criteria. Many organizations have benefited tremendously from initiating a thoughtful dialogue with customers, engaging them in the process of identifying performance behaviors or outcomes that can both guide performance planning and serve as a basis for soliciting customer feedback. Often, this dialogue takes an organization beyond the knowledge it had accumulated through ongoing market analysis and customer satisfaction data, and opens up new opportunities for meeting customers' needs.

Unfortunately, research has shown that many organizations that use 360-degree feedback programs for managerial and leadership assessment fail to put these programs into a strategic context (Schneier, Shaw, and Beatty, 1991). Without a clear link to what drives competitive advantage, an organization will not be making the most of what a well-designed 360-degree feedback process with customer involvement has to offer.

The Downside of Customer Involvement

A few caveats about the use of customer feedback should be mentioned. First, customers are focused on what is important to them, and their criteria for an effective encounter may change with time and experience or vary across customers. To some degree this limitation can be addressed by aggregating data across an array of customers and periodically reassessing the relevance of the criteria. Customers may also have a limited range of interactions with managers or service providers, and as a result may be constrained in the types of feedback they can provide. Thus, a well-designed process might allow the customer a "no opinion" response option for each criterion and try to ensure that customers who are invited to give feedback are in a good position to do so. Anonymity may be an important consideration for customers, and their relationship with the manager or service provider may be affected by the feedback process, especially if some of the feedback is negative. Often, anonymity may be difficult to maintain, especially if few customers are invited to participate in giving feedback, or if their feedback is potentially identifiable because of its uniqueness. Finally, customers may have limited time or interest in providing feedback, and the likelihood of their responding may be affected by the extent to which they have especially positive or negative input to provide. Fortunately, the effect of this limitation is likely to be diminished if customers have the opportunity to be involved in the planning and design of the feedback process from the beginning. Even with these limiting factors, the potential payoffs of customer involvement are considerable and worth the investment in designing a process that will be fair and reliable.

Case Study

First Union Corporation provides an exceptional example of the competitive benefits of customer involvement in an industry that is both product- and service-based. First Union's approach to customer involvement is exceptional because it reflects a high degree of alignment from corporate strategy to the teller window. According to Brett Lauter, vice president and director of service quality marketing (and the architect behind the First Union model), the customer is the beginning and the end of First Union's strategy for success.

First Union is one of the largest financial service companies in the United States. In May 1997, First Union had $137 billion in total assets and over forty-five thousand employees serving twelve million customers through nearly two thousand retail offices and numerous other access channels along the East Coast. In its quest for competitive advantage, First Union has historically chosen to pursue a strategy emphasizing its ability to serve customer needs better than its competitors. In the 1980s this pursuit was characterized by a strong emphasis on service quality, relying on mystery shoppers with carefully designed behavioral checklists to measure service quality excellence. In the early 1990s, First Union held its own in-house pilot of the Malcolm Baldrige Award competition, which led to a corporatewide TQM focus. Consistent with its commitment to the customer, First Union has also led the field in its use of marketing research, building a customer knowledge base that is a leader in its industry.

First Union's business strategy today can best be summed up by its belief that customer loyalty, earned only through the highest levels of customer satisfaction, may be the single most important driver of long-term financial performance. First Union has challenged itself to capitalize on its core competencies in market analysis, service excellence, TQM, and business-process analysis to achieve its strategic and financial objectives.

First Union's Model

In developing its customer-focused business strategy, First Union has built on, and gone beyond, the "balanced scorecard" approach to measuring competitive advantage and success (see Kaplan and Norton, 1996; Kurtzman, 1997). A basic understanding of the balanced scorecard is a good starting point for understanding the advanced approach used by First Union. As an approach to strategic management, the balanced scorecard has three defining attributes. First, it calls for identifying the specific criteria the organization will use to define strategic success. Generally, a balanced scorecard will include financial measures of business performance. However, the notion of balance is to recognize that other outcomes may also be critical to the longer-term strategic success of an organization. These may include criteria such as customer or employee satisfaction, innovation, or other factors relevant to the industry in which the organization competes. A second attribute of the balanced scorecard approach is that it requires the identification of "key drivers" of successful performance for each criterion. Key drivers may include any number of factors that influence (drive) performance against these criteria. For example, job satisfaction may be a key driver of overall employee satisfaction. Product or service quality may be a key driver of customer satisfaction, and overhead expense levels may be a key driver of financial performance. Finally, to achieve balance, the approach assumes an understanding of the potential trade-offs that may occur among the strategic success criteria. Determining the appropriate balance among these criteria and then maintaining that balance becomes the strategic work of the organization.

With its clear focus on the customer, First Union has taken the balanced scorecard idea a step further. Its scorecard defines four strategic success criteria, all shaped around its recognition of the customer as the focal point for competitive performance. The success criteria built into First Union's model (see Exhibit 5.2) are (1) financial performance (defined by customer-based profitability measures), (2) employee satisfaction, involvement, and loyalty (employee measures designed to recognize the integral role of employees in the product and service delivery process), (3) customer satisfaction, involvement, and loyalty (as significant customer outcome measures), and (4) business process measures (focused on business processes that have a direct impact on customers, such as time required to open or access an account). The model that results—CSRI (Customer Satisfaction & Retention Information)—represents a state-of-the-art integration of these criteria into a comprehensive, data-based approach to achieving competitive advantage through a balanced assessment of performance, defined in terms of their impact on customer satisfaction and retention.

At the broadest level, the CSRI can be viewed as a 360-degree, strategic-management process in which the organization itself is the focal point for feedback. Customers and employees provide input on factors that drive their satisfaction and loyalty, and the organization assesses itself using key business process and financial performance indicators. Unlike a traditional 360-degree feedback process, each set of measures in the CSRI focuses on the unique process and outcome factors of greatest interest to First Union's most important constituency group: customers.

One audience for the CSRI data at the corporate level is the Corporate Quality Council, consisting of members of First Union's senior executive team. Like a 360-degree process, the CSRI provides the Quality Council with a comprehensive, multiconstituency assessment of their overall job performance (that is, how well the bank is doing against the CSRI key customer indicators). The criteria that form the basis of this assessment are the key drivers of

**Exhibit 5.2. First Union Corporation's
Customer Satisfaction & Retention Information (CSRI).**

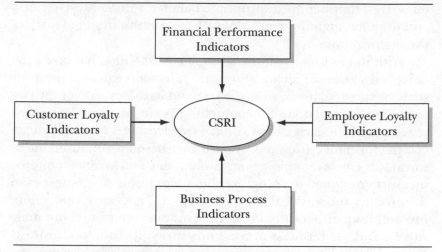

Source: First Union Corporation.

success for each of the areas of the CSRI model (customer loyalty, employee loyalty, business process effectiveness, and financial performance, respectively). Other key audiences for the CSRI data are teams who are responsible for the management, design, and development of products, delivery channels, and pricing and service strategies for the corporation.

The CSRI is also being used to provide multiple-perspective feedback to leaders of strategic business units. Here, in contrast to the more traditional 360-degree feedback instrument focusing on leadership behaviors, the CSRI is heavily focused on the measurement of this balanced array of strategically relevant, customer-based performance outcomes. These outcome measures will form a valuable complement to any additional behavior-oriented feedback process that First Union might choose to employ.

CSRI as a Strategic Management Process

First Union envisions the CSRI as a holistic and integrated strategic management system built around the customer. According to Brett Lauter, "Using the customer as the strategic focus, CSRI allows First

Union to assess its 'return on quality' by tying business process quality, customer service quality, and people management quality to financial results." With the added sophistication of a statistical technique called *conjoint analysis,* the CSRI goes beyond the balanced scorecard approach to determine specific performance-profitability relationships among the variables in the model. This capability provides First Union with the exceptional ability to make informed projections and trade-off decisions regarding how to maximize performance across important and sometimes competing performance criteria. For example, CSRI data allow First Union to accurately assess the customer satisfaction versus profitability trade-offs related to customers' requests for service process improvements, or to set appropriate price-to-product ratios for customers' preferred delivery channels (for example, phone access). In addition, ongoing tracking and competitive data allow First Union to anticipate changes in customer attrition and to assess the impact of business decisions on this key indicator of strategic performance.

To enhance its value for strategic decision making, First Union has done the research necessary to define the specific interrelationships among the measures in the CSRI model. For example, First Union is able to measure the impact of improved product quality on customer satisfaction and loyalty, and, ultimately, on product profitability. They are also able to assess the anticipated impact on profitability associated with alternative investments in improved business processes. In the future, they hope to be able to measure the payoff in customer satisfaction and loyalty that should result from higher employee satisfaction and reduced turnover. Thus, First Union's investment in developing a comprehensive and strategically relevant organizational assessment process will provide a foundation for information-based organizational learning at all levels of the company and will allow for strategic decision making and action planning in response to ongoing data.

Developing the CSRI

Brett Lauter's service quality marketing team, with the involvement of several consulting organizations, developed the CSRI model after years of research, thought, and experience with a variety of service quality, TQM, human resources, and financially driven strategic-measurement processes. Although the CSRI model is straightforward, actualizing it requires a significant investment in building the necessary information bases and a commitment to using them as a framework for strategic management. Currently, the customer indices are developed, validated, and in place. Customer-based measures of financial and business process performance have been defined, and analysis of the interrelationships among these measures is under way. The criteria and measurement process that will define the employee satisfaction and loyalty indices are currently under development.

To develop the CSRI measures and indices, data from over fifteen thousand customer surveys and interviews were used to identify the twenty-nine key drivers of customer satisfaction, retention, and loyalty. In general, key drivers can be defined as product, price, delivery or access-related characteristics that drive or predict customer satisfaction, loyalty, and so on. The key drivers include traditional service-quality factors such as friendliness, staff product knowledge, and wait time; product-related characteristics such as rates of return and transaction fees; and factors related to key customer-access channels such as opening an account and accessing an existing account. These key drivers were used to identify the specific critical business processes and areas of employee involvement that have a direct impact on customers' perceptions and level of satisfaction.

Once the twenty-nine key drivers of customer satisfaction and loyalty were identified, conjoint analysis was used to determine the relative importance weighting and expected performance level of each key driver. Further analysis was performed to define customers' minimal expected level of performance for each key driver. This information allowed First Union to understand how customers value each set of the price, product, distribution or access characteristics, and at what level of performance customers would become dissatisfied or defect to another company. Using their customer knowledge base, First Union was able to establish a Customer Loyalty Index, reflecting a composite of customer satisfaction, customer retention, and likelihood of a customer's purchasing new or additional products.

These data also allow First Union to examine the relative impact of performance on each of these key drivers of customer loyalty on overall customer profitability. These relationships can be tracked on an ongoing basis by continually gathering feedback from customers on their perceptions of current performance. In addition, the accountability for each key driver can be identified and appropriate performance expectations established. As a result, the key drivers provide an important focal point for aligning organizational and individual level performance management and development efforts to the strategic priority of building and maintaining customer loyalty.

Implementation of the CSRI

Full implementation of the CSRI process will allow First Union to

1. *Communicate the important factors that will lead to competitive success.* The ability to identify and communicate, throughout the organization, the key drivers of performance on the strategic success criteria used in the CSRI model will be a significant outcome of First Union's investment. This information serves to focus the attention and resources of the organization on the product development, service improvement, and channel enhancement activities that are of greatest importance to customers. Further, the CSRI allows First Union to identify what product, service, or delivery characteristics have the greatest impact on customer profitability. Potentially, First Union can use this information to ensure that human and capital resources are focused on these characteristics. In addition, the CSRI gives First Union a common language, based on a common set of customer-based measures, with which to talk about strategic and operational issues and performance throughout the organization and across business units, regions, and product lines. This common language and measurement process strengthen management's ability to capitalize on potential synergies within and across business units.

2. *Integrate feedback from all important constituencies in defining and measuring success.* The CSRI allows First Union to systematically gather and integrate input from customers and employees with current data on business process performance and financial results. This multiple-perspective assessment of the strategic performance of the organization allows First Union the ability to track and monitor the results of interest to all of its important constituencies.

3. *Facilitate alignment of corporate strategy and implementation throughout the organization.* A significant benefit of the CSRI is that it will allow First Union to align implementation planning to the strategic priorities captured and defined in the model. Goal setting, performance planning, coaching, training, and organizational development activities at the corporate and business unit levels will be focused on building the capability to deliver performance on the key drivers identified in the CSRI model.

4. *Examine the interrelationships among critical organizational performance variables and their relative impact on overall competitive advantage and shareholder value.* With the data and analysis capabilities underlying the CSRI model, First Union can effectively balance its scorecard results, making any necessary trade-offs among the competing interests of its various constituency groups in a way that is far more informed than its competitors are able to. This will be a significant aid in making strategic choices of where and how to invest its internal resources.

At the corporate level, the customer aspects of the CSRI are in implementation for several business units and product lines. Relationships among these measures and financial performance and business process indicators are being further analyzed.

Key to the implementation of the CSRI is the continual tracking of current performance against the key drivers and performance indicators. At the corporate and business unit levels, these data are being continually collected; customers are surveyed on an ongoing basis regarding current performance on the twenty-nine key drivers and to assess the Customer Loyalty Index. The data further enhance First Union's ability to use the information to examine customer defections and perceptions of competitors.

First Union has completed pilot testing the tactical-level application of the CSRI in two business units. At this tactical level, management feedback and performance measurement can occur and become part of a strategically relevant 360-degree assessment process.

The utility of the CSRI as a performance management and development tool will rest in First Union's ability to apply its strategic elements in a tactical measurement process at the level of the individual branch or business unit. According to Rhonda Miller, a relationship excellence coordinator in First Union's customer direct access division, the CSRI takes First Union "beyond the end of the paved road" in terms of making use of information from customers and employees. CSRI data from customers, linked to managers' quality goals, are rolled up to the division level on a daily basis. Employee CSRI data will replace semiannual climate surveys and, along with ongoing profitability and business process performance data, will provide a comprehensive approach to performance measurement and feedback for division managers.

One of the important characteristics of the CSRI as a performance feedback tool for managers is that it provides feedback based on key drivers of customer loyalty, including factors related to the manager's and employees' roles in the delivery of business processes that affect customers. This focus on key drivers of strategy-critical customer outcomes is what separates this process from the traditional 360-degree feedback model.

What Can an Organization Learn from First Union's Experience?

Although First Union's approach to gaining competitive advantage through customer feedback may be difficult for all organizations to replicate, several learning points may be of value:

1. *Customer involvement enhances strategic alignment.* Customer input and feedback can play a critical role in linking a 360-degree feedback process to an organization's business strategy. Again, customer involvement in both defining performance criteria and providing feedback is critical to establishing that important strategic linkage.

2. *Customer involvement may redefine the feedback criteria.* The First Union example encourages the expansion of our thinking to encompass a variety of methodologies to capture input for a 360-feedback process. All constituencies who are to provide feedback do not need to do so using the same assessment instrument and criteria. In fact, the criteria may need to be tailored to the interests and priorities of the feedback givers, to the differences in the behaviors or outcomes they are likely to observe or experience, or to the competitive value of the information to the organization.

3. *Customer involvement facilitates top-to-bottom focus.* The First Union example demonstrates the potential benefits of having 360-degree

feedback and development processes aligned from the organizational to the individual level. Top-to-bottom alignment may be achieved by using an integrated set of validated feedback criteria for the 360-degree program throughout the organization. These criteria should be based on the organization's understanding of what will drive its competitive advantage and success. Achieving this alignment enables the 360-degree process to focus the entire organization on one set of strategic priorities.

4. *Customer involvement requires investment.* Finally, the First Union example illustrates the extensive investment that can be made in developing a measurement and feedback process capable of refocusing the organization on its strategic priorities. In the First Union case, they were able to integrate and build on their earlier commitment and investments in market research, service quality, TQM, and business-process analysis. At a minimum, involving customers in a 360-degree feedback process will always require the extra effort of bringing them into a more intimate relationship with the organization. However, this investment in boundary spanning has the potential of enhancing both organizational and individual learning and effectiveness.

Conclusion

The First Union example is rich with insights for how an organization can take a strategic approach that can lead to a strategically relevant 360-degree assessment and feedback system with applicability at the corporate, business unit, and individual levels. However, such a comprehensive approach is not the only way of reaping the benefits of customer involvement, and if an organization is not ready for such an investment, a more modest approach should be considered. The level of customer involvement can be varied by simply including a sample of customers in the respondent pool for an off-the-shelf, validated assessment tool or by engaging some valued customers in the process of defining effectiveness criteria for inclusion in a tailored, 360-degree feedback instrument. Whatever the approach that fits an organization best, outreach to customers should be planned with care; their willingness to participate should be assessed, and they should be allowed to influence both the process and the conditions for their involvement.

This chapter has focused on the competitive advantage of involving customers in maximizing the value of 360-degree feedback for individuals and for organizations. The next chapter will consider how value can be further maximized through its contribution to a more systemic condition that underlies organizational development: a continuous learning culture.

Chapter Six

360-Degree Feedback in the Establishment of Learning Cultures

Patricia O'Connor Wilson
Cynthia D. McCauley
Lily Kelly-Radford

The process of 360-degree feedback is important not only because it can contribute directly to organizational development but because it can help create a general learning culture that will make ongoing development possible. This in fact may be its maximum value. But to do so, 360-degree feedback must move beyond being a tool primarily used to examine individuals as performers. It must also help individuals understand themselves as learners and as members of learning groups. The concept of 360-degree feedback for individuals must be expanded to include 360-degree feedback for groups and for organizations.

To understand what we mean, consider the following two scenarios:

Bob attends his company's management-development workshop and receives 360-degree feedback on the fifteen managerial competencies that make up the company's "success profile"— things such as strategic thinking, motivating subordinates, and building positive relationships with customers. By carefully analyzing the feedback, mentally connecting it to things he already knows about himself, and discussing the feedback with the workshop facilitator and some of his fellow workshop participants, Bob gains a clearer picture of his strengths and weaknesses as a manager. He targets a few areas where he is motivated to improve, starts outlining an action plan, and goes back to talk to his boss about what he has learned and where he wants to go. The discussion leads to a refinement of his goals and action plans, as well as to a commitment from his boss to help him work toward these goals. Bob is one of several hundred managers in the company who go through the workshop in a year. In following up with the workshop participants eight months after the program, the workshop staff finds that most participants have made noticeable progress in improving the competencies they identified as the focus of their development efforts.

Ann has been in a new job for about a year. She is starting to feel as if she is on top of things but at the same time senses that it would be a good time to get some formal feedback. Her motivation stems from at least three sources. First, although her boss has given her ongoing feedback in the first year of this assignment, she sometimes isn't sure what her colleagues and subordinates think about her. And although the group she manages has been publicly praised on several occasions for its performance, she has informally heard some grumbling about how her group reacts to requests from other functional areas in the organization. Finally, the organization just completed a review of the competencies its managers will need as it moves to a flatter, more team-based structure. Ann would like to see in what ways she may need to learn and grow in order to be effective in the new environment. As she begins her second year in this job, Ann thinks it's time for some feedback and setting of new learning goals.

She goes to the 360-feedback system on her company's intranet. From a menu of competencies, she picks out the ones she wants to get feedback on and selects the people from whom she wants to get feedback. In addition to choosing some of the managerial competencies that are critical to her job, she chooses several team-based skills and several learning competencies that she understands the organization to have prioritized: analysis of new problems, openness to diverse viewpoints, and use of multiple learning tactics. The system notifies the raters and sends them the appropriate form that can be completed anonymously on-line.

Ann next arranges a meeting for her group with one of the company's group feedback specialists. Together they design questions that they would like feedback on from several other groups whose work is closely linked to their own. The feedback specialist collects and summarizes this feedback for the group.

Ann gets her individual feedback a week later. She shares her highest- and lowest-rated items with her boss; they discuss both the personal and organizational implications of the data and work toward the creation of a development plan that supports both individual and organizational learning. She also shares this information in a meeting with her subordinates. They discuss how her individual feedback is related to the feedback the group received from other groups. They make development plans as a group. As a result of this meeting, Ann refines her own personal development plan.

The first scenario describes a typical, well-designed 360-degree feedback process: a manager receives feedback on a set of competencies important for success in the organization. He has time to reflect and make sense of the feedback, creates development plans, and gets the support of his boss. The organization is supporting this important assessment-and-feedback process for a critical mass of employees and is following up to evaluate the impact of its efforts. This organization is encouraging and supporting individual development, particularly the development of competencies needed to perform well as a manager.

But encouraging and supporting the development of managerial competencies isn't enough to create a learning culture, that is, a culture "in which organizational members share perceptions and expectations that learning is an important part of everyday life" (Tracey, Tannenbaum, and Kavanagh, 1995, p. 241). The second scenario captures some of the ways 360-degree feedback processes can be expanded to contribute to a learning culture. For example, the manager seeks out feedback when she feels a need for it; she is able to get feedback on herself as a learner, not just on herself as a manager; she knows where the organization has certain development needs and is able to get feedback relative to those needs; her feedback is more widely shared and discussed; and feedback is not limited to the individual. Group-to-group feedback is available.

This chapter will show how 360-degree feedback can be an integral part of establishing a learning culture. We first provide an overview of what a learning culture is. We then look more closely at the role of 360-degree feedback in establishing a learning culture.

Learning Culture

The values, expectations, and norms that are shared by organization members define an organization's culture. The culture represents the shared mind-set that allows organization members to perceive and understand events and activities in similar ways. In a *learning* culture, the key mind-set is that individual, team, and organizational learning is a necessary part of the work of the organization. Thus, the organization's work is not focused entirely on creating products and services but also on creating them in ways that support continuous learning and improvement.

This focus on learning has evolved fairly recently in organizations and represents a shift from traditional organizational cultures that emphasize performance—maximizing organizational productivity through the efficient use of resources directed toward meeting defined needs in the marketplace. The shift toward learning is in response to a business and social environment that is seen as increasingly complex and uncertain. Flexibility and adaptation are the keys to survival in this environment. Not focusing on learning, changing, adapting, and improving as critical aspects of organizational effectiveness puts the sustainability of the organization and the vitality of its members at risk. Although performance is still centrally important in a learning culture, ongoing learning is viewed as an equally necessary condition for achieving high levels of sustained performance.

Despite the fact that in the past five years corporate leaders have talked more about learning and development than in the previous fifty (Senge, 1996), few systems have attempted to craft a sustained learning culture. Organizations that have begun the process are viewed as experimental and cutting-edge. How can we recognize the beginnings of a learning culture in these organizations? In other words, how is a learning culture manifested in things we can see—the behaviors of organizational members and the practices of the organization as a whole?

We see at least three places to look for the signs of a learning culture: (1) in the learning behaviors of individuals in the organization (Do they demonstrate the ability and willingness to learn?); (2) in the learning behaviors of groups or teams in the organization (Do they demonstrate the ability and willingness to learn together as a collective?); and (3) in organizational processes and systems (Do they encourage and support individual and collective learning?). Establishing a learning culture thus requires changes in behaviors and organizational practices; these changes go hand in hand with the changes in the underlying mind-sets shared by organization members. We will briefly describe each of these elements or signs of a learning culture before focusing more specifically on 360-degree feedback as an organizational practice in a learning culture.

Individual Learning

Organizations with learning cultures establish and sustain them by attracting and developing people with the ability and motivation to learn. These employees are the foundation of a learning culture. They demonstrate their ability and willingness to learn by seeking feedback, getting outside their comfort zone, approaching problems in a learning mode, adapting to organizational transitions and change, and monitoring their learning (Bunker and Webb, 1992; Lombardo and Eichinger, in press; Noer, 1996; Spreitzer, McCall, and Mahoney, 1997).

Seeking feedback. They want to understand their strengths and weaknesses. They look for the impact of their behaviors and the effectiveness of their strategies. They are open to criticism and are motivated to improve based on feedback from others.

Getting outside their comfort zone. They take advantage of opportunities to do new things. They are willing to take the risk of engaging in activities that challenge their skills and abilities. Setbacks and mistakes are expected and viewed as opportunities to improve.

Approaching problems in a learning mode. They experiment and test out their thinking. They realize that they don't have all the answers and thus seek out others to provide data and input. They examine problems from multiple perspectives.

Adapting to organizational transitions and change. They are optimistic about transitions and find the silver lining in the dark clouds of change. They relinquish the need to control the chaos and ambiguity of change. They are willing to leave old attitudes and previous situations behind.

Monitoring their learning. They pay attention to how one learns "in the moment." They monitor their progress toward learning goals. They easily engage in reflection about themselves as learners.

Collective Learning

A learning culture is also characterized by people learning together. In such a culture, learning is no longer viewed as just an individual activity but also as a collective one. Work groups, project teams, task forces, and the organization as a whole become learning units. The following activities, carried out in an ongoing cycle, demonstrate collective learning (Dixon, 1994):

Seeking information. Group members seek out information both inside and outside the group. It is the responsibility of all members, rather than just the responsibility of people in specialized roles (for example, the leader, the market researcher), to generate this information.

Sharing information. Group members share information with each other, not just with the leader or manager of the group. People are committed to the accurate and timely reporting of information rather than for screening out negative information, holding information to a more favorable time, or keeping information in silos.

Interpreting information. Group members share how each understands and interprets the information. Through this process of collective interpretation, they see more complexity and multiple points of view. The group may not reach a completely shared understanding but will have a broader and deeper understanding of the information as a result.

Taking action. Group members act on the knowledge they have gained through the joint sharing and interpretation of information. They have enough discretion to make changes that they see are in line with the new knowledge and understandings they have developed.

Collective learning also calls for certain values and skills to be developed in the group (Dixon, 1994; Isaacs, 1993; Schein, 1993; Senge, 1990): (1) freedom to speak openly without fear of punishment or coercion; (2) the ability to listen to others, respect their ways or understanding, and work to understand their perspectives; (3) willingness to reflect on and challenge one's own thinking and actions; and (4) equality of ideas—that is, no individual's ideas are more correct than anyone else's simply because of the individual's position or status.

Organizational Practices

Finally, an organization's learning culture is manifested in its practices, that is, in the processes and systems that encourage and support learning at the individual, group, and organizational levels. Numerous practices can support learning; however, it is not the purpose of this chapter to go into detail about these. In general, these practices are aimed at

Generating data and information. This includes formal processes that allow individuals, groups, and the organization as a whole to get feedback and put it into the context of organizational goals and values; also included are systems for the sharing of intellectual property throughout the organization.

Providing opportunities to learn. These practices include processes for accessing coaches and mentors, for identifying developmental job assignments, and for engaging in ongoing course work and self-study. Events and forums that bring organizational members together to share multiple perspectives and work on challenging organizational issues provide opportunities at the group and organizational levels.

Providing managerial support. In learning cultures, managers dedicate resources to learning activities; they make learning a part of the strategic activities of the organization and model a learning orientation. Organizational systems reward managers who play the roles of coach, translator, and gate-opener to organizational knowledge.

Holding individuals and groups accountable for learning. In learning cultures, individuals and groups are rewarded for learning, not just for performance. Managers engage in development planning with all employees, and individual development plans support the needs of the organization.

Of course, the major premise of this chapter is that 360-degree feedback is one of the key organizational practices for establishing and maintaining a learning culture. We will now examine how 360-degree feedback can be designed to maximize individual and organizational learning.

360-Degree Feedback in Learning Cultures

In order for 360-degree feedback to play a role in enhancing learning cultures, it must contribute to the development of continual learning behaviors and organizational practices such as those just described. As such, applications of 360-degree feedback should (1) include feedback on learning competencies, (2) be readily accessible to employees, (3) incorporate new perspectives, (4) encourage more sharing of feedback, and (5) provide clear links between individual and organizational development. In this section we will describe five emerging applications of 360-degree feedback that encourage the development of a learning culture.

1. Providing feedback on self as a learner
2. Empowering individuals to seek the kind of feedback they need when they need it
3. Encouraging collective learning and sharing about individual strengths and weaknesses
4. Allowing groups within the organization or the organization itself to gain multiple perspectives on strengths and weaknesses as collectives
5. Linking individual and group development to the organization's development needs

Feedback on Self as Learner

The content of traditional 360-degree feedback instruments focuses on end-state skills—otherwise known as managerial or executive competencies such as business knowledge, interpersonal skills, or commitment (Spreitzer and others, 1997). But individuals also need feedback on their learning competencies. For example, do they seek feedback? Do they take advantage of opportunities to do new things? Do they adapt to organizational transitions and change? Just as individuals are not always the best judge of their end-state competencies, they also need the perspective of others to understand their skills and abilities as learners.

There are two key reasons for providing feedback on learning competencies. First, end-state competencies, whether derived from research or experience, focus on what has made leaders and managers successful in the past. Future challenges will likely require managers to develop and adapt new skills beyond those that made them successful in the past. Because those new skills are to be used in the future and are not yet clearly defined, the only competency we can assess clearly now is the ability to learn. Our assumption is that people with the ability to learn will be more likely to develop the skills that are called for in the future.

Second, by understanding and improving their learning competencies, individuals' belief in their ability to do something about their weaknesses, and thus their sense of control, is enhanced. With traditional 360-degree feedback instruments, which focus on end-state skills, individuals become aware of the gap between where they are and where they need to be, relative to the set of competencies measured by the instrument. Although it is undeniable that knowing about a performance gap enables a person to begin the process of correcting it, it is unfair to hold individuals accountable for changes they do not yet have the skills to make happen. In other words, is the individual equipped with an understanding of his or her ability to close the gap? Imagine the frustration of having an awareness of a skill or performance deficit if, at the time of this heightened awareness, it is unclear what actions are needed or can be taken to fix it. Using instruments that facilitate learning about the way you learn can provide the critical element needed to develop personal strategies for closing the gap. Through insight and techniques for closing the gap, individuals will also experience an enhanced sense of belief in their ability to develop in the areas that are demanded of them, whatever they may be. The resultant sense that they are in *control* of their perceived deficit contributes greatly to the motivation to work on their development. Further, research has shown that enhancing the level of belief in one's ability increases the likelihood of goal attainment, which is a key measure of developmental progress over time.

Two examples of 360-degree feedback instruments that provide feedback on self as learner are Prospector and Learning Agility: The Learning II Architect. Prospector (McCall, Spreitzer, and Mahoney, 1996) assesses learning ability and a person's willingness to take advantage of growth experiences. This instrument assumes that leadership potential involves the capacity to extrapolate significant personal learning from experience. Key experiences that, by their very nature, cause an individual to stretch beyond his or her comfort zone of proven skills and perspectives are referred to as developmental experiences. From these experiences, a person can glean the greatest learning. Prospector examines a person's propensity for recognizing the opportunity to learn from those experiences, both through reflection on past experiences and learning "in the moment" while engaging in the experience. Individuals receiving feedback on such an instrument develop an enhanced sense of learner behaviors and thus increase the likelihood of their success within environments that require continual learning. Prospector assesses individuals on such dimensions as "seeks opportunities to learn," "adapts to cultural differences," "has the courage to take risks," and "learns from mistakes."

The Learning Agility instrument (Lombardo and Eichinger, 1996) assesses the willingness and ability to learn new competencies in order to perform under first-time, tough, or different conditions. It assumes that people high in learning agility do five things well: (1) think through problems carefully and are comfortable with complexity, ambiguity, and explaining their thinking to others; (2) know themselves well, treat others constructively, and value experimentation—personally and at work; (3) push for change and accept the consequences of being out ahead of others; (4) get results under tough conditions and inspire high performance in others; and (5) use a variety of learning sources. Individuals taking the instrument receive feedback in these five areas: mental agility, people agility, change agility, results agility, and source agility.

Instruments that provide feedback on an individual's learning competencies can be used in a number of ways. First, the instrument can be used in conjunction with a traditional end-state, 360-degree feedback instrument. Individuals can then create development plans that outline not only development goals but learning behaviors for attaining the goals. They will know which learning behaviors are their strengths (and can immediately start applying these behaviors to their development goals) and which behaviors they need to start using more regularly in order to improve their ability to close the gap between where they are now and where their development goals suggest they should be in the future.

A large training organization used a learning competency instrument in this way. Managers held individual one-hour interviews with their staff to discuss the insights gained by staff members from a traditional 360-degree feedback instrument and to identify their developmental needs and set development goals. The results of a learning-competency instrument were added to the discussion to provide a more complete picture—one that encompassed the staff member's ability to learn. In a second meeting, managers and staff members structured assignments to help the staff members achieve their development goals in light of their learning ability and the organization's learning goals. For example, one staff member was put in charge of a task force working on a major organizational issue. One of her development goals was to become more skilled at leading in situations where she did not have direct authority. But both she and her manager knew that she was also weak in seeking feedback from others—a deficit that could hamper her from getting the most from this developmental assignment. Thus, a feature was added to this assignment: a colleague that she trusted a great deal was added to the task force and asked specifically to be a source of feedback about her work with it.

During the fifteen months that followed the assessment-and-feedback phase, managers provided ongoing coaching for their staffs. The coaching focused not only on the individuals' development goals but on the learning strategies needed to reach those goals. An understanding on the part of the manager and his or her staff of each individual's strengths and weaknesses as a learner not only improved the coaching process but became a visible sign in the organization that the ability and willingness to learn was an important attribute.

A 360-degree, learning-competency instrument can also be used by itself to focus specifically on improving a person's ability to learn. Here, the emphasis is less on learning competencies as a means of developing other end-state skills and abilities than on competencies that deserve, in and of themselves, focused developmental efforts. The instrument might be embedded in a training program designed to improve learning skills and strategies, or it could be used when individuals are placed in a developmental assignment to help them understand how their ability and willingness to learn will affect the degree to which they will develop from the assignment. Finally, it could be part of an organization-wide intervention that emphasizes to all organizational members the importance of being a learner.

On-Demand Feedback

Traditional 360-degree feedback processes tend to be initiated by the organization. They are often one-time or annual events, and every manager uses the same feedback instrument. Predetermined sets of competencies, specific windows of opportunity for individuals and groups to receive feedback, and one-point-in-time measurement are characteristic of most processes. In order to support a learning culture, organizations need to have 360-degree feedback processes that give employees more control over when they can seek and receive formal feedback. Such processes can provide access to data at the exact time the individual can most benefit from receiving it. For example, feedback is particularly important when a person is tackling new challenges, when things are not going well, or when a person is faced with decisions about career directions. Giving employees more control over the timing of their feedback also sends the message that the organization expects them to use learning tools on an ongoing basis.

Feedback can be made more directly relevant to the individual's current situation by allowing some choice in the competencies included in the instrument. As in our example, Ann was able to customize her feedback to focus on competencies particularly relevant to her job challenges and areas she sensed were important for her continued development in the organization. Feedback is more likely to be acted on when the information is clearly transferable to on-the-job challenges and relevant to areas where the individual is motivated to improve.

The evolution of 360-degree feedback instruments from paper-and-pencil formats to on-line computer technology makes possible the kind of on-demand and customized feedback that we are describing. Although this evolution was driven primarily by the need for organizations to find more efficient ways to administer 360-degree feedback instruments to large numbers of employees, computer-based systems also created flexibility in how and when feedback is sought. Some organizations are already beginning to take advantage of this flexibility by giving employees more direct access to 360 instruments. Tailoring the instruments to their own needs is also possible with computer technology, including the ability for raters to receive the feedback instrument in their preferred language. By making on-demand feedback possible, employees can track their improvements over time. (See Chapter Nine for a broader discussion of the processes and issues in measuring behavioral change over time with 360-degree feedback instruments.)

Even if they provide on-demand feedback systems, organizations may still want to have 360-degree feedback processes that involve large numbers of employees receiving feedback on a standard instrument on a regular basis. An on-demand, customized process does not preclude a more regular, standardized process, and vice versa. A more standardized process can ensure that all employees receive feedback (some may be more hesitant to seek it on their own), that they have an opportunity to receive feedback on a broad set of competencies, and that the organization has comparable data across employees.

Open Sharing of Feedback and Collective Learning About Group Members

With traditional 360-degree feedback applications, individuals tend to interpret their results in relative isolation—either by themselves or with a feedback specialist. The development of a learning culture can be supported by expanding this interpretative process to include all members of a work group. Instead of each individual trying to make sense of his or her feedback in isolation, the group is involved in interpreting the feedback and taking action that supports development as a result of the feedback. Such a process promotes collective learning about each person's strengths and weaknesses as a group member.

We earlier defined the collective learning process as being characterized by group members sharing information with each other and sharing how each understands and interprets the information. Although traditional 360-degree feedback processes encourage individuals to discuss their data with others, particularly where there is disagreement among raters, these practices do not quite capture the sharing and openness of collective learning. Traditional practices not only leave these activities up to the discretion of the individual but also position the individual as the key—and often sole—interpreter of the data. Clearly, there are learning limitations to single-perspective interpretation. Sharing data themes and promoting others' involvement in interpreting the feedback not only gives a person insight to the meaning of the data but also enlists support from others for ongoing development efforts. In a culture that supports collective learning, there are systems and processes that allow for the more public sharing of data about individuals' strengths and weaknesses, for clarifying what the data mean, and for deciding what actions should be taken—by the individual and the collective.

In many organizations it would be foolish to suddenly mandate more sharing of 360-degree assessment information about individuals. A number of these organizations are still command-and-control environments where decisions are made at the top of the hierarchy and passed down with the expectation that employees will implement and not ask questions. Engaging a wide segment of the organization in collective learning would be a foreign concept. Sharing assessment data with others could be detrimental in such an organization; it could be used as another way of controlling or even coercing employees. In other organizations there may be little trust and a great deal of competition among peers or within work groups, creating an unsafe environment for sharing feedback. But for organizations that are trying to create more collective learning norms, 360-degree feedback should not be overlooked as one avenue for encouraging and supporting those norms. Although we are not aware of any organization where 360-degree feedback is handled in a completely shared fashion, we have seen evidence of organizations taking steps in this direction.

One example comes from the research and development group of a consumer products company. This group is working to create a culture that emphasizes a customer focus, continuous improvement, and employee empowerment. As part of this effort, the top management team and their direct reports (that is, functional and project leaders) participated in a four-day leadership development program. Receiving feedback from a 360-degree instrument was a key part of the program. As part of the design, each member of the top team told the group as a whole (1) what he or she learned about self from the 360-degree feedback, (2) a development goal set as a result of the feedback data, and (3) the kind of support needed from the group to achieve the development goal. The process was designed to model openness in sharing knowledge about strengths and weaknesses, commitment to personal development, and the need for co-worker involvement in work toward development goals. Although there was no collective interpretation of data, this example illustrates more sharing of information and relating it to the organizational context. This process was also congruent with structured dialogues held during the program between the top team and their staffs about what each group needed from the other in order to create the kind of organizational culture they were trying to achieve.

Two of our colleagues at the Center for Creative Leadership have worked with an international company for several years, facilitating and documenting the organization's purposeful efforts to move from a traditional mind-set toward one that creatively faces current and future challenges (Palus and Rogolsky, 1996; Raabe and Palus, 1997). A feedback-intensive strategy is used for individual and organizational development and includes individual 360-degree feedback, group feedback sessions, climate surveys, employee-manager dialogues, and action research. It is in the group feedback sessions where we see evidence of attempts to more widely share and interpret evaluative information about co-workers. In a group feedback session (held three times a year), a manager and his or her direct reports meet, and each person verbally gives feedback to each other person in the group. The nature of the feedback varies across groups and evolves over time. In a session, the feedback might focus on three strengths and three weaknesses in doing your work or on special issues within the group. The sessions are based on the organization's stated management principle of honesty and frankness, and they provide opportunities to better integrate the work of the group and to support each other's development. This example illustrates a more open sharing of evaluative data: each person is aware of every other person's evaluation of every group member. And because there is face-to-face sharing, collective interpretation can more easily take place.

A final example comes from an evolving 360-degree feedback process in a large financial services corporation (Heckler, 1997). The feedback process was designed to be part of a vigorous development effort; it was championed by senior executives, with high involvement of bosses and support from the participants' teams. The process started at the top, with the CEO deciding that all thirteen senior executives (including himself) would rate each other and then review individual data in a group setting. After reviewing their own data, each executive prepared a presentation for the group that included highest-rated items (strengths), lowest-rated items (development needs), and how his or her talents and contributions to the company could be enhanced. After each presentation, there were reactions and ideas for action from the group. As one might expect, tension was initially quite high, but as the meeting progressed, the insights and support offered by the group became apparent. And during the session, the idea of the executives being coaches to each other emerged. This group debriefing process was not forced at the next level, but some groups chose to adopt and, in some cases, expand upon it. This process meshed well with the movement in the organization to become more team-oriented. In their team-building work, they had learned that teams need members with diverse and complementary skills. Their reasoning was, How will we know if we have complementary skills if we don't share information about each other's assets and downsides?

It is important to keep in mind that in all of these examples, there were conscious attempts to act on values pointed out earlier as essential for collective learning. The R&D group had just completed a list of values they wanted to live by that included straightforward communication, respect for each other, and openness. The international organization is striving for honesty and frankness. The financial services company had a culture that emphasized integrity and trust and a history of employee participation in decision making. Also, these feedback efforts did not stand alone as isolated attempts at collective learning. In each case, the mind-set of learning together fit with other initiatives in the organization.

Multiple Perspectives on Groups and Organizations

Traditional 360-degree feedback processes focus on the individual as the subject of the rating. But what if the processes allowed groups within the organization or the organization itself to be the subject of the feedback, allowing them to gain multiple perspectives on their strengths and weaknesses as collectives? We view group and organizational applications of 360-degree feedback as an important supportive process for the development of a learning culture. Just as individuals need to understand how they are perceived by others, collectives need outside perspectives on themselves as groups. As 360-degree feedback to individuals can promote greater understanding of their strengths and weaknesses, multiple-source feedback about the group as a whole can help group members better understand themselves as a group and the impact they have on their constituencies. We view this application to be potentially valuable on two levels: (1) *groups within organizations* receive feedback from raters outside the group, and (2) the *organization itself* receives feedback from multiple perspectives— groups both within and outside the organizational boundaries.

Although numerous surveys allow groups to examine their own functioning from their own internal perspectives, the Campbell-Hallam Team Development Survey (Campbell and Hallam, 1994) is an example of one that measures team effectiveness from the perspective of both team members and outside observers who are familiar with the team. (See Chapter Four for an example of this instrument.) Observers could be customers, other work groups that the team interacts with or coordinates their work with, or management. Ratings of effectiveness are made on a number of items clustered into eighteen dimensions (for example, commitment, mission clarity, innovation, and quality of work). Although observers rate the team on a set of more global items than those used in team-member ratings, just as with individual 360-degree feedback, team self-ratings can be compared with ratings from observers. Differences in perceptions between the two groups signal areas in need of further examination.

Organizations can also create their own systems for multiple-perspective feedback for groups. We encountered the beginnings of such a system in the credit-card division of a large bank. Each function in the division worked with each of the other functions to create stakeholder agreements. These were mutual agreements about what functional groups expected from each other—for example, what the credit-application group expected from marketing, and vice versa. Expectations were around the interdependencies between the groups—for example, timelines for projects, what information was to be shared on a regular basis, what issues required joint decision making, who needed to sign off on what, how services would be delivered, and how each group expected to be treated by the others.

Every six months each group rated the other groups in terms of the degree to which expectations were met. The process included numerical ratings as well as qualitative feedback. Various group leaders were experimenting with different strategies to arrive at the ratings. Some spent considerable time having the whole group discuss and arrive at the ratings and qualitative feedback; some worked mainly with their supervisors to generate the information; and some assigned the evaluation task to a particular group member who was responsible for getting input from a variety of people in the group. The groups held a joint debriefing session after the feedback was exchanged in order to clarify the meaning of the feedback and renegotiate expectations. Again, various debriefing strategies were tried, ranging from meetings between the group managers to larger joint meetings that included many members from the other groups.

This division was still in the early stages of experimenting with stakeholder agreements. The process was by no means running smoothly. There was some resistance to giving low ratings or to giving ratings at all (some wanted to provide only qualitative feedback), and the process was proving to be time consuming. Yet most people interviewed about the process reported learning a great deal about the priorities and contexts in which other groups had to operate. The process required groups to find common ground, facilitated the surfacing of differences in points of view so they could be discussed openly, and had already led to some adjustments in how groups interfaced with each other.

Multi-rater feedback can also be designed so that the organization itself becomes the subject of the feedback. Just as individuals need to understand how they are perceived by others, and collectives need outside perspectives on themselves as groups, organizations need to understand how they are perceived by, and thus affect, their various stakeholders. Organizations need information on their weaknesses in order to highlight potential capability deficits, as well as information on the impact of their strengths in order to better leverage organizational learning and support the development of the weaker areas. This application is truly emerging, and although we are not aware of any organizations that have experimented with this process, we point to the merits apparent in one scenario.

Case Example

An international pharmaceutical company has come to face the challenging side of rapid growth and success: a thinning pipeline of individuals prepared to take on the leadership positions required to guide the burgeoning organization into the future. The company had traditionally grown leaders from within. Then it grew as an organization through acquisition and began integrating newly acquired units through the assimilation of a historically based mission, a strong code of conduct, and an enduring commitment to the customer. Although the acquired companies were assimilated, they were also allowed to operate fairly independently, so long as their individual success continued.

Teams throughout the organization—both leadership and operational—now dialogue and reflect on the key individual and organizational attributes that will allow them to remain competitive and successful in the future. As a result, a set of standards, supported by the CEO, is being devised to guide the development of those future leaders needed so urgently by the organization. The standard with the largest implication for learning—and organizational development—is that of "interdependence." Although it is believed that this practice will eventually yield greater learning across the boundaries of the operating companies, the past practices stand in stark opposition to the tenets of interdependence. The organization realizes that the costs of nurturing interdependence among the operating companies may be high but that the cost of allowing learnings to remain in separated collectives throughout the organization is prohibitive. The competitive nature of the industry demands that learning be brought to the organizational level if the conglomerate is to stay alive. But do the operating companies understand their strengths and their areas of vulnerability well enough to see value in engaging more interdependently with the other operating companies?

In order for the operating companies in this conglomerate to better understand how they are perceived by their constituencies, the organization has chosen to expand the use of its organizational effectiveness survey, which measures such dimensions as communication, visioning, planning, and innovation. Although the surveys were traditionally distributed only to employees, with the results reviewed separately by each operating company, the organization has decided to expand the rater population to reflect more of a 360-degree process. The organization itself has become the subject of the feedback, and multiple perspectives have been sought. Data are gathered on each company's effectiveness from all of its constituencies—including past and present employees, customers, board members, suppliers, alliance partners, competitors, governmental agencies, and other operating companies within the conglomerate. A composite report of the entire organization, as well as individual feedback reports, is created for each operating company.

As a next step, the organization could employ *organizational self-study* as a way to focus the areas of organizational development. This is a developmental activity in which members systematically look together at the organization's successes and challenges—as reflected in the 360 as well as informal experiential data—its goals and its values, the relationship of its present state to its ideals, and possible future directions and ways of achieving its goals. It's a self-directed, self-motivated look at where the organization is and where it wants to go (Rogolsky and Drath, 1997). The goal of such a study is to build an ongoing self-exploration, self-assessment, and reflection capability in the organization and its members. In this way, gaining multiple perspectives on the organization's strengths and weaknesses would become an ongoing process—as tied into the planning cycle as budgeting or other key processes. Organizational self-study presumes that certain knowledge doesn't exist, doesn't come into the consciousness of the individuals, until the dialogue is held. In other words, this dialogue brings the data and the information gleaned from the 360-degree feedback process to a level of usable organizational knowledge.

Certainly, this application presents new challenges to full disclosure of organizational weaknesses, but the implications for learning, and thus competitive sustainability, could be significant. Each of these rater groups holds a perspective on the organization's relative effectiveness and thus helps paint a portrait of the organizational development that needs to occur to reach higher levels of efficacy and performance. Such data could lend valuable strategic insight into stakeholder satisfaction, perception of the organization as a desirable place to work, strength in the marketplace, and, primarily, current and future capabilities that need to be strengthened through development.

Linking Individual and Group Development to the Organization's Development Needs

Traditional 360-degree instruments measure global competencies that have been deemed important for an individual's continued success in the organization or within a specific role. The competencies are usually drawn from research, experience, an organizational audit, or some combination of these sources; they tend to have face validity. What is less apparent is whether these dimensions represent competencies that are important for the organization's continued success. Most traditional 360-degree processes also incorporate a planning stage in which individuals set goals and design strategies for the attainment of those goals. These goals often represent the closing of a perceived gap in one or more competency areas deemed important for the individual's development. Goals tend to be selected and prioritized by examining the demands of the individual's current responsibilities and linking development areas to those competencies that will make him or her most effective in carrying out those responsibilities. Although the selection of, and progress toward, goals is critical to learning and development, the traditional perspectives used to select critical competencies and prioritize goals may be limited. We suggest that in order for this process to enhance a learning culture, individuals need to receive feedback on dimensions and design developmental strategies that are critical to the organization's development needs. The same is true when the 360-feedback concept is applied at the group level: groups need to know about the organization's development needs as context for setting their own development goals.

We illustrated this concept in our opening example. Ann's organization is moving to a flatter, more team-based structure. The change is intended to help the organization be more flexible, respond to customers more quickly, and share information more readily across functional areas. But the change is also a developmental challenge for the organization: old practices and ways of behaving will clash with this new structure. The organization will have to develop new practices, and members will have to behave in new ways. The organization makes an effort to understand and communicate to employees what new competencies will be needed. Individuals and groups can then use that information in their own feedback-seeking and development-planning activities.

Changes in the organization, such as flatter structures, more global operations, or the increased use of technology, are not the only factors that determine an organization's development needs. As we pointed out in the previous section, just as individuals have strengths and weaknesses, so do organizations. For example, some organizations may have developed cultures that value slow, careful analysis of problems. This organizational strength may become too dominant, paralyzing the organization when quick decisions need to be made. The organization can become aware of this bias or weakness through an organizational 360-degree feedback process, as described in the previous section. This knowledge can then become more widely shared, alerting members that the skills for making decisions with less complete information are a high priority for the organization.

Inherent in this application is the assumption that the organization is willing to explicitly share and interpret potential areas of weakness. If information and knowledge concerning the organization's strengths and weaknesses are not shared openly, individuals and groups will not be able to customize their feedback to include dimensions critical to the organization's development. This application also goes beyond linking development to strategic imperatives, which tend to broadly interpret where the organization is going; rather, it looks at where the organization needs to be strengthened in order to get there.

A second assumption of this application is that all learners must be accountable. In order for organizational 360-degree processes to be effective, individuals and collectives must take it upon themselves to expand their learning in those areas most required by the organization overall. This moves accountability for learning from an individualistic or collective focus to one in which learning contributes to those areas critical to the survival, sustainability, and competitiveness of the organization.

Two benefits that accrue from linking individual and group development to organizational development needs are (1) the leveraging of the organization's human capital and (2) the increased likelihood that individual and group development will be supported by the organization. It has often been said that an organization's greatest assets are its people. From a developmental and learning perspective, people are its *only* assets. This being the case, determination of the organization's development and ongoing sustainability rests in the individual and collective learning of its members. From a resource standpoint, if individual and group development plans do not support the organization's development needs, this represents a serious lack of human-capital utilization that could weaken the organization.

Lack of support for ongoing development is one of the more common problems in organizations. Although continuous efforts are made to help individuals and groups receive developmental feedback and devise development strategies, often the ongoing support required for goal attainment is missing. In our view, an organization is more likely to enhance its support of development, through systems and other resources, if individuals and groups define their development strategies in the context of the capabilities the organization needs to develop to remain vital. Without this connection, individuals and groups may be left to their own devices for making progress toward goals, thus weakening the chances for goal attainment that is of organizational relevance.

Conclusion

We described five evolving 360-degree feedback processes that support and reflect movement toward a learning culture. In reflecting on how your organization could begin using these processes, it is important to consider (1) the degree to which the organization is ready to engage in these processes, (2) the evolutionary nature of the processes, (3) the challenges inherent in application, and (4) what 360-degree feedback can and cannot contribute to the enhancement of a learning culture.

1. *Organization readiness is critical to assess before engaging in any of the five 360-degree feedback processes.* In describing the various processes, we have referred to some of the organizational values and practices that underlie the success of each of these processes. In Exhibit 6.1, we provide specific questions to ask in determining the organization's readiness for a particular process.

Although managers may not find readiness factors present in an entire organization, they may note the emergence of such elements in pockets throughout the organization. Is the organization working toward making these characteristics more prominent, as reflected in the strategic priorities set by senior management? If so, managers can build on the early work of emerging groups by giving these processes and characteristics more visibility, positioning them as pilot groups, and slowly enhancing the organization's awareness of the critical role of learning in supporting organizational sustainability.

2. *All of the processes discussed here are evolutionary in nature.* This means taking small steps, designing experiments, monitoring outcomes and reactions, and building the trust that is core to making individual and collective learning work. Certainly, more is understood in research and practice about individual learning than collective learning. We believe that individual learning and the understanding thereof is a prerequisite to collective learning, in that a critical mass of individual learners is needed for a collective to yield the same benefits. Collective learning requires a greater stretch of perspective, resources, and systems understanding. Organizations should thus begin by focusing on the development of individual learners. Although creating understanding of the interrelationships between individual learning and organizational success makes the knowledge garnered through 360-degree feedback processes more useful and purposeful, it is not yet completely within our grasp. Given what we still have to learn about leveraging learning, the next advances in the understanding of learning cultures will occur through thoughtful experimentation and trust that the desired end-state will deliver the benefits of greater sustainability.

3. *There are also a variety of challenges inherent to instituting 360-degree feedback processes that enhance continuous learning.* Managers need to protect the organization from "360 weariness." This phenomenon occurs when organizations repeatedly use 360 applications that lack a definitive purpose. When this is the case, raters

**Exhibit 6.1. Questions to Assess
Organizational Readiness for 360-Degree
Feedback Processes That Support a Learning Culture.**

Feedback on Self as Learner	• Do the organization's hiring criteria and reward systems reflect that it values active learners?
	• Does the organization encourage employees to work outside their comfort zones, experiment, and take risks?
On-Demand Feedback	• Do employees value feedback to the extent that they will seek it on their own?
	• Does the organization have a technology infrastructure to support on-line feedback systems?
Open Sharing of Feedback	• Is there enough trust in the organization for people to share their views openly and to take a nondefensive stance toward feedback?
	• Are public dialogues about issues and conflicts within the organization encouraged?
Multiple Perspectives on Groups and Organizations	• Do groups in the organization see themselves as having interdependent relationships with other groups?
	• Does the organization value outside perspectives?
Linking Individual and Group Development to Organizational Development Needs	• Is the organization willing to point out its development needs?
	• Are individuals and groups willing to align their development needs with those of the organization?

tend not to be thoughtful and insightful in giving their feedback, instead rushing through the practice and rendering the process ineffective—if not invalid. This also occurs if the organization gathers information but then fails to either share it or act upon it or both. Given the time and effort required to institute 360-degree feedback processes effectively, managers should be prudent in the frequency and timing of such applications.

Another challenge managers must be aware of and work to reverse is the influence of the hierarchy effect. This effect holds that learning capabilities, particularly of teams, tend to deteriorate steadily the higher one goes on the corporate ladder (Senge, 1996). In addition, the higher one goes, the less individual feedback one tends to receive. Thus, it is imperative that managers find processes by which to identify and subdue this effect before it frustrates the efforts of individual learners and negatively affects the learning culture.

Finally, organizations will find specific barriers to learning embedded in their systems and processes. By engaging learners and other stakeholders in dialogue, managers can identify those influences and manage them accordingly. For example, did the organization not "listen" when information on a potential organizational weakness came from an outside stakeholder? What blocked that information? And can a system be created to capture that information, no matter how dissonant, and give it the visibility it requires? Are groups unwilling to openly share feedback with each other? What is preventing openness from occurring, and what does this imply about trust levels within the group?

4. *The 360-degree feedback process is not a panacea for organizations seeking to establish a learning culture.* The 360-degree feedback process should be viewed as but one tool needed to promote the creation of such a culture. Other organizational processes and capabilities—reward, education, information, and control systems; dedication of material resources; and stakeholder modeling of learner behaviors—should be examined for their relative support of learning in the environment.

Given what we have illustrated here and the demonstrated roles that 360-degree feedback can play in supporting a learning culture, we are left with the following challenge: How should we develop 360-degree feedback processes that will better fulfill this role? This is a question we continue to examine. Certainly, developing systems and collectively learning present clear challenges, but we feel they also hold the great promise of enhancing an organization's ability to be adaptive, competitive, and future-focused amid the turbulent forces acting on today's organizations.

Thus far, this book has focused on how to maximize the value of 360-degree feedback for individuals (Part One) and for organizations (Part Two). In Part Three the chapter authors will consider these topics simultaneously, looking at them from the technical and administrative perspectives of design, implementation, and measurement.

Maximizing the Value of 360-Degree Feedback Through Design, Implementation, and Measurement

Designing 360-Degree Feedback to Enhance Involvement, Self-Determination, and Commitment

Ellen Van Velsor

This chapter focuses on standard 360-degree feedback instruments, although much of what it covers can be applied to customized instruments as well. More specifically, I will focus on the methodology and the administrative aspects of the 360-degree instrument process. These can be summarized as (1) the questionnaire, (2) the scored feedback (or results), and (3) the administrative process used to get the organization started and to reach beyond the feedback process to the ongoing support for individual development.

Each of these aspects will be covered, and guidelines that will help create involvement, self-determination, and commitment will be offered. The guidelines are drawn from research done at the Center for Creative Leadership (CCL) and elsewhere, as well as from CCL's experience in offering 360-degree feedback over the years.

Because the administrative process is critical for setting the context for the entire 360-degree feedback experience, it will be considered first. We will return to the administrative process, with regard to its role in providing support for development planning and change, at the end of the chapter.

Setting the Context: The Administrative Process

In general, the administrative process should be one that serves to increase trust by providing all participants with sufficient information about the purpose of the intervention, as well as about what people can expect along the way. It is useful to think in terms of several guidelines. These will be presented throughout the chapter, and each will be discussed.

GUIDELINE 1: THE PURPOSE OF THE PROCESS SHOULD BE CLEAR TO EVERY MEMBER OF THE ORGANIZATION.

A 360-degree feedback instrument is typically chosen or developed for use because the capacities assessed in the tool are those that the organization wants its managers to develop over the long run. The decision to focus on the specific capacities assessed by the 360-degree instrument can be made based on their fit with the organization's strategic goals. Or a particular instrument may be chosen because of the leadership research or theory from which an instrument is derived (research may have shown that the capacities assessed in the instrument are related to effective leadership in similar types of organizations or industry contexts). In either case, managers should be made aware that the leadership capacities or management skills are ones that are seen as critical; skills and capacities should be linked to organizational goals and strategies and should be focused on in current and longer-range development-planning sessions.

Also, development-planning and implementation systems should be set up to help people improve their skills or performance in those key areas after the feedback. Knowing that dimensions important for continued success and effectiveness are being assessed and knowing that support for improvement will be forthcoming should motivate managers to be truly involved in the process.

One factor that may raise anxiety and work against the commitment and motivation of raters and ratees is the possibility that the data will be used for other than individual development planning (that is, for performance appraisal, salary action, or promotion decisions). Although private evaluations may differ from what raters choose to communicate in a 360 process used for development purposes (Murphy and Cleveland, 1995), it may be that when ratings affect a ratee's salary or job assignment, raters are less motivated to express their honest opinions of another's performance. To the extent that ratings are skewed, either positively or negatively, and do not accurately reflect the views of the raters, they are no longer useful for development or appraisal purposes and, in fact, work to sabotage the very processes they are meant to support. (For more on the issues surrounding the various uses of 360-degree feedback, see Chapters Three and Four.)

Because trust in how the data are used can be an issue for managers and raters alike, some organizations are beginning to find that it may be a mistake to initiate a 360-degree process for performance appraisal in an organization in which 360 tools do not have a history of being used for development. But once a 360-degree feedback system has been used for development purposes—once people have become comfortable with the process and have become used to using the data as a means for improving their skills and capacities (with the support of other systems put in place for this purpose), it may be possible to move to the successful use of 360 instruments for appraisal. If ratings become more lenient during this change, this can be picked up by comparative analysis of newer data with ratings from prior (development only) years, and the use for appraisal can be reconsidered if individual ratings rise or fall significantly.

Several benefits can accrue from integrating feedback for development with its use for performance appraisal, once people feel comfortable with the process. First, from a systems point of view, it may be easier to administer a 360 process that can provide information on strengths and development needs during a performance review. Second, multiple perspectives probably have added value, in terms of getting the most accurate and comprehensive view of performance. Although traditional performance-appraisal practices would suggest that the ratings of bosses are, in general, the best predictors of job performance, peers and direct reports are better observers of some leadership capacities such as relationship orientation or coaching skills. And, finally, if 360-degree feedback has been used for development over time, people can be identified who have shown the ability to work with this feedback and to develop in areas where improvement is needed. If we want to reward and retain people who have the ability to learn and adapt to change and feedback, the identification and reward of successful development over time is probably more important than rewarding the kind or number of strengths an individual displays at a single point in time. (For more information about comparing ratings from different points in time, see Chapter Nine.)

GUIDELINE 2: COMMUNICATE CLEARLY ABOUT THE LIMITS TO CONFIDENTIALITY AND ANONYMITY.

Confidentiality and anonymity are often confused, although they are both significant issues in a 360-degree process. *Confidentiality* refers to the limitations placed on how a target manager's data are shared, whereas *anonymity* refers to the extent to which a rater's identity is revealed. Although ensuring that adequate safeguards are applied is critical to both confidentiality and anonymity, in most 360-degree processes both confidentiality and anonymity have limits, and these need to be made clear to participants in the process.

Issues related to confidentiality and anonymity are almost always issues of trust. The effective use of 360-degree feedback for development or for appraisal depends on creating an environment that is seen as supportive of individuals, respectful of their needs for privacy, and concerned about their development (Chappelow, 1998). When raters' responses are not anonymous or when adequate safeguards have not been developed to protect the anonymity of rater identity, fears of retribution may arise and may result in a lack of candor in their responses or, in fact, to complete nonresponse.

To create or maintain trust, the process should be perceived by managers as supportive and by raters as not revealing their individual responses, particularly in feedback reports. In large part, ensuring rater anonymity is a matter of distributing the forms to an adequate number of raters in each rating group and ascertaining (from the vendor) that feedback from a rater group will not be provided unless a minimum number of forms (usually three) are scorable for a group (for example, direct reports, peers). Once assured of this safety net, most raters will be comfortable completing forms and will provide honest and helpful responses.

Even beyond the data collection process, however, it is important to make sure that raters will not lose their anonymity as a result of how results are displayed. This aspect of the process is not likely to be visible to raters in the beginning but can work to seriously undermine the process in the end. For example, some instruments display, in the scored feedback reports, item frequencies by rater, using rater numbers or some other code as a cover for rater identity. The rationale for this is that managers like to see the distribution of responses in addition to the average scores and find it helpful to know whether a certain score was produced by rater responses that were similar to each other or whether there were some unique or extreme responses (very high or very low) that factored into the resulting score. In a setting where there is already a significant amount of trust and a genuine desire to create a supportive developmental experience with the 360-degree feedback, the display of item frequencies by rater will probably not be an issue. But where trust is not high or feedback is new, the display of individual rater responses, even when disguised by codes, might be more detrimental to the goal of getting honest results than it is beneficial to the feedback process.

An increasing number of 360-degree feedback processes provide ratings from the manager's immediate boss as a separate category, thereby eliminating the anonymity of the boss's responses. Although most managers are keenly interested in what the boss has to say and find these ratings one of the most compelling features of their feedback, it is important that bosses be made aware that responses will be reported directly to the manager and not combined with others' responses.

There is some evidence in feedback research that ratings may be affected by lack of anonymity. In a study of upward feedback (that is, ratings of the supervisor by subordinates only), Antonioni (1994) found that subordinates whose ratings were not anonymous felt less comfortable and rated their managers significantly higher than subordinates whose ratings were anonymous. In CCL's research on data from Benchmarks (a multi-rater questionnaire assessing a variety of leadership skills and perspectives in which a boss's responses are not anonymous), boss ratings tend to be higher, on average, than ratings from peers or from direct reports. Although it may be that an individual's manager is a better evaluator of skills and perspectives than are co-workers, another view is that this rating "leniency" may result from the bosses' knowing that their responses will be available in the feedback reports. This phenomenon has been a longstanding dilemma in performance appraisal and represents a trade-off to be considered in a 360-degree feedback process—the value of receiving the supervisor's evaluation directly versus the degree to which the supervisor can be candid in evaluating the manager. In any case, the supervisor should be made aware before completing the questionnaire, through a clear explanation of the process, of how the data will be displayed in the feedback report when the intent is to display boss data as a separate category. And managers, as well as those responsible for facilitating the feedback, should be aware of the leniency effect usually present when anonymity is compromised.

GUIDELINE 3: RATERS SHOULD BE CHOSEN BY THE TARGET MANAGER.

In a 360-degree feedback process, a manager will typically receive a packet of questionnaires. In that packet will be one form the manager will use to record self-ratings on a variety of behaviors and skills, along with a number of forms for others to complete. These forms are usually almost identical in content to the self form and are to be distributed to the manager's boss, direct reports, peers, customers, or others who are in a position to rate the skills and behaviors included in the questions or items on the questionnaire. It is important that forms be distributed to an ample number of potential raters because some raters may not complete and return their forms. In order to ensure the anonymity of raters who do so, the responses of any rater group (for example, peers, direct reports, customers) having fewer than three raters should not be presented to the feedback recipient unless combined with the responses of another rater group.

One line of thinking with regard to choosing raters is that in order to ensure that the manager gets feedback from a balance of people able to see both the manager's strengths and development needs, raters should be chosen by an objective third party. Yet the trade-off to believing that each manager has a good mix of raters may very well be a loss of a sense of ownership of the resulting data by the target manager. That is, if someone other than the target manager chooses who should rate that manager, the manager is probably more likely to reject the validity of any negative results. Receiving negative feedback is difficult in the best of circumstances, and taking away managers' self-determination in the choice of raters will surely have a negative impact on attending to the feedback from those raters. On the other hand, the credibility of ratings may be questioned by a manager's boss or co-workers if there is doubt about how a manager self-selected raters. This issue could be a serious one if the supervisor's ratings differ significantly from others' ratings or when performance appraisal is a goal of the 360-degree feedback process.

Because many managers will not know how to choose a rater, guidelines should be provided for the selection of raters. For example, managers should be advised to

1. Look over the items on the questionnaire, and choose only people who know them well enough to rate the items presented in the questionnaire.
2. Choose a balance of people, some of whom they see as supporters but also some they know may be more critical; select people the manager feels will provide candid, constructive feedback, regardless of whether it is negative or positive.
3. Solicit information from an adequate number of people in each rater category (for example, peers, direct reports), recognizing that all raters may not return their forms. This is important because if the number of forms returned from a group is not adequate, the responses of different group members are usually combined rather than broken out in the feedback (results) report, making that report much less rich in the perspectives represented and in the total information presented.
4. Seek the input of their boss or another significant and objective third party with respect to who could provide useful ratings of the manager's skills and behaviors.

GUIDELINE 4: CUSTOMER INPUT CAN BE VERY USEFUL, BUT THE QUESTIONNAIRE SHOULD CAPTURE THEIR UNIQUE VIEWS.

On some instruments, raters can include both internal and external customers. Because internal customers can overlap with peers, managers should be advised to select raters with as little overlap as possible in order to get feedback from both groups separately and to thus maximize the richness of the resulting feedback report.

Different constituencies will have different perspectives on a manager's skills. Items should be relevant to the domains of behavior that different constituencies can observe. Input of external customers can be extremely valuable in that they see a somewhat different set of skills and perspectives than direct reports or bosses see in a manager. Yet, they may not be able to answer some of the questions that a direct report or internal peer would find easy to respond to. Questionnaire items that assess aspects of performance unique to the relationship between managers and external customers should be present if the intent is to use it with customers. In addition, external customers may interact with the target manager irregularly or indirectly. The frequency and intensity of the manager's direct work with external customers should be taken into account in deciding whether to ask them to act as raters. (The value and uses of customer input on 360 instruments is discussed in more detail in Chapter Five.)

GUIDELINE 5: SUPPORT FOR DEVELOPMENT SHOULD BE SUPPLIED.

Finally, in order to enhance involvement of both the manager and the manager's boss in the development process, support for the manager's development should be supplied in several forms. The expectations for what managers should do with the feedback (how it should be used) should be clear to both managers and their bosses before the process begins. Expectations related to a manager's sharing development goals with his or her boss, as well as the responsibilities of the boss for developmental coaching following the assessment process, should be clearly articulated. The manager should have at least one person available to act as a coach, both during the feedback process and in the period beyond feedback when managers are working on self-improvements. This coach could be the supervisor, a trained facilitator or human resources consultant, or a trainer in a leadership development program. Follow-up surveys can be administered to provide additional feedback on change. (See Chapter Nine for more information on assessing change as a result of feedback.)

Some organizations take a systems approach to human resources development. A key feature of this approach is linking development strategies within an overall framework of development planning rather than engaging in the use of a single strategy, like 360-degree feedback, as an isolated event. A development systems approach likely has greater potential to result in lasting change than does the approach that treats a single tool, like 360 feedback, as the complete solution (McCauley and Hughes-James, 1994; McCauley, Moxley, and Van Velsor, 1998).

In summary, an administrative process that supports managers' involvement, ownership, and self-determination is characterized by (1) good communication about the purpose of the 360 program, (2) managers choosing their own raters, guided by information on how to select good raters, (3) the thoughtful implementation of potentially valuable customer feedback, and (4) the provision of support adequate to the challenges individuals will face in receiving and integrating their feedback.

The Questionnaire: Input to the Process

The choice of a questionnaire is a critical step in the 360-degree feedback process. The quality of the feedback that participants will receive is very much determined by the quality of the questionnaire (or instrument) used. Listed next are several guidelines to keep in mind in reviewing or developing a 360-degree feedback instrument. For more detailed information, the reader is referred to Van Velsor, Leslie, and Fleenor (1997) and to Lepsinger and Lucia (1997).

GUIDELINE 6: INSTRUCTIONS SHOULD BE CLEAR.

Typically, in a 360-degree feedback process, a manager will receive several kinds of instructions related to the process of completing the questionnaires. He or she will receive instructions or guidelines about how to choose raters and distribute forms, what to communicate to raters about the process, and how to return forms for scoring. The manager also will receive instructions on how to complete the forms—how to think about and respond to the items on the questionnaire.

Instructions on all questionnaires and accompanying materials should be clear and complete. Given the large volume of information the manager receives and the importance of understanding the processes of questionnaire distribution and item response, all instructions should be written clearly and be as easy to follow as possible to reduce the likelihood that raters will fail to respond or will respond incorrectly. The accuracy and completeness of data are critical to quality feedback and continued ownership and involvement in the process.

GUIDELINE 7: QUESTIONNAIRE ITEMS SHOULD BE WELL DESIGNED.

After the instructions, the first thing managers and their raters see are the items on the questionnaire. These are typically behaviors, skills, or perspectives on which the manager is to be rated. Usually, a questionnaire contains many items that assess several skills or perspectives. For example, SkillScope (Kaplan, 1997), a multi-rater skills assessment for managers, contains items such as "adept at disseminating information to others," "makes his or her point effectively to a resistant audience," and "strong communicator on paper."

Each rater's responses to items are typically averaged across the group of items that measure a single skill or perspective (thus creating a scale score); then the scale scores for groups of raters are averaged. For example, the responses to the SkillScope items listed (in addition to several other, related items) would be averaged for each person who rated the manager to get a scale score from each rater for the scale "Communicating Information." Then, the scale scores for "Communicating Information" from all raters in a particular rater group (for example, peers or direct reports) would be averaged to get the different rater group scores for that scale.

Because raters' responses to the items are the raw material making up the feedback that individuals will receive, it is essential that items be well constructed. Several aspects to item construction should be noted in developing or selecting a questionnaire. These include the nature of item content; the clarity of item language; the unidimensionality, face validity, and observability of items; the extent to which items are free of unnecessary qualifiers; and the test-retest reliability (or stability over time) of items.

The Nature of Item Content

Although the trend over the past twenty-five years has been to move away from a trait-based approach to understanding leadership (traits of people in leadership positions, sometimes without regard to their effectiveness, are studied in order to discern what leads to good leadership) toward a more behavioral approach (what effective leaders do is studied), a mix of approaches continues to be evident when we survey existing 360-degree instruments.

Some items in use on instruments available today relate more to stable traits than to skills or behaviors (for example, "high level of aspiration," "unhurried," "dependable"). Yet, many items are behavioral in nature, focusing on specific ways of behaving or on leadership practices. For example, items such as "I praise people for a job well done" or "plans what resources are needed to carry out a task or project" would be more behavioral in their approach. Some items are more accurately described as skill- or competency-based, such as "speaks effectively to a large group" or "is good at visualizing ways to improve." And finally, items may focus on attitudes or values if the authors believe that leadership effectiveness or others' willingness to follow a leader is based on attitude or values agreement. SYMLOG (Bales, 1991) is an example of a multi-rater assessment instrument focusing on values, as well as on behaviors (in two separate questionnaires), with raters responding on the values instrument to items such as "equality, democratic participation in decision-making" and "individual financial success, personal prominence, and power."

The different types of item content have implications for how the feedback is used and how much the feedback recipient may buy into the feedback. In general, the greater the inference a rater has to make (that is, the less observable an item or the more the item attempts to measure an internal state), the easier for the manager to reject the feedback if it is negative. In the face of negative feedback, others cannot know what we feel or the values we hold dear unless we have expressed those in conversation or in our behavior. Also, developing or changing values or character traits is more difficult than modifying behaviors or building skills. Inasmuch as 360-degree instruments are intended as tools to foster development, feedback may be most readily accepted when items on the questionnaire relate to, or can be linked with (as in SYMLOG), observable behaviors as much as possible.

Clarity

The wording of items should be clear. If the wording of an item confuses the rater or if raters are likely to respond differently to an item because it is ambiguous, then the instrument will not do a good job of measuring the intended skills and perspectives. One common example is the use of the word *organization* in an item. The meaning or intended referent for the word can be hard to interpret and can produce multiple interpretations if different raters have a different mental picture of what the word is supposed to mean. Another kind of item that can have multiple meanings is a single adjective, used without any definition; the word *conservative* is an example. An item such as that can produce very low agreement among raters if each rater is thinking of something different when responding. For example, does the item mean fiscally conservative, conservative in religious beliefs, generally not a risk-taker, or politically conservative?

Unidimensionality

If an item is unidimensional, it focuses on only one aspect of a skill or one behavior. An example of an item that is *not* unidimensional would be, "is perceptive of just how much influence he or she has and works to enhance that influence." It is entirely possible that an individual could be perceptive but not working to enhance influence, making this item impossible for raters to respond to accurately. If both of these behaviors are important to measure, an item like this should be broken into two items ("is perceptive of just how much influence he or she has" and "works to enhance his or her influence"). Separating the two behaviors will allow raters to rate people who are either perceptive and not working to enhance influence or not perceptive yet still working to enhance influence.

Face Validity

Face validity is important in that it relates to the manager's first impression of the instrument and, thus, can have a negative impact if it is lacking. High face validity means that the items make sense to people; behaviors seem relevant to leadership or management performance. However, most 360-degree instruments do not suffer from a lack of face validity because they are based on behaviors or skills that managers need, especially if the instruments have been developed from solid research and leadership theory.

Observability

Items need to relate to observable phenomena. Asking raters to rate behaviors that they do not generally observe can be a frustrating experience for the rater and can provide data to the manager that are impossible to interpret. Feedback on items that cannot be directly observed by raters will be easy for managers to dismiss, given that raters have to infer unobservable qualities from outward behaviors not directly assessed by the items or to assess qualities they have not had the opportunity to observe.

In addition, items should either be ratable by all rater groups or targeted toward specific rater groups. The advantage of using the same items across rater groups is that it allows for comparison of the different rater views. Yet some behaviors or practices are relevant only to people whom a manager supervises; others may be more adequately assessed by peers; and other aspects of a manager's skills are perhaps seen primarily by the boss. Having different items for different rater groups can focus managers on the key dimensions that define their relationships to the different rater groups. Probably the best strategy is to include some items that are rater-specific and some that focus on areas that can be compared across raters. To the extent that items are included that are not necessarily ratable by all rater groups, response options such as "no opportunity to observe," "not applicable," or "don't know" can be used. This and other properties of good response scales are addressed more fully in the section that follows.

Free of Unnecessary Qualifiers

A well-constructed item is generally free of qualifiers; that means it doesn't contain words like *very, extremely,* or the like. Qualifiers make an item more difficult to respond to and sometimes conflict with the dimensions of the response scale. The response scale is the set of choices that raters use to rate an individual on an item (options for response scales are discussed later in this chapter). For example, the item, "This manager has extremely good general management skills," with a response scale of "strongly agree," "agree," "slightly agree," "slightly disagree," "disagree," and "strongly disagree" would be difficult for the rater to answer or the feedback recipient to interpret. In this example the interpretive problem results not only from the use of a qualifier but also from the lack of fit between the way the item is worded and the response choices the rater is given. Although to "strongly agree" or to "strongly disagree" that a manager has extremely good general management skills is unambiguous in its meaning, it is less clear what should be inferred from a response such as "slightly agree" or "slightly disagree" (that a manager has extremely good skills). Does the manager have good but not extremely good skills? Does he or she display extremely good skills but only on occasion? Clearly, it would be up to the recipient of this feedback to decide.

Test-Retest Reliability

Finally, items should have adequate test-retest reliability, which relates to the stability of items over short periods of time and is important because we want to know that, given no change in the target manager's skills or behaviors, raters will respond similarly to the items at different times. If they do not respond similarly under conditions of no change, it means that the items are ambiguous in their meaning and interpretable in different ways at different times. Ambiguous items (that is, items with low test-retest reliability) are useless in assessing a construct because we can never be sure what they are measuring.

Test-retest reliability is established through a series of special pilot tests of the questionnaire. The general procedure is as follows: (1) The questionnaire is administered to a group of people (fifty is usually enough) who are asked to rate themselves and possibly to get ratings from others (to simplify the pilot study process, test-retest reliability studies are sometimes conducted only with self-ratings); (2) these individuals do *not* receive feedback on their scores until after the test-retest process is complete; (3) after a short period of time (usually four to six weeks), the *same* people who completed the questionnaire the first time are asked to complete it again; (4) the earlier ratings are compared, item by item, to the second ratings, typically using a correlational analysis; (5) correlations of .4 (between Time 1 and Time 2 ratings for each item) are usually considered minimally acceptable, with correlations of .6 or .7 being more desirable (correlations can range from 0 to 1).

Although the test-retest process feels repetitive to the people who are asked to participate, they should be advised that repetition is exactly the point, because the goal is to test the integrity of the questionnaire items. It is critical that the same people complete the items the second time around, because the focus of this study is the consistency of their responses over short periods of time. It is therefore unacceptable to substitute new respondents for ones who may drop out for the second administration of the questionnaire.

Although some argue that test-retest reliability is not important when a questionnaire is designed to measure qualities on which people can improve, it is even more important that test-retest reliability be high with instruments such as these. If raters' responses to items fluctuate significantly over periods of time too short for real change to have taken place (for example, two to six weeks), then we can suspect that the items are poorly written and that raters are responding differently, not because the target manager has changed but because the meaning of the items is ambiguous. When we attempt to track change over longer periods of time, it is important to know that items are reliable or stable so we can attribute any response shift to real change rather than to poor item construction.

GUIDELINE 8: CONSIDER DESIGN
ALTERNATIVES FOR RESPONSE SCALES.

The response scale refers to the choices given to raters for framing their responses. There are two kinds of response scales used in most 360-degree instruments: frequency and mastery. Frequency response scales prompt the rater to respond according to *how often* a behavior is seen or how frequently a statement is true of the manager. Mastery response scales prompt the rater to respond with an assessment of *how well* a skill is developed or a behavior or practice is executed.

In current 360-degree instruments, frequency scales tend to be the norm. Frequency response scales may be easier for the rater to use, in that raters are asked to describe something that is concrete and observable (how often a behavior occurs) rather than to evaluate something that may be more abstract (how well developed a capacity is). As discussed earlier, observability is a desired characteristic for items; knowing that raters are reporting on behaviors they can actually see can help managers accept negative feedback and set goals for change.

Yet, one disadvantage of a frequency response scale is that, by itself, it implies that more frequent use of a behavior or a skill is better, without taking into account whether this is actually the case. For example, an item such as "pays attention to detail" with a response scale running from "1 = not at all" to "5 = very frequently" would allow a manager to get a high rating (for example, 5) on a behavior that can be ineffective if overdone. In fact, some recent research (Eggars, Leahy, and Churchill, 1997) has shown that when items from the same instrument are compared, the criterion validity of scores based on responses to a frequency scale may be less than that of scores based on a mastery scale.

A second issue with frequency responses is that the frequency with which a manager uses a particular leadership practice or behavior may vary across subordinates but might be the correct frequency for each of those subordinates. Therefore, direct-report ratings of a behavior might vary across raters, but there may be no need for the manager to change behaviors or improve skills. In addition, because most instruments provide averaged scores across raters on the leadership domains assessed, appropriate variations of managerial behavior across a group of direct reports may be hidden from view by the aggregation of rater data. In summary, although frequency scales do have some desirable properties and perhaps lend themselves to easier completion by raters, when used alone they may not provide as much useful or valid information as mastery scales and should be supplemented by other frameworks for helping the manager interpret the meaning of his or her scores.

Another way response scales vary is on the number of points on the scale. Response scales on instruments typically range from 2 points—for example, (1) strength, (2) development needed—to 10 points; a 5-point scale is the most frequent. One objection to the often-used 3- or 5-point scales is that these scales have a midpoint response that allows raters to provide vague or noncommittal responses. For example, the 5-point response scale, 1 = very satisfied, 2 = satisfied, 3 = neither satisfied nor dissatisfied, 4 = dissatisfied, and 5 = very dissatisfied, might work to encourage a rater who did not want to put much thought or energy into the task to respond right down the middle with "neither satisfied nor dissatisfied" responses. For this reason some people favor a 6-point scale over a 5-point scale. An example of a 6-point scale is 1 = very satisfied, 2 = satisfied, 3 = slightly satisfied, 4 = slightly dissatisfied, 5 = dissatisfied, and 6 = very dissatisfied. Using this scale would force a rater to choose between two middle alternatives and to commit to a position of either satisfied or dissatisfied, to some extent. Generally, it can be demotivating to receive feedback that is consistently mid-range, especially if the mid-range response is something like "neither satisfied nor dissatisfied." But the impact of feedback on any response scale can be enhanced through the use of various strategies to facilitate interpretation, such as comparison to norms, highlighting important data, and the like. These strategies are discussed later in this chapter.

Many people favor a shorter response scale because of its simplicity and ease of use. In rating a manager, it is probably easier for raters to choose between two or even five choices than it is to choose between ten alternatives. And it is easy for the manager to interpret responses on a short response scale (for example, [1] "strength," [2] "development needed"). But if one desires to assess change in managers' behaviors over time, generally a longer response scale is better, in that it can potentially pick up smaller increments of change. For example, at the extreme, a 2-point scale that allows raters to indicate "strength" or "development needed" in response to a number of items would be inadequate for assessing change because a person would have to change a great deal in the mind of the rater to move from one category to the other. On the other extreme, a longer scale could potentially pick up the level of change individuals can be reasonably expected to achieve as a result of most leadership development interventions (for example, a movement from 5 to 6 on a 10-point scale). For a more in-depth discussion of this and other topics related to change, see Chapter Nine.

A final issue having to do with response scales is the inclusion of opportunities for raters to register a "no opportunity to observe" or "not applicable" response to one or more items. If these choices are available, raters should be instructed to use them when they feel they cannot rate the particular skill or behavior because (1) the rater believes the skill or behavior is not required in the target manager's job, (2) the rater interacts with the target manager too infrequently to assess the skill or behavior, or (3) the rater has not had the opportunity to observe the skill level or behavior because the rater and target manager are geographically remote from each other.

There are both costs and benefits to the inclusion of these choices in a response scale. One cost is the possible loss of data in that people who want to get through the rating task in a hurry may overuse these categories. They may use them rather than spend the time to make another, more considered choice. Basically, responses in these categories become "missing data" in the scoring process because they can't be assigned a value. A potential advantage to having this choice for raters is that it allows raters to register a meaningful response when they do not feel an item relates to the target manager's job or when they have not had the opportunity to observe the behavior because they interact with the individual too infrequently, are geographically remote, or work outside the manager's organization. That information may be useful in helping a manager interpret his or her data, in that a large number of "don't knows" could signify that the raters did not feel they knew the manager very well (although some instruments do collect data directly on how well the rater knows the target manager). Multiple "don't know" responses can also be a piece of feedback if the items in question are behaviors or practices that the manager believes he or she is using with great frequency or mastery.

Similarly, "not applicable" as a response choice can be especially advantageous on 360-degree instruments, especially when there are raters who are internal and others who are external to the organization (for example, customers). In this case, the availability of a "not applicable" choice can give an alternative to raters when an item is really not relevant to their relationship with the target manager. In the absence of this choice, raters must either leave the item blank or hazard a guess based on a set of experiences that may be far removed from the item(s) in question.

Output: The Feedback Report

Often, a request to know more about a 360-degree feedback instrument is a request to see a copy of the instrument itself. Yet, the instrument is simply the input to a process. What the manager actually receives as a result of the process is scored output or a feedback report. On this report, the manager sees the assessments made by his or her boss, peers, direct reports, and others on whatever valued skills and perspectives the process is designed to address.

As explained earlier, groups of questionnaire items typically are averaged to create scale scores. Each scale score represents a single skill or capacity. Because these scale scores are usually the main dimensions on which managers receive 360-degree feedback, and because we want individuals to take this feedback seriously, it is important that the feedback scales be well constructed.

In addition, the way in which feedback is displayed can vary greatly from one instrument to another, reflecting the many choices available for designing and formatting output. Regardless of whether one is creating a customized instrument or buying a ready-made product, it is important to consider design alternatives to report formats. These two issues (construction of feedback scales and design of report format) are addressed in the next two guidelines.

GUIDELINE 9: FEEDBACK SCALES
SHOULD BE WELL CONSTRUCTED.

Any evidence that scales are poorly constructed can be reason for individuals receiving feedback to reject the information or lose commitment to development goals. In general, each scale should represent only one construct; the construct should be defined, and both internal consistency reliability and construct validity should be established. As administrators of a 360-degree process, we should know that items in a given scale are interrelated and that the scores measure what they purport to measure or that they are related to other measures of effectiveness.

Sometimes, factor analyses are used to determine how the proposed items group together to form scales. When factor analytic methods are used for scale development, we are allowing the actual correlations among the items we've written to tell us what scales, if any, exist within the "item pool" (the total group of items we have on the instrument). To the extent that items do not "load" on a scale, we would typically discard them in favor of other (existing or rewritten) items, continuing the process of writing and rewriting items until we had a sufficient number of items loading directly on a number of desired dimensions or scales.

Another way of making decisions about the dimensions to assess and the items that can assess those dimensions is to build on the instrument developer's experience or on organizational needs or strategies. When this method is used, the desired dimensions are usually identified first, with the writing of items (several items for each dimension) occurring only after scale domains are identified. When this approach is taken, factor analyses may be used to check the extent to which items do form scales as expected. But sometimes, analysis of these "a priori" scales is limited to checking to see whether the internal consistency of the resulting scales is acceptably high.

Like items, scales need to be properly constructed in order to be meaningful and useful. Well-constructed scales have some of the same properties as well-constructed items; they also have some unique properties. As with items, test-retest reliability is an important quality of scales and is usually established by ensuring that all items included in a scale have adequate test-retest reliability.

Another aspect of reliability that comes into play for the dimensions or scales on which managers will receive feedback is called internal consistency, which relates to the homogeneity of the item content within feedback scales. Internal consistency measures are based on the average correlation among items and the number of items on the scale. Fundamentally, it asks whether all the items that make up a single scale are, in fact, measuring the same thing (as inclusion on a single scale would suggest). If they are, then managers who exhibit one of the behaviors that define the scale should also tend to exhibit the behaviors described by other items on that scale (or should exhibit them to the same degree). If this coefficient (usually Cronbach's alpha) is low (less than .7), either the scale contains too few items or the items have little in common. If the coefficient for a scale is very high, there may be more items than are really necessary to adequately measure the construct. Typically, we try to develop scales that attain the highest internal consistency with the fewest items. An example of a scale having high reliability (alpha = .97) would be the following items (some are abbreviated) to assess "decisiveness," taken from Benchmarks (Lombardo and McCauley, 1994):

1. Displays a real bias for action
2. Is quick and approximate rather than slow and precise
3. Is action-oriented
4. Does not hesitate when making decisions

However, if the item "quickly masters new technical knowledge" were added, scale reliability might decrease because the additional item goes outside the domain of decisiveness and into the domain of learning.

In addition to understanding scale reliability, it is important that we know something about the validity of the scales on which feedback will be received. Basically, validity relates to the degree to which we know that an instrument is measuring what it claims to be measuring and that the main inferences underlying its use are supported by empirical data. Obviously, the degree to which validity has been established is critical to maximizing the ownership of data by the manager receiving it. Any manager who is asked to devote time and energy to addressing leadership development needs as a result of a 360-degree feedback process has a stake in knowing that it is, in fact, measuring what it claims to be measuring and that those capacities do, in fact, relate to effective performance in leadership roles.

Typically, in a validity study for a 360-degree feedback leadership instrument we need to establish that scores on the scales have been shown to be related to independent assessments of performance or effectiveness as a manager or leader, because the inference underlying the use of these tools is usually that higher scores are better scores (that is, people with higher scores are better leaders or higher performers). A simple validity study often has the following elements: (1) ratings are collected, from self and from others, on the questionnaire; (2) data are also collected on other kinds of performance assessment—these can be performance-appraisal ratings, responses from a separate questionnaire that asks general questions about effectiveness or performance, or relative rankings of managers (top 20 percent, middle 60 percent, bottom 20 percent) in terms of their recent past performance; (3) statistical analyses are conducted that compare the ratings on the instrument to the other kinds of performance assessment. The correlation between the performance ratings and the instrument scores should be statistically significant and at least moderate in magnitude (.4 or above).

In summary, if validity is weak or if no such evidence is available, a manager would be right to question the need to invest time and energy in trying to change or improve, because there would be no certainty that more skill or different behaviors would be attainable or even beneficial.

GUIDELINE 10: QUALITIES ASSESSED SHOULD BE DEVELOPABLE.

On a 360-degree feedback instrument, regardless of whether it is used for development purposes only or for performance assessment, the items and scales should represent qualities that are developable. Although it is useful to gain self-knowledge about aspects of character that are stable (and therefore not changeable), it is important for managers to know that characteristics being assessed are also amenable to development, especially when improvement is the goal. Behavioral or otherwise observable items forming scales that relate to practices or perspectives one can change are the most useful form for 360-degree feedback, in that it enables managers to engage in a goal-setting and development-planning process that enhances involvement and self-determination.

Knowing that an instrument used for development is assessing qualities that are, in fact, developable can be seen as a type of validity. The kind of validity study that is important in this case is a study showing that scores on the instrument can be changed through development planning and effort on the part of the manager. Studies that look at change as a result of feedback are not as numerous as those focusing on other aspects of reliability and validity because of the many problems and pitfalls inherent in measuring change over time. The interested reader is referred to Chapter Nine for more information on these issues.

Finally, the scales on which managers receive feedback also should be aligned with the vision and values of their organizations. Managers should perceive that the dimensions on which they are being assessed are related to skills and perspectives valued and rewarded in their organizations. Managers are not likely to be motivated to work on development goals if those goals do not relate to valued skills and practices seen as effective in their workplace.

GUIDELINE 11: CONSIDER DESIGN ALTERNATIVES FOR REPORT FORMATS.

The design of a report format can have a significant impact on how readily managers can interpret the data they receive, as well as on how motivated they are to take action based on the feedback. The phrase *design alternatives for report formats* refers to the strategies and frameworks for data presentation that are built into the feedback report. All 360-degree feedback presents self-ratings and ratings from others on a variety of items and scales. People need help sifting through, prioritizing, and interpreting the large amount of data that can be produced in a feedback report of this type. For example, knowing that the average rating, across all raters, on a particular competency was 3.0 (on a 5-point scale) is not very informative and is hard to interpret. Yet, this score takes on more meaning if we know that the mean score for all other managers who have ever been rated is 2.5, and even more so if we know that direct reports rated the manager 2.5 and peers rated the manager 3.5.

Types of Feedback Display

The most common types of feedback display used in 360-degree feedback instruments are graphic displays and narrative. Graphic displays are charts, graphs, or tables showing numeric scores, whereas narrative is typically a detailed, textual description and interpretation of the results, which is personalized to varying degrees.

Graphic displays can provide an excellent visualization of how managers view themselves in comparison to their raters and instrument norms (comparison to norms is discussed later in this chapter). Commonly used visual displays include bar graphs, line graphs, grids or plots, and circumplexes. Many instruments use a combination of types of graphic display in a single feedback report. Exhibit 7.1 presents an example of a line graph. Other exhibits later in the chapter (Exhibits 7.4 and 7.6) show examples of bar graphs.

Narrative reports are used to varying degrees in many instruments, especially those that are PC-based (that is, instruments using disk-based computer technology for administration or scoring or both). Narrative reports are generated from standard blocks of interpretive text written into program code. In the scoring process, scale scores within certain ranges are linked to specific blocks of text, and the appropriate combinations of text are combined; a narrative report is generated. Narrative reports differ from the development materials that sometimes accompany 360-degree feedback in that development materials are usually off-the-shelf manuals, workbooks, and readings; narrative reports are personalized interpretations of an individual manager's scores on the instrument.

In some settings the narrative report can be an especially powerful tool, in that it provides a level of interpretation not readily available without a facilitated, face-to-face, individual feedback session. Narrative can prove useful over time, as well, because it allows the manager to reread the descriptive and interpretive material rather than revisiting graphical data and relying on memory for meaning.

Breakout of Rater Responses

Separate mean ratings for different groups of raters (for example, peers, direct reports, customers) is a key feature of 360-degree instruments. It is, in fact, the distinguishing feature and the reason for the "360" (views from all around) label. The intent of this type of instrument is to give the manager good information about how skills and behaviors are seen by people with whom he or she has differing relationships. Knowing, for example, that direct reports see the manager as very good in the area of leading subordinates will mean more to the manager than seeing a moderate rating on such a dimension from peers or from all rater types grouped together.

Exhibit 7.1. Example of a Line Graph.

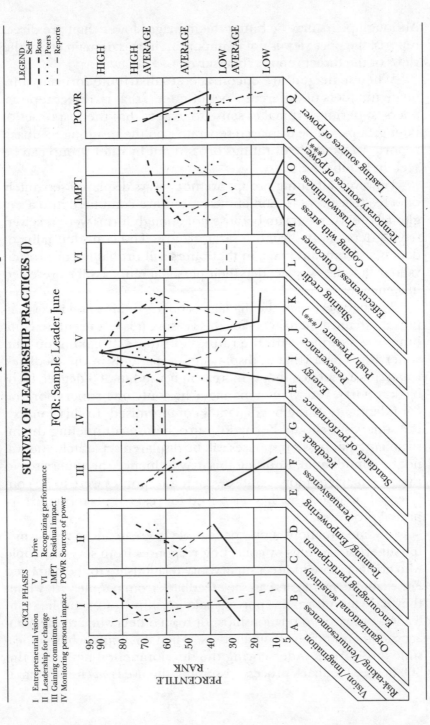

SURVEY OF LEADERSHIP PRACTICES (J)

FOR: Sample Leader June

CYCLE PHASES
I   Entrepreneurial vision   V   Drive
II Leadership for change   VI   Recognizing performance
III Gaining commitment   IMPT Residual impact
IV Monitoring personal impact POWR Sources of power

LEGEND
Self ——————
Boss -- -- --
Peers ·········
Reports — — —

Source: Copyright © 1996 by The Clark Wilson Group, Incorporated. Printed with permission of the publisher.

Although peers may be rating the manager lower than are direct reports, the peer view is not as important in this domain as are the views of the direct reports themselves.

When managers are encouraged to distribute forms to adequate numbers of different types of raters (that is, direct reports, peers, superiors), it makes sense to expect that the responses of rater groups will be displayed separately on the resulting feedback report. An example of ratings broken out by rater group can be seen in Exhibit 7.2.

However, all rating groups are not always displayed separately on a feedback report. Sometimes, raters are combined into a single "all observers" group because not enough forms were received from raters in one or more rater groups. The confidentiality of data is a significant issue, in that raters will probably not provide valid data if they suspect that their personal ratings will be revealed in some way.

The perspective of the manager's boss is unique and is very important to most managers. For this reason, it is less useful to combine boss's ratings with the ratings of others. Breaking out the supervisor's data (that is, displaying it separately in the feedback report) is a practice that is increasingly used in 360-degree feedback reports. Yet, when a manager has only one supervisor, the confidentiality of the boss's data is compromised. In this context, the supervisor should be made aware, before completing the instrument, that boss's responses will be displayed separately and will not be confidential. Knowing this may influence the supervisor to rate the manager more positively than if responses were to be confidential, an effect that has been seen for years in performance appraisal processes.

In some situations it may be feasible to create more anonymity for supervisor ratings by collecting responses from several people who are in a more indirect supervisory relationship to the manager. For example, managers can seek feedback from people with whom they have an informal reporting relationship (for example, team leaders or matrixed relationships) or from others who are the managers of their immediate supervisors. When this approach is not feasible or desired, underscoring the developmental nature of the 360-degree feedback process (assuming the use is *not* for appraisal

Exhibit 7.2. Example of Breakout of Rater Data.

	Your Score	Low	Mid-Range		High
Self	4.00			S	
All Observers	3.56		O		
Boss/Superiors	4.75				B
Peers	3.42		P		
Direct Reports	3.40		R		

Most Important for Success

All Obsvr	Boss	Self
8	✓	✓

	Self	Boss/Sup	Peer	DRpt
36. Displays a real bias for action, calculated risks, and quick decisions.	4.00	[5.00]	3.00	3.60
37. Is quick and approximate rather than slow and precise in making decisions.	4.00	4.00	3.67	3.20
38. Is action-oriented.	4.00	[5.00]	4.00	3.20
39. Does not hesitate when making decisions.	4.00	[5.00]	3.00	3.60

Higher Ratings Preferred

Key:

[ ] = 15 highest rated items (plus ties) for each rater group.

___ = 15 lowest items (plus ties) for each rater group.

 *   = Gap of at least 3 points between raters from one category.

Source: Benchmarks®, copyright © 1994, Center for Creative Leadership.

or selection) may help to influence the manager's boss to provide candid ratings of behaviors and skills.

One additional concern about the breakout of boss data has to do with the impact of these ratings on the manager's reaction to the feedback. Many managers will place disproportionate weight on the boss's ratings and will tend to pay less attention to ratings of peers or direct reports. This can and should be addressed in a facilitated feedback session (that is, a session, led by a person qualified to present feedback on the instrument, in which scores are presented and explained). Such a session should emphasize the value and importance of peer and direct report views in light of the impact that the manager's behaviors have on these individuals and with respect to the implications for the effective leadership of these important constituencies.

Although the anonymity of raters needs to be protected if not enough forms are completed, feedback that is broken out by rater group is more informative than feedback that combines the responses of different rater groups. In order to lead most effectively, a manager needs to have the most comprehensive view of how he or she is perceived. The richness and complexity of a manager's interpersonal world is diluted when data from different rater groups are lumped together. Different types of raters will observe different behaviors. Because no one observes a manager in all possible situations, feedback from multiple groups gives the manager greater quantity and quality of information about his or her behavior and skills.

In addition, the interpretation of a behavior will often vary, depending on the rater's relationship to that manager. Direct reports not only see things that the boss may not see (and vice versa), but they often will interpret the same things differently, perhaps because they need different things from the manager. For example, a behavior such as "keeping others informed" may get very different responses from a manager's boss and direct reports if the manager places more importance on upward communication than on communication with direct reports, especially if those direct reports depend on the manager as a main source of information.

At least seven other strategies are frequently used for creating focus for development in 360-degree feedback reports. Typically, a combination of two or more strategies is used in any one feedback report, sometimes in combination with narrative interpretation and sometimes not. The remainder of this section describes, in some detail, each of these seven additional strategies.

Comparison to Norms

Next to the breakout of rater data, the comparison of individual scores to norms is the most widely used context for presenting scores on standard 360-degree instrument feedback reports. Comparison of this sort helps managers answer the question, How are my scores, relative to the scores of other managers? For example, in Exhibit 7.3 the norm group is represented by the shaded bar, self-ratings are represented by solid dots, and combined others' ratings are represented by an open square.

For most instruments the norm base is composed of all managers who have taken the instrument over time. When an instrument has been developed for general use by many organizations and has been administered to groups of managers over time, the norm base can be quite large and diverse. Sample sizes of norm groups on some of the most well-known instruments range from about four hundred to over one hundred thousand managers (Leslie and Fleenor, 1998). However, scores are increasingly presented, not in comparison to a "public" database of all managers but in comparison to smaller and more targeted norm groups. When there is reason to believe that management skills or leadership capacities might be specific to an industry group, organizations often want the scores of their managers compared to scores of managers in comparable industries. When an instrument has been developed within a specific organization or has been customized for use by a single organization, the norms used will sometimes be limited to those collected from managers who have completed the survey from that one organization. The advantage of these more specific norms is that each manager's scores are being compared to others who share similar circumstances (same organization or same industry), allowing the managers to know how their scores compare to those of other managers in their company or industry. When an instrument is being used to assess and develop organization-specific or industry-specific skills and competencies, it may be more useful to know how each manager is doing relative to others in the organization or how the organization

Exhibit 7.3. Example of Comparison to Norms.

SKILLS OVERVIEW

Pat Manager	PDI Norm
Name	Norm group

SKILLS	Extent to which skills are used					DISK	IMP
	1 not at all	2 little	3 some	4 great	5 very great		
THINKING FACTOR Analyze Issues				●□			S
Use Sound Judgment				□–●			S B
ADMINISTRATIVE FACTOR Establish Plans			●□				
Manage Execution			●–□			●–□	S
LEADERSHIP FACTOR Provide Direction			●——□			●–□	S B
Lead Courageously			□●				B
Influence Others			●□				B
Foster Teamwork			□——●		□–●		S
Motivate Others			□●				
Coach and Develop			◉				
Champion Change			□●				B
INTERPERSONAL FACTOR Build Relationships			□——●		□–●		
Display Organizational Savvy			◉				
Manage Disagreements			●				

Respondents:		Key:	
	Boss = 1		□ Boss, Direct Reports, Peers/Colleagues
	Direct Reports = 3		● Self ▬ Norm Group
	Peers/Colleagues = 4		●–□ Self/Other discrepancy
			S Self critically important
			B Boss critically important

as a whole compares to other organizations in that industry. If, however, the goal is general leadership development, a comparison to more general norms may be advantageous, in that the numbers of managers to which a manager is compared will be much larger and more diverse and will allow managers to know how their scores compare to those of effective leaders from all kinds of organizations.

Whatever norms are used, it is important to know that they are appropriate for the level of manager to whom the feedback will be given. Comparing the scores of middle managers to a norm base of senior managers, for example, may cause middle managers to draw inappropriately harsh conclusions about their leadership competency, if the instrument is one on which senior managers usually score higher.

Most of the instruments whose audience is a general one (for example, managers from many different levels, organization types, industries) use a norm group that has data from managers at all levels, many organization types, and various industries. However, if there is reason to believe that the manager is working in an industry, an organization, or a job in which the leadership demands are unique or unusual, organizational or industry norms may be more useful than norms drawn from a general managerial population.

Comparison to norms generally takes one of two forms: standard scores or percentile rankings. A standard score is a computation that allows individual scores to be compared to a distribution of scores by taking into account the mean and standard deviation of the total population. The use of standard scores allows the user to know what, in relation to the population distribution, is considered a high score and what is considered a low score—regardless of the specific rating-scale format used for the instrument. An example of the use of standardized scores, from the Campbell Leadership Index (Campbell, 1991), is included in Exhibit 7.4.

A percentile ranking represents the percentage of people in the norm base who have lower scores than the individual being ranked. Exhibit 7.5 shows a feedback display that uses a percentile ranking.

Comparison to an Ideal

Comparison to an ideal is based on a somewhat different philosophy than comparison to norms. Although comparison to norms assumes that it is most useful for managers to see how their skills

Exhibit 7.4. Example of Use of Standard Scores.

CWO CAMPBELL LEADERSHIP INDEX INDIVIDUAL PROFILE

NAME: CLI APP B SAMPLE

DATE SCORED: 03/19/91

ORIENTATIONS (Scales)

NUMBER OF OBSERVERS: 5

PROFILED STANDARD SCORES

LEADERSHIP ORIENTATIONS		Std. Score	Score 25---30---35---40---45---50---55---60---65---70---75	This Score Is:
LEADERSHIP	Self	66		Very High ++
	Observers	63		Very High ++
Ambitious	Self	62		Very High ++
	Observers	66		Very High ++
Daring	Self	65		Very High ++
	Observers	62		Very High ++
Dynamic	Self	67		Very High ++
	Observers	60		Very High ++
Enterprising	Self	67		Very High ++
	Observers	58		High +
Experienced	Self	63		Very High ++
	Observers	59		High +
Farsighted	Self	59		High +
	Observers	55		High +
Original	Self	61		Very High ++
	Observers	57		High +
Persuasive	Self	51		Mid-Range =
	Observers	61		Very High ++

◆ = Your Score   ◇ = Observer Average

Exhibit 7.5. Scores on the Leadership Practices Inventory.

	PERCENTILE	CHALLENGING	INSPIRING	ENABLING	MODELING	ENCOURAGING
H I G H	99	30 29 28	30 29 28 27	30	30 29 28	30
		27	26	29	27	29 28
			25	28	26	27
	90	26			25	26
			24			25
	80	25	23	27	24	24
	70	24		26		
M O D E R A T E			22		23	23
	60	23	21	25	22	22
	50	22	20	24	21	21
	40	21	19			20
	30			23		
L O W			18		20	19
	20	20	17	22	19	18
		19	16			
				21		17
	10	18	15		18	16
		17	14 13	20 19	17	15 14 13 12
		16 15	12 11	18 17	16	
	0	14	10	16 15	15 14	

compare to other managers, comparison to an ideal assumes that it is most useful to compare oneself to a goal-state or to a theoretical "best." An example of an instrument that is theoretically based and that uses comparison to an ideal as one interpretive device is SYMLOG (Bales, 1991), which is shown in Exhibit 7.6.

Comparing scores to an ideal can lead to drawing different conclusions than when scores are compared to norms from other managers. For example, using normative comparison, a percentile rank of 80 percent (meaning that score is better than that of 80 percent of managers) would seem quite good and may leave a ratee feeling that no improvement is needed. However, a score of 80 percent in relation to an ideal would push one to conclude that the development job is not yet finished, because the ideal is still at some distance. Although normative feedback may be more encouraging for most managers, some may be more drawn to the idea of stretching themselves toward an ideal, be it their own ideal or one set by the theory on which an instrument is based. Comparison to an ideal is one of the least frequently used strategies for interpretation of scores, but it has the advantage of giving managers a "higher bar" against which to calibrate their personal development goals.

Item-Level Feedback

In order to act on their feedback, managers need the concrete behavioral information inherent in items. Without these, it is hard to know how to improve scores or increase competency in the sometimes abstract domains that scales can represent. Items define the meaning of scales, which are often too global to provide the kind of detail necessary in planning an individual development strategy. So, item-level feedback can have great utility.

However, the use of item-level feedback in 360-degree instruments presents an interesting dilemma in that, statistically speaking, items are unreliable. In fact, that is one reason items are grouped into scales; scales have a stability that items lack. Feedback on items can be more useful but less reliable, whereas feedback on scales can be more reliable but less useful.

Although some instruments avoid item-level feedback, most 360-degree instruments provide both item- and scale-level feedback to managers. Often, the item feedback is nested within the scale feedback—a strategy that is particularly helpful in that it provides

Exhibit 7.6. Example of Comparison to an Ideal Score.

Bargraph of the average of all ratings made on: CTM
Rating question: **In general, what kinds of values does your team** *currently* **show in behavior?**

Type: UF
Ratings: 15
Final Location: 6.0U 1.9P 10.6F

the bar of X's = the average rating on each item
E = the *optimum* location for most effective teamwork

RARELY   SOMETIMES   OFTEN

1 U	Individual financial success, personal prominence and power.	XXXXXXXXXXXXXXXXXXEXXXX
2 UP	Popularity and social success, being liked and admired.	XXXXXXXXXXXXXX — E
3 UPF	Active teamwork toward common goals, organizational unity.	XXXXXXXXXXXXXXXXXXXXX — E
4 UF	Efficiency, strong impartial management.	XXXXXXXXXXXXXXXXXXXXXXXXXXXXXXEXXXX
5 UNF	Active reinforcement of authority, rules, and regulations.	XXXXXXXXXXXXXXXXXXXXXXXXEXXXXXXXXX
6 UN	Tough-minded, self-oriented assertiveness.	XXXXXXXXXXXXXXXXXXXEXXXX
7 UNB	Rugged, self-oriented individualism, resistance to authority.	XXXXXXXXXXEX
8 UB	Having a good time, releasing tension, relaxing control.	XXXXX — E
9 UPB	Protecting less able members, providing help when needed.	XXXXXXXXXXXXX — E
10 P	Equality, democratic participation in decision making.	XXXXXXXXXXXXXXXXX — E
11 PF	Responsible idealism, collaborative work.	XXXXXXXXXXXXXXXXXX — E
12 F	Conservative, established, "correct" ways of doing things.	XXXXXXXXXXXXXXXXXXEXXXXXXXXX
13 NF	Restraining individual desires for organizational goals.	XXXXXXXXXXXXX — E
14 N	Self-protection, self-interest first, self-sufficiency.	XXXXX E
15 NB	Rejection of established procedures, rejection of conformity.	XXXXX — E
16 B	Change to new procedures, different values, creativity.	XX — E
17 PB	Friendship, mutual pleasure, recreation.	XXXX — E
18 DP	Trust in the goodness of others.	XXXXXXX — E
19 DPF	Dedication, faithfulness, loyalty to the organization.	XXXXXXXXXXXXXXXXXXXXXXXXXXXXX — E
20 DF	Obedience to the chain of command, complying with authority.	XXXXXXXXXXXXXX — E
21 DNF	Self-sacrifice if necessary to reach organizational goals.	XXXXXXXX — E
22 DN	Passive rejection of popularity, going it alone.	XX — E
23 DNB	Admission of failure, withdrawal of effort.	X — E
24 DB	Passive non-cooperation with authority.	X E
25 DPB	Quiet contentment, taking it easy.	XXX — E
26 D	Giving up personal needs and desires, passivity.	X — E

immediate concrete examples (in the item feedback) of why a particular capacity (that is, a scale score) was seen (rated by others) as high or as low. Examples of this strategy from two different sample feedback reports are presented in Exhibits 7.2 and 7.8.

Highlighting High and Low Items and Scales

Many 360-degree feedback reports highlight high and low scores on items and scales as a way of helping the individual sift through the large amounts of data that are provided and set developmental priorities. Highlighting the highest and lowest scores at the scale level can be useful, especially when there are many scales on which feedback is received and when the interpretation of scale scores does not depend on the interaction of scales (that is, no additional interpretive power is gained by looking across the scores provided on different scales).

Formatting the feedback so as to bring the best of a manager's strengths to light is a way of enhancing ownership of the data and adding to the manager's motivation to learn from the feedback experience. There are several processes for accomplishing this objective, including ordering scale scores so that strengths appear first or listing the top ten strengths as seen by self and by observers. In addition, highlighting the lowest items and scales can help managers set developmental priorities.

Yet, a problem with presenting high and low scores on items is that the listing may be made up of a smattering of items from many different scales and may thus provide a very unreliable summary of the most significant data. Although the *set* of items making up a scale adequately assesses the capacity named by the scale (if the scale reliability is adequate), any individual item is an incomplete representation of the capacity measured by the scale. As such, concentrating efforts to improve on a single item may not result in significant improvement on the capacity overall. A low score on a single item may also be misleading because it may be an item from a scale on which the overall score was average and extraordinary development efforts are not needed. Again, items are best used for illustrative purposes—as concrete examples of behaviors and skills that are related to a particular competency and not necessarily as pieces of actionable feedback in and of themselves.

Highlighting Largest Self/Rater Discrepancies

Although all 360-degree instruments compare self-view to the views of others, not all feedback reports use the graphic display to highlight the greatest or most significant discrepancies. Some feedback reports provide a list of items or scales following the graphic display that shows the largest self/rater difference. Another strategy, illustrated in the Executive Leadership Survey (Exhibit 7.7), is to sort the data into groups using self/rater discrepancy as a sorting mechanism. For example, when self-rating is high and others' ratings are high, those items and scales can be seen as visible strengths. When self-ratings are lower than others' ratings, we may be dealing with unrealized strengths. Items and scales that relate to acknowledged areas for improvement are identified as those on which both self- and others' ratings are low. Finally, blind spots are represented by those items and scales on which self-ratings are higher than others' ratings (Wilson and O'Hare, 1989). When narrative interpretation is used in a computer-scored instrument, patterns of difference can be tracked by the scoring software and discussed in the computer-generated narrative comments.

Other Approaches to Highlighting

As with many other aspects of feedback design, there are both benefits and downsides to coding aspects of a manager's feedback using color, underlining, or bolding. On the positive side, such highlighting can help a manager sort through large quantities of information more quickly, focusing directly on scores that show the greatest self/rater discrepancy or on scores that are particularly high or low in relation to norms. On the negative side, any mechanism used to direct the attention of managers to certain facets of the feedback may be taking evaluative responsibility away from the manager because the feedback report determines what is more and less important for the manager to focus on. The balance between the benefits and risks of these attentional devices probably depends on the complexity and length of the feedback report. In a shorter, simpler report, and when skilled facilitation of feedback will be provided, it is probably unnecessary to have the feedback report direct a manager's attention to certain aspects of the feedback. However, when a report is long or complex or when no one supports the

Exhibit 7.7. Example of Highlighting Self/Rater Discrepancies.

Self ratings from the previous page are compared to others by these rules:
Visible strengths (V. Strength): Both you and others rated you Average, High Avg or High
Unrealized strength (U. Strength): Self = Low or Low Avg; others = Average, High Avg or High
Acknowledged soft spot (Soft): Both you and others rated you Low or Low Avg
Blind spot (Blind): Self = Average, High Avg or High; others = Low or Low Avg

Executive Competencies	Self	Boss	Associates	Reports
I. Forward Thrust				
A. Leadership vision	Low	Soft	Soft	U. Strength
B. Risk-taking/Venturesomeness	Average	Blind	Blind	V. Strength
II. Executive Perspective				
C. Financial and operational analysis	Average	Blind	Blind	V. Strength
D. Marketplace savvy	Average	V. Strength	Blind	V. Strength
E. Organization savvy	Low Avg	Soft	Soft	U. Strength
F. Judgment	Low	Soft	Soft	U. Strength
III. Executive Implementation				
G. Decisiveness	Low Avg	Soft	Soft	U. Strength
H. Team growth and development	Low	Soft	Soft	U. Strength
I. Cultural appreciation	Low Avg	Soft	Soft	U. Strength

IV. Drive

	Average	Blind	Blind	Blind
IV. Drive				
J. Standards of performance	Low Avg	Soft	Soft	U. Strength
K. Executive energy	***	***	***	***
L. Push/Pressure (***)	High Avg	V. Strength	V. Strength	V. Strength
M. Coping with stress				
V. Acknowledging Contributions				
N. Sharing credit	Low	Soft	Soft	U. Strength
Outcomes				
Impt. Personal Impact				
O. Effectiveness/Outcomes	Low Avg	Soft	Soft	U. Strength
Powr. Power Sources				
P. Temporary sources of power (***)	Low	Soft	Soft	U. Strength
Q. Lasting sources of power	Low	Soft	Soft	U. Strength

(***) Interpretation of these dimensions depends on their relationship to up-front skills.

manager's attempt to interpret his or her data, highlighting of various parts of the feedback is probably necessary and useful.

Importance to Job or Success

Providing feedback on the perceived importance of the skills and capacities represented by items and scales can provide a powerful way of prioritizing which parts of the feedback may need the greatest attention, especially when the manager and the boss agree on the level of importance of different behaviors. When the manager and the boss do not agree, importance data can provide a relatively nonthreatening way to begin a conversation about what skills and behaviors need attention, given the characteristics of a manager's job and organization.

When an instrument is developed for use within a single organization, the importance of the different skills to managers' jobs may vary by department. Knowing how different skills are perceived in terms of relative importance in different departments or functional areas can help managers prioritize what parts of their feedback deserve the most attention.

Collecting and presenting ratings on the importance of a capacity or skill to the manager's job is another way to help managers understand which development goals they should focus their energy on. For example, a low score on a scale such as "balance between life and work" may be something a manager wants to work to improve, but the manager should do that in the context of knowing that balance between life and work is (or is not) seen as important to the job, or may be in fact deleterious to success.

There are concerns around the use of importance data, however. One argument is that the importance of different domains of leadership behavior should be ascertained as part of the processes of selecting the domains on which the instrument will focus and developing the scales that measure these domains rather than asking a manager to rate the importance when the instrument is completed. The question is, Why waste managers' time responding to items and scales if we don't know for sure whether they are important in that organization?

Second, for instruments that do include ratings of importance in a job or organization, there has been concern that nothing much was known about the validity of the importance data. That is, although all instruments that meet high-quality standards for instrument development[1] contain scales on which the relationship to effectiveness is known, few have tested the assumption that responses to "importance" questions produce useful information. In other words, can that information be related to the likelihood that someone with high scores on the "more important" scales will be more successful (effective or promotable) than someone with high scores on the "less important" scales?

For the past three years, researchers at CCL have been studying how importance ratings relate to ratings of managerial success in organizations. To date, they have found fewer and weaker relationships than expected. "Importance" ratings may be picking up raters' views about ideal leaders (that is, what they value in a leader) or those values to which an organizational culture may pay lip service but not reward with actual promotions. In many organizations, to perform effectively means to produce a favorable bottom-line result quarter after quarter and year after year. The behaviors that lead to this kind of effectiveness are not always the same as the behaviors that raters want to see in their leaders. These findings suggest that more validity testing needs to be done with a variety of instruments using importance ratings.

"Do More/Do Less" Information

When a frequency-type response scale is used on an instrument, the assumption built into the responses is that more of a behavior or skill is better than less of a behavior or skill. Although the same can be said for a mastery-type response scale (that is, more mastery is better than less mastery), mastery tends to mean that the individual is both good at the skill and knows when to employ it. Frequency, by itself, does not capture all that is important in the use of competencies.

For example, with some management practices, what leads to effectiveness can be related to situational, organizational, or individual needs. Effective managers may have low ratings from some raters on items or scales because lower ratings are desired in a specific context or because the individuals with whom the manager works do not need the manager to display higher frequencies of some behaviors. A low-to-moderate score on the degree to which a manager structures subordinates' work may mean that the manager is not structuring enough or that the manager is not doing much structuring and not much is desired.

When a frequency response scale is used on a 360-degree instrument, it is helpful to have some additional framework in the feedback delivery format that can report raters' views as to whether the observed frequency is the desired frequency or whether it should be greater or less. Only a few instruments in use today ask raters to indicate whether a manager should "do more" or "do less" of the rated behavior. An example of a report (Yukl, 1995) that uses this framework is provided in Exhibit 7.8.

Although this additional response can add to the sometimes onerous task of completing an instrument, especially if it is a lengthy instrument, the feedback can provide another useful way for the manager to prioritize work on development goals. In the previous example, a "do more/do less" option would allow the manager's raters to give the manager a low (frequency) rating on the degree to which he or she structures subordinates' work but also allow them to leave the "do less" option blank (meaning the low amount of structuring is just right) or even to register a feeling that they might like the manager to do even *less* structuring.

Verbatim or Write-In Comments

Verbatim comments have become especially popular and easier to produce with the advent of PC-based instruments and instrument scoring. The advantage of write-in comments is in the richness they can add to the quantitative data presented in scores. Using write-in methods, raters are allowed to describe, in some detail, the impact of certain behaviors on them or to give examples of how particular behaviors play out. In addition, they can register their views with respect to skills or behaviors they see as important but that may not be reflected in the items provided.

Yet, over the years there have been several concerns about verbatim text on 360-degree instrument feedback as well. One concern—that a rater's handwriting may reveal his or her identity—can be overcome if the input process is PC-based (that is, if raters input their verbatim responses directly into the computer). However, in some cases, the nature of the comments or examples given may still

Exhibit 7.8. Example of the Use of "Do More/Do Less" Information.

CONSULTING

Key ■ □ = Self   ■ ○ = Colleagues
     ■ △ = Direct Reports   □ ◇ = Boss

OVERALL FREQUENCY

		NEVER 1	SELDOM 2	SOMETIMES 3	USUALLY 4	PERCENTILE	NOTES
Consulting	3.4= □						
	3.3= △					60th	
	3.1= ○					50th	
	3.3= ◇					70th	

SAMPLE BEHAVIOR ITEMS

NEVER 1	SELDOM 2	SOMETIMES 3	USUALLY 4	RESPONSES 1 2 3 4 NA ?	NOTES

17. Encourages people to suggest improvements and innovations (e.g., better ways to do the work, new or improved products).

4.0= □
4.0= △
3.7= ○
0.0= ◇

RESPONSES: 3: ①(○); 3: ① (□), Ⓐ (△), ② (○); ?: ◇①

18. Consults with people to get reactions and suggestions before making major changes that will affect them.

3.0= □
3.5= △
2.7= ○
3.0= ◇

RESPONSES: 2: ②(○); 3: ① (□), Ⓐ (△); 4: Ⓐ (△), ① (○), ◇①

19. Encourages people to express any concerns or doubts that they may have about a proposal that is under consideration.

3.0= □
3.0= △
3.0= ○
3.0= ◇

RESPONSES: 2: ①(○); 3: ① (□), Ⓐ (△), ① (○), ◇①; 4: ① (○)

RECOMMENDATIONS

	DO MORE	DO SAME	DO LESS	NOTES
Consulting	△3	△1	△0	
	○2	○0	○0	
	◇0	◇0	◇1	

Key △ = # of Direct Reports   ◇ = # of Bosses
     ○ = # of Colleagues

allow the receiving manager to know, or to feel he or she knows, who provided the comments. A second risk is that the power of the written responses will override the impact of the actual scores. That is, managers may pay more attention to what people have said than to the ratings they have provided on items and scales, when the scores should be the most significant piece of the data. The item and scale data are focused on the behaviors and dimensions on which feedback is desired and, in a high-quality instrument, will be the part of the feedback that has known reliability and validity.

Although verbatim comments can provide useful additional understanding on the part of the manager, these comments should not be given priority in the overall feedback experience. They are most useful when facilitated feedback sessions are held and the consultant can guide a manager's attention. When feedback is un-facilitated, it may be important to restrict or eliminate verbatim responses lest people focus on them too much. Given these potential downsides of verbatim response, it is probably wise to use this method only in organizations that have some prior positive experience with multi-rater feedback, where trust in the process and in each other is high, and where feedback will be facilitated. In that kind of setting the value can be extremely high.

Support for Development Planning and Change

The impact of 360-degree feedback will be limited if the process ends as soon as the manager receives his or her feedback report. Research on the impact of 360-degree instruments has shown that in order for managers to use the information to enhance their development as leaders or to improve their performance, they need support. The more support they receive, in terms of variety and quantity, the more likely they are to implement change as a result of feedback.

Support can come in the form of an ongoing developmental relationship with the feedback consultant, other human resources staff, or with an employee's own manager. With supportive relationships can also come the possibility for development that can result from new challenges, which can be planned and arranged by the manager and whoever is playing the role of coach in the relationship (McCauley and others, 1998). Finally, support for goal setting and development planning can come in the form of written materials that may accompany the degree instrument.

GUIDELINE 12: BE FAMILIAR WITH THE CHARACTERISTICS OF GOOD DEVELOPMENT MATERIALS.

Although a clear graphic display, built around several strategies for interpretation and perhaps narrative support, will allow managers to know what scores they received and will give some guidance as to what to pay attention to, managers may still lack awareness of all that these scores can mean. They will have the "What?" but still lack answers to the "So what?" and the "Now what?"

With any feedback process, the "So what?" question can be addressed by interpretive material, presented either one-on-one or in a printed development guide. Most of the instruments in use today do come with development planning materials of some sort. This may be in the form of a detailed interpretive and planning guide. The guide may contain background on the domains measured by the instrument, explanations of how the scales are related to one another, details on how the instrument is scored, and exercises to summarize and organize the feedback, along with goal-planning forms to use. In addition, developmental workshops for managers are also offered with many instruments so that feedback can be received and processed in a setting that provides good developmental support. This service is especially valuable for the individual from an organization that may not have these support systems available internally or where there is no internal staff trained to provide feedback on 360-degree instruments.

GUIDELINE 13: BE AWARE OF ISSUES IN POSTASSESSMENT.

The ability to check on progress toward goals is an important feature of any good development system, and many 360-degree instruments now provide postassessment services. PC-based instruments often have the capability of comparing data from different administrations of the instrument, allowing managers to track their scores over time.

The integrity of postassessment data, however, depends on several features of the instrument and the process. First in importance is knowledge of the instrument's test-retest reliability. If test-retest reliability is low or is not known, then we cannot know whether change that shows up in postassessment is real change or whether it is an artifact of item or scale instability. Unfortunately, many of the instruments offering postassessment do not provide test-retest information on their instruments (Leslie and Fleenor, 1998; Van Velsor and Leslie, 1991). Another concern has to do with the process used to measure change. Because this issue is covered in depth in another chapter in this book (see Chapter Nine), it will not be covered here.

Conclusion

In order to design 360-degree feedback so that it enhances involvement, self-determination, and commitment, at least four things must be done. The first is to build trust. To build trust in the process and to protect the quality of ratings, steps must be taken to ensure the anonymity of raters and the confidentiality of the target manager's data.

The second is to focus on development rather than on superficial types of change. To focus on development, the process needs not only to assess observable phenomena but also to employ strategies that allow the individual to link those observables to deeper processes, competencies, and frameworks.

The third is to enhance understanding, during both the input and the output phases of the process. To enhance understanding, materials should be unambiguous in their instructions, in the items to which people will respond, in the way data are fed back, and in materials that help people take the information forward into the rest of their lives.

Finally, because impact is always something that is desired from a 360-degree feedback process, the feedback itself needs to be linked to development plans and action plans.

If the guidelines in this chapter are followed, the process of 360-degree feedback should provide constructive information to the individual in a way that minimally threatens self-esteem and maximally increases a person's sense of self-confidence and commitment to development. It should also improve the developmental climate of the organization.

The next chapter will focus on the issues associated with applying 360-degree feedback cross-culturally.

Note

1. Quality standards for instrument development are published by the American Psychological Association (1992) and are often referred to by psychologists as APA Guidelines. The reader is referred to these guidelines for more detailed information on standards for the development and use of tests.

Chapter Eight

Understanding Cultural Influences on the 360-Degree Feedback Process

Jean Brittain Leslie
Nur D. Gryskiewicz
Maxine A. Dalton

Although the use of 360-degree feedback is flourishing in the United States, its application is not widespread in other parts of the world. One reason for this is that most of the currently available instruments were developed in the United States, and there are many technical problems associated with applying 360-degree feedback across cultures.[1] Maximizing the value of the process in the cross-cultural context found in multinational organizations thus requires an understanding of two essential areas: (1) cultural assumptions underlying the use of 360 instruments and (2) cultural influences on the interpretation of instrument scores.

In the discussion that follows, these two areas will be explored, and guidelines will be offered that can help in the application of the 360-degree feedback process in multinational organizations. But first, in order to get a sense of the problems encountered in cross-cultural 360-degree feedback, consider the following case and commentary.

Case Study

Johnathan Rento's first assignment as a newly hired human resources executive of a U.S.-based multinational firm was to assess the development needs of the firm's worldwide senior executives and design a training program to help them begin the development process. There was no doubt in Johnathan's mind that a 360-degree assessment was the way to go; he contracted with a training organization to handle the administration, scoring, and delivery of a 360-degree feedback survey.

It was not long before Johnathan realized that this strategy was not as simple as he had thought. First came a telephone call from the managing director of the food-processing plant in France. The caller said, "I am to use a number-two pencil to fill out this questionnaire. But what is a number-two pencil? And surely you cannot mean that I am to ask my peers to complete this assessment of my skills!" Just as Johnathan hung up the phone, a call came in from the senior human resources manager in Germany. The caller said, "I have a situation here that I do not know how to handle. Most of the direct reports of Herr Frommer speak only German. He has been sent only English forms. Furthermore, Herr Frommer says that his peers are located in Spain, Belgium, and Austria. Should he ask them to complete the forms? And what about their ability to rate him?" Weeks later, Johnathan resolved as many issues of the 360-degree feedback implementation process as he could and had begun the final preparation for the week-long training program of which the 360-degree feedback was the most critical piece. The day had arrived, and as the executives were reviewing their feedback, questions started rolling in about how they could compare their results to each other and to others in their respective countries.

Although this situation is fictional, similar problems arise whenever the 360-degree process is implemented cross-culturally. The use of instruments in the United States is well supported by its culture. Young children are socialized to believe that they can grow, change, and develop. They become accustomed to taking tests that benchmark progress or stages of development. Among their first experiences in school are with taking standardized achievement tests. Within a short period of time they learn that these tedious tests have great implications for their future. By the time they are ready for college or graduate school, they have come to respect the power of test taking and the implications of the feedback the test results produce. For most individuals in the United States the process of completing standardized tests has become so commonplace that they know what a number-two pencil is and how to fill in a bubble answer sheet correctly. Consequently, the increasing popularity of using instruments in the workplace is not surprising. Other cultures may not be accustomed to instruments, especially not to instruments in the workplace, and certainly not to 360-degree feedback instruments. The transportation of 360-degree instruments across cultures undoubtedly raises challenges in translating, validating, and implementing these instruments (Dalton, 1995).

What assumptions in management development are made, perhaps in error, because 360-degree instruments written for U.S. audiences are not readily transportable across cultures? To what extent is the notion of development for managers using the 360-degree feedback process shared by other cultures? What about the cultures where trait theories drive the leadership philosophies? Given that management development itself has a short history in the United States, can we assume that some of the differences encountered across the globe might be the result of a lag in the diffusion of the technology rather than the result of cultural differences? In other words, is it a matter of time or readiness before 360-degree feedback instruments become a common tool in other countries for management development? What about cultures where discrepancies are discouraged and congruence is encouraged? Besides 360-degree instruments, are other feedback processes equally popular and effective in other cultures?

The belief adopted by a majority of U.S. corporations that national values are becoming more homogeneous and therefore managers and management practices are readily transferable has been challenged (Bigoness and Blakely, 1996). "While there is much to be learned from exemplary management practices in other cultures, the differences between cultures limit the transferability of management practices from one to another" (Newman and Nollen, 1996, p. 774). However, once the awareness and the impact of these cultural differences on the management practices are established, 360-degree instruments and feedback thereof can become valuable tools for management development in multinational corporations.

Cultural Assumptions Underlying the Use of 360-Degree Instruments for Development

U.S. managers accept certain assumptions about using 360-degree instruments for development: (1) the process of growth and development within the workplace is ongoing; (2) constructs (indicators based on models of effective management and leadership) measured by 360-degree instruments are appropriate for most workplaces and cultures; (3) it is both acceptable and valuable to ask bosses, peers, direct reports, and customers for developmental feedback; (4) managers will accept test results as accurate and truthful when the 360 data are kept confidential and when the raters are guaranteed anonymity; and (5) psychometric instruments, or instruments that reliably and validly measure individual differences, are a known and appropriate strategy for candidly describing people and for explaining their behavior. These assumptions may well be challenged outside the United States because they are culturally bound. The following section discusses these U.S.-based assumptions in detail.

Growth and Development Within the Workplace Is Ongoing

The popularity of 360-degree feedback instruments in the United States is embedded in the assumption that they provide recipients valuable information that can guide their development. The notion of development for managers may be viewed as distinctly and optimistically a U.S. belief. In other cultures, ascribed characteristics such as lineage or social class may be considered a more appropriate method of selecting managers, or a meritocracy may be used to ensure that the most talented become leaders. Large French companies, for example, recruit from the Grandes Écoles (schools set up to provide education geared to technical, administrative, and business needs). Competition to get into these schools is fierce, and only those with superior mathematical skills and abstract, logical thinking are accepted (Randlesome, Brierley, Burton, Gordon, and King, 1993). The French elite make up a substantial proportion of the management class, and many of the elite are Parisian graduates of the Grandes Écoles. Attending the right schools and being born into the elite class can have a powerful impact on French managers' careers.

The belief that managers are born, not made, is accepted in many parts of the world. In fact, this belief was held in the United States until not too long ago. In the 1930s and 1940s hundreds of studies were published to support trait theories of leadership (Yukl and Van Fleet, 1992). This line of research failed to uncover a universal set of characteristics that distinguished leaders from nonleaders. An evolution of thought in leadership research, from trait theories to behavioral theories, has driven the current management development philosophies in the United States. Trait theories may still drive leadership philosophies in other countries, however. Italy, for example, has a relatively small number of business schools, and very little money is spent on public- and private-sector management development training (Randlesome and others, 1993).

Why do differences exist across countries in the notion of management development? A possible explanation rests in the values of a culture (Hampden-Turner and Trompenaars, 1993; Hofstede, 1980, 1991; Hoppe, 1990; Kim, 1994; Kluckhohn and Strodtbeck, 1961; Triandis, 1986). One value difference lies in individuals' source of identity—individual or collective. People from individualistic cultures such as the U.S. culture look after their own interests and those of their immediate family. They are expected to be self-reliant, show initiative, and take responsibility for their own careers (Wilson, Hoppe, and Sayles, 1996). It is not surprising then that U.S. managers believe that self-development is a worthwhile goal, and the 360-degree feedback process is often considered a step to enhancing development.

By contrast, people of collectivistic cultures attend to the interests of the family, clan, or ethnic group. They are expected to show loyalty and support to the group, including the company, in return for a sense of belonging and lifetime employment. In Japan, for example, group accountability is the norm. In other cultures of the Far East, such as those of China and Korea, competition with peers and rewards for personal gain are not considered proper (Wilson and others, 1996).

Another value difference may lie in the extent to which the less powerful accept that power is distributed unequally. Low power-distance cultures such as that of the United States may expect that power will be distributed equally and that everyone essentially has the same chance to better themselves. In reality, however, racial, ethnic, religious, social class, and gender prejudices still exist, preventing equal access to opportunities. Also at the core of this value is the belief that promotion and the resulting privileges should be based on achievement or track record, as opposed to family, social class, seniority, or age. Yet, an informality exists between those who have power and those who do not. In cultures where individual power is minimized, asking for and accepting 360-degree feedback from peers and subordinates may be a more readily accepted practice.

Cultures that accept an unequal distribution of power grant privileges to those born into the aristocracy. In cultures where status by ascription prevails, managerial prowess may be considered predetermined. The use of 360-degree feedback for the purpose of development may not be considered a customary practice. Thus, it is imperative that we understand where 360-degree feedback might fit within the overall cultural framework of development in the country of interest. Only then can we examine the compatibility of the constructs these instruments attempt to measure.

Constructs Measured by 360-Degree Instruments Are Applicable in Most Cultures

It is important to determine if the model of effectiveness described by the instrument is culturally appropriate. It is naive to assume that management and leadership models are transferable across all cultures—that they are not culture-bound. Even 360-degree instruments that have been painstakingly validated for use outside the United States need evidence that the constructs being measured are considered to be reflective of effective management in the culture of choice. Take, for example, the concept of decisiveness. Both U.S. and French managers may consider decisiveness to be a strength. However, the ways in which decisiveness is implemented in those cultures may differ. In the United States, decisiveness may mean trading off the benefit of complete information with the need for action, whereas in France it may mean taking a firm position based on a thorough review of all relevant information (Dalton, Lombardo, McCauley, Moxley, and Wachholz, 1996).

Wallace, Sawheny, and Gardjito (1995) make up one of a few research teams that have examined the relationship between culture and effective leader characteristics. Using mixed-gender panels of different nationalities and reviews of indigenous academic and historical literatures pertaining to leader characteristics, Wallace and his colleagues identified forty-seven characteristics that people are inclined to follow. Questionnaire surveys conducted in Japan, India, Indonesia, and the United States with 409 business employees indicated important national differences. For example,

Japanese employees are significantly more inclined than employees from any of the other countries to follow a leader who is seen as profound. Indians are significantly more inclined to follow a leader who is seen as ambitious or pragmatic. Indonesian employees are significantly more inclined to follow a leader who is seen as religious or as having an authoritative bearing. And U.S. employees report more inclination to follow leaders seen as openly and directly expressing opinions. Wallace and others also found that forty-two leader characteristics (89 percent) are related to national indices of work-related values, eighteen (38 percent) are related to national economic indicators, thirteen (28 percent) are related to religious beliefs, seven (15 percent) are related to industry, five (11 percent) are related to gender, and eleven (23 percent) are related to family structure, ethnicity, or education. Wallace and others' work suggests followers' expectations of effective leaders do not generalize to other countries. Their work also suggests that specific combinations of work-related values and economic variables may explain most of the variance in desired traits of leaders.

One way to begin assessing the fit of a 360-degree instrument within a culture is to ask knowledgeable insiders if the concepts measured by the instrument make sense, if the items are culturally appropriate for the workplace, and if high scores describe someone who would be considered an effective manager. MacLachlan, Mapundi, Zimba, and Carr (1995, p. 647) suggest acceptability of a reliable and valid Western instrument be examined in non-Western cultures by asking managers to rate the following statements on a scale of 1 to 5: (1) "I enjoyed completing the questionnaire," (2) "I found the questionnaire interesting to complete," (3) "Many questions were difficult to understand," (4) "The questions were relevant to my work," (5) "All the questions were relevant to the culture," (6) "I believe that the results of the questionnaire might help to identify training needs," (7) "I don't know how the questionnaire can detect relevant personality traits for personnel selection and development," and (8) "I was put off because the questionnaire was too long." We would, in addition, go through the instrument item by item, asking (9) "Is it acceptable to ask this question in the workplace?" and (10) "An individual with a high score on these questions would describe an excellent manager in our company." Looking at responses to these statements can help determine whether the 360-degree instrument being offered will be accepted as a reasonable standard to aspire to.

It Is Acceptable and Valuable to Ask for Feedback

Asking bosses, peers, direct reports, and customers for feedback is not an accepted practice in all cultures. Cultural differences exist in the perceptions of whose feedback (bosses, peers, direct reports) is considered most meaningful. In certain Latin American cultures, U.S. managers have reported that it is difficult to get direct reports to give them negative feedback (Wilson and others, 1996). In these cultures, conflict is avoided for the sake of social harmony. Saving face in Japan is one expression of this belief. U.S. managers working in these cultures might find a request for direct feedback to be shocking or even offensive.

The acceptance of peer feedback has also come into question in some cultures. A team of researchers was told by several French managers that they did not trust feedback from peers because they have been competing with them since the first years of school. These managers did not believe that their peers could rise above a competitive mode to provide them with objective information (Dalton, 1992). On another occasion, a Japanese focus group discussing the concept of 360-degree feedback remarked that objective evaluations from an office of many females cannot be used because women tend to respond according to their subjective likes and dislikes; they lack the capacity to be objective.

Before using a 360-degree feedback instrument internationally, a first step would be to sit down with knowledgeable company insiders in the country and discuss the concept of multi-rater feedback and development. The 360-degree process needs to be perceived as valid, accurate, and legitimate for the feedback to be meaningful.

Confidentiality and Anonymity Must Be Maintained

It is a common U.S. belief that managers have a stronger sense of acceptance and ownership of their feedback when the 360 data are confidential (Burd and Ryan, 1993; Dalton and Hollenbeck, 1996). When the data are confidential and used for development, 360-degree feedback goes only to the participant and a trained facilitator, with the expectation that only the development plan will be discussed with others.

The idea of confidential feedback is not equally accepted across all cultures. In cultures characterized by a high power distance (for example, Philippines, Mexico, Venezuela, India, Yugoslavia, and Singapore), bosses may feel that they have a right to see results, and employees may accept this belief. *Power distance* refers to one of the main dimensions on which Gerte Hofstede's research (1976, 1980) showed national cultures to differ. *Power distance* is generally defined as the extent to which a society accepts the unequal distribution of power. People from larger power-distance cultures tend to share values and beliefs that (1) dependence on higher-ups is accepted and desired, (2) directive and persuasive superiors are preferred, (3) authority is not to be questioned, (4) managers are entitled to privileges, and (5) the use of coercive and referent power is accepted (Hofstede, 1980). Hofstede's conclusions were based on an examination of data from 372 managers from fifteen nations attending management development programs in Switzerland and from a second sample of 60,000 respondents from a large multinational business organization in forty countries.

Of course, the belief that the one who pays for the assessment has the right to the feedback is also present in some U.S. organizations. The United States is, however, considered a low power-distance culture. It may be that in organizations where threat and fear are used to motivate employees, direct reports may not believe that the data will be kept confidential.[2]

Additionally, survey results may violate or interfere with nonverbal feedback given to group members in ways not visible to the uninitiated Westerner. According to Hall (1966, 1976), there are remarkable differences between communication patterns of people from low- and high-context cultures. Hall's theoretical framework for understanding cross-cultural communication classifies world cultures into low-context (including the U.S. and Northern European cultures) and high-context (including East Asian, Arab, African, Southern European, and Latin American cultures). In low-context cultures, meaning is derived from spoken words. People in low-context cultures tend to emphasize rationality and assume that events can be explained and reasons for their occurrence determined.

Thus, an emphasis is placed on explicit meaning (Kabagarama, 1993). High-context cultures derive meaning from the context in which the communication has taken place. Implicit and metaphoric associations are key methods of communication. A high value is placed on the persuasive power, rhythm, and sound of words to heighten the impact of the message (Kabagarama, 1993). It can be important not to overlook nonverbal communication (substituting gestures for words) as an ongoing method of relaying feedback to groups.

In general, it is important to be aware that there may be cultural differences regarding who owns the data and that practices considered "the best" in the United States may be considered bizarre in other cultures.

For 360-degree feedback to be effective, we in the United States tend to believe that anonymity of the raters is crucial. Research shows that data gathered for developmental purposes are more accurate when raters believe that their ratings will not be used to hurt and punish the persons they are rating (Farh, Cannella, and Bedeian, 1991; McIntyre, Smith, and Hassett, 1984; Zedeck and Cascio, 1982). The flip side of anonymity is that, for some raters, it can be an opportunity to pay back "old debts." In either case, it is a good practice to have managers who will receive the feedback select the raters whose judgment they trust. However, some raters may not believe the promise of anonymity. One of the authors had the experience of giving feedback to a manager from mainland China whose direct reports had given him a perfect score on all of the scales in the survey. When asked what he thought this meant, the manager replied, "I think they did not believe that it was anonymous."

Psychometric Instruments Are a Known and Appropriate Strategy for Describing Behavior

Using psychometric instruments to describe human behavior is quite common in the United States, Canada, and parts of Europe. It is not as common, for example, in France. It may surprise U.S. managers that graphology (the study of handwriting) is a common selection and placement practice in French organizations (Doron and Parot, 1991). Whether a job candidate, for example, dots her i's, closes her cursive a's (top closed or open), or makes a big loop in her t's are considered indications of her personality. Clearly, understanding the role of instruments within a culture is critical to the introduction of 360-degree assessments outside the United States.

A recent study of 437 participants, including managers, human resources professionals, and consultants from twenty-nine countries, found the following assumptions underlying the use of 360-degree instruments across cultures: self-improvement, honesty, anonymity, motivation, feedback, and acceptance (Gryskiewicz, 1995). The lack of use of 360-degree instruments in participants' respective cultures was attributed to newness or lack of organization or country readiness, going against tradition, lack of know-how, lack of resources, and issues of trust and acceptance. The respondents, who were users of 360-degree instruments, were positive in their reception of these instruments as long as they were used "wisely," honestly, and in an organization that supported the process. As we conclude our discussion of the cultural assumptions that are associated with the use of 360-degree feedback, we present two actual cases as exemplars of the worst and the best scenarios of application within multinational corporations.

Worst-Case Scenario

A renowned U.S.-based consulting firm received an assignment from a U.S. corporate customer to fly to Japan and conduct a management training program for their Japanese affiliate. The consultants flew into town to deliver their always-popular, three-day management-development program. On the first day of the program, the Japanese managers listened attentively to the outline of the program and participated, politely and quietly, in all of the activities. The agenda for the second day included the 360-degree feedback activity. Only two of the twenty-four Japanese managers returned to the course on the second day. No one came back on the third day. They all called in sick. The consultants were embarrassed and the corporate sponsors were aghast. They had never thought to ask about the cultural appropriateness of this form of management development and thought that sending this expensive consulting group to Japan was a way to bring the Japanese affiliate into the fold.

Best-Case Scenario

A European multinational organization held an annual management-development program for its high-potential managers from all over the world, including representation from every continent. These high-potentials were slated to become both expatriate and multinational managers in the organization and so needed to be effective within and across cultures. The purpose of the meeting was to allow these future managers to meet each other and to meet senior executives in the corporation. Another purpose of the meeting was to let these future managers and leaders know what was expected of them as expatriate and multinational managers rather than local managers; 360-degree feedback was the tool chosen to introduce this model of management and leadership. The 360-degree feedback was introduced to the class participants six months in advance as a tool that represented the model of effectiveness on which the high-potentials would be evaluated when they were working cross-culturally. Translations of the surveys and instructions were provided for the target individuals' raters as needed, and norms were available for all the countries represented. The feedback report itself was in English—the official business language of the company at the international management levels. The feedback session started with a discussion of the concept of 360-degree feedback and its cultural fit for each participant; this information was folded into the feedback session. The feedback did not "work" in all cases, and the individual had support from the facilitator to reject what did not fit due to the cultural context of his or her raters. A longitudinal validity study is under way with this organization to determine the efficacy of this tool cross-culturally and over time in predicting managerial success in the organization.

Cultural Influences on the Interpretation of 360-Degree Feedback

The previous section encourages the reader to challenge assumptions associated with U.S.-developed 360-degree instruments and their implementation outside the United States. In this section, we continue to highlight ways in which culture influences the 360-degree feedback process but focus on interpreting the feedback of a culturally diverse group. Here, we explore what we consider to be particular concerns in the interpretation of 360-degree feedback across cultures: (1) finding an appropriate norm group, (2) interpreting the differences between self- and others' ratings, and (3) dealing with language differences to ensure comparability of scores.

Comparing the Target Manager to a Reference Group

For feedback to be meaningful, it is common to compare individual scores to an appropriate external reference group—a norm group. When feedback is being administered within a specific country, it is important to use country-based norms with an instrument that has been translated and validated for use in that country. This is necessary because countries have different conventions about the use of response scales. A response scale refers to the choices people have when they answer items on a 360-degree instrument. Response scales range from 2 points (Yes or No) to 5 or more points (Never, Occasionally, Sometimes, Usually, Always). Cultural differences have been found, for example, between Hispanics' and non-Hispanics' use of the response scale (Hui and Triandis, 1989). Hispanics were found to exhibit extreme checking when answering questions on a 5-point response scale. Replacing the 5-point response scale with a 10-point scale eliminated the difference between Hispanics and non-Hispanics.

The issue of comparability becomes more complex with a multinational manager who works across several borders with peers in multiple countries, a boss in still another country, and direct reports in yet another country. In this situation, determining the appropriate norm group becomes a puzzle and language becomes a critical issue. Surveys in several languages may be needed, and the equivalence of meaning for each language group must be demonstrated by the test publisher. Appropriate normative comparisons are critical, and the test publisher may choose to provide a multinational norm group rather than a country-specific norm group.

Interpreting the Gap Between Self and Others

Normative comparisons relate managers' scores (self-reported and others' ratings) to similar groups. Another core comparison is that of managers' scores to the ratings of their observers (superiors, peers, direct reports, and customers). The magnitude of the gap between where participants say they are and where others say they are is used to indicate the potential need for development (see Chapter Seven for more details). Reviews of top U.S.-developed 360-degree feedback instruments showed that highlighting self and other differences was the most common source used to suggest a developmental opportunity (Leslie and Fleenor, 1998; Van Velsor and Leslie, 1991).

Although the use and production of 360-degree instruments has grown over the years, research interpreting the gap between self- and others' ratings (self-and-other differences) has not kept pace. The absence of research on self-and-other differences, as they relate to culture, is even more stark. The research that exists explores differences in cultural patterns in the use of response scale ratings and self-rating modesty or leniency. These studies are often contradictory and subject to methodological flaws, a problem that commonly plagues cross-cultural research. However, they can offer some insight into interpretations of 360-degree feedback within multinational settings.

Determining Cultural Effects on Ratings: Use of Extremes and the Middle

Hofstede (1980) was among the first researchers to report cultural differences in rating patterns. This phenomenon, commonly called *acquiescence,* refers to the tendency within cultural groups to answer questions similarly, regardless of content—as "yea-sayers" (true or yes), "nay-sayers" (false or no), or "middle-sayers" (sometimes or occasionally)—of the response scale (Couch and Keniston, 1960). Hofstede reported that countries located near the collectivism end of the individualism-collectivism dimension tend to show acquiescence more often than other countries. Hofstede described collectivist countries such as Venezuela, Peru, Taiwan, Singapore, Mexico, and Greece as those with a "we" consciousness. As mentioned previously, people born into these cultures rely on extended families or clans to protect them, in exchange for unquestioning loyalty. Since service to the in-group is more ideal in collectivist cultures, modesty in ratings may be a more accepted practice.

Zax and Takahashi (1967) found similar evidence when they discovered repeated use of the middle of the rating scale among

Asians. Chen, Lee, and Stevenson (1995) more recently found that Japanese and Chinese students were more likely than American or Canadian students to use the midpoints. To use the extremes of the scale, in collectivist cultures, may be considered in poor taste and boisterous (Hui and Triandis, 1989). Or perhaps Asians are influenced by the virtues of moderation prescribed by Confucian philosophy.

In contrast, Hui and Triandis (1989) and Marin, Gamba, and Marin (1992) found that Hispanics tended to use the extreme points of a response scale in an attempt to make their feelings known. Research indicated that Americans, too, tend to respond in extremes (Chen and others, 1995).

These studies suggest that cultural patterns exist in the way people respond to questions. Self-other gaps in the feedback may be larger for managers from some countries—not because of their raters' inability to rate certain skills or abilities or because of performance differences but because of cultural influences in rating patterns. It might be helpful to begin a feedback session by discussing the use of response scales within the country or the company. This kind of discussion will help provide a context for interpreting feedback as well as highlight the importance of selecting a culturally appropriate comparison group. Additionally, educating the rater on the use of response scales—a practice finding increasing use in the United States—might provide raters with a better understanding of how to complete the survey. The key to this discussion is emphasizing how the feedback will be used, if it is confidential, and how valuable it will be for the feedback recipient if the rater uses the whole response scale.

Determining Cultural Effects on Rating Self and Others

Research in Western settings has shown that self-ratings tend to be higher or more lenient than ratings obtained from supervisors or peers (Farh and Werbel, 1986; Fleenor, McCauley, and Brutus, 1996; Harris and Schaubroeck, 1988; Meyer, 1980; Thornton, 1980). Studies comparing Taiwanese workers' ratings have found evidence of modesty in self-ratings (that is, self-ratings are lower than ratings from peers or supervisors). These results suggest that rater bias may be explained in cultural terms (Farh, Dobbins, and Cheng,

1991). An attempt to replicate this research among mainland Chinese samples did not support the latter. In fact, Yu and Murphy (1993) found a similar pattern to that of Western managers. Mainland Chinese workers rated themselves significantly higher than either their peers or their superiors rated them. Yu and Murphy caution the reader: their failure to replicate Farh and others' (1991) research does not suggest that the research should be dismissed. Instead, Yu and Murphy argue that Eastern cultures are, in fact, distinct from each other and that Taiwan may be more conducive to modesty than mainland Chinese culture.

Although the research on self-and-other differences is inconclusive, several cautionary considerations can be drawn. Those 360-degree development strategies that focus *international* managers on discrepant scores may erroneously encourage managers to interpret the discrepancy as an indication of a development opportunity. It may, for example, be inappropriate in Japan to praise the self highly, but others may be expected to do so. Or it may be considered inappropriate to use the entire response scale when rating others. It may be best to interpret the meaning of 360-degree feedback within the culture of the participant as well as the culture of the raters.

Dealing with Language Differences to Ensure Comparability

Language expertise (in both the source and targeted language) and knowledge about instrument development are keys to successful instrument translations. Back-translations, that is, translating a piece back to the original language in order to ensure accuracy, are a critical first step to assessing how well an instrument is being adapted. Among their multiple purposes, back-translations can help avoid unwanted error and embarrassment. For example, a back-translation of a survey translated into French Canadian revealed that the item "has not adapted to the management culture" had been translated to read "has not adapted to the culture of the organization." A back-translation of an item that in English read "has left a trail of bruised people" revealed that the literal Japanese translation depicted a much gorier situation than was intended by the U.S. use of the word "bruised." The literal back-translation of the Japanese version read "has left a trail of mangled and bloody people." One of the causes of poor 360-degree instrument translations may be that the original-language version contained business jargon, such as "puts out forest fires," that were difficult to translate accurately. Another cause of error may be that concepts, expressions, and ideas used in the source language version do not have equivalents in the target language (Hambleton, 1993). Back-translations can also reveal if the vocabulary is comparable in terms of the level of difficulty, readability, grammar, writing style, and punctuation. For example, a back-translation of the English item that used *patient* as an adjective—"patiently allows good people a chance to develop"—yielded this two-part statement in Norwegian: "is patient and grants good fellow workers the opportunity to develop themselves."

Knowledge about instrument development is particularly important when translating instruments for multiple languages. Specific answer formats for questions (for example, multiple-choice, forced-choice, essay), certain conventions and procedures in giving instructions (for example, language use in test rubric, layout, use of graphics), and presentation (for example, paper and pencil, PC-based software, computer scannable and scoreable sheets) may not be equally familiar to all populations. To ensure fairness, it is important that all procedures associated with 360-degree feedback instruments be familiar to all populations for whom adaptations of the instruments are intended.

The conditions under which 360-degree instruments are administered should be as similar as possible to eliminate unintended score variations. Instructions should be in the source and target languages and should be communicated in the native language of the country of choice. In countries where the 360-degree process is new, special care should be given to explaining the ideal conditions in which to fill out the instrument.

It is sometimes important for multinational organizations to be able to compare employees from different parts of the world on the same instrument. Translating instruments into the languages of those who are to be compared is not sufficient for a claim of comparability. Only test adaptation that includes the process of (1) translating, (2) back-translating, (3) testing instruments for reliability, and (4) testing for validity can lead to comparable feedback for managers within one company representing many cultures and language groups. In multi-language regions (for example, Quebec and Belgium), test publishers may be required to demonstrate comparability among different language versions of the same test.

The easiest way to ensure comparability of scores across cultures is to select a publicly available instrument. The burden of proof that multiple-language forms are comparable rests on the test publisher. When selecting a 360-degree feedback instrument, look for empirical evidence in the technical manual to support a claim of comparability. For those needing to evaluate a publisher's claims or wishing to develop their own cross-cultural surveys, the procedures for adapting instruments will be outlined next.

Documentation should include (1) a detailed account of the procedures, (2) the design used, (3) methods employed to assess equivalence between the original language and translated versions, (4) identification and selection of translators, (5) inclusion of items as well as information about those items that were modified or not included, (6) some of the major problems encountered and how they were solved, (7) aspects relating to the administration of tests including the selection and training of administrators, and (8) the interpretation of results (Hambleton, 1993).

Implementation Guidelines

Many of the ideas presented in this chapter have implications for applying a 360-degree feedback process in multinational organizations, for cross-cultural training, for the selection of an instrument for use with a multicultural audience, and for further research. Successful implementation of 360-degree feedback in multinational companies to a large extent depends on prior preparation. Reading, conducting focus groups, interviewing organizational insiders and expatriates, and collaborating with colleagues from the country of interest are helpful ways of developing such a cross-cultural perspective. Based on our collective learnings from our research and experiences with 360-degree feedback in numerous countries, we offer the following guidelines:

1. In preparing for implementation, find out whether (1) individuals in the country of interest believe that adults can develop, learn, and improve their situation through this process; (2) the

individuals in the country of interest believe that the workplace has a role in providing developmental feedback and developmental opportunities for individuals; (3) the psychometric instruments are an accepted convention in the country where 360-degree feedback is to be used; (4) the individuals in the workplace accept the idea of soliciting information from their superiors, peers, direct reports, and customers as appropriate and useful; (5) the individuals in the country of interest accept and believe that the feedback will be kept confidential and the raters will remain anonymous; (6) the model of management or leadership represented in the 360-degree instrument is sensible and useful for the target organizational level and culture; (7) each question in the survey is culturally appropriate (see MacLachlan and others, 1995, p. 647); and (8) mechanisms for postfeedback reaction to the 360-degree process are currently in place. The more affirmative the answers are, the easier it will be to apply the 360-degree feedback in a cross-cultural context.

2. When buying an instrument from a vendor, review the test manual to find out whether (1) the appropriate normative comparisons are available; (2) the test adaptation procedures are appropriate and sufficient for the intended use; and (3) there is evidence of ongoing international research with the instrument to address the unanswered questions.

3. Enter the country and the feedback session as a respectful colleague and partner to the person receiving the feedback. Learn from each other the usefulness and limits of the process for that person in his or her organization and country.

4. Provide training to raters and feedback givers on (1) how the instruments will be used; (2) cultural influences on the use of response scales; and (3) the value of using all the points on the scale.

5. Acquire knowledge in cross-cultural training on (1) how compatible the theoretical frameworks of development are in the host culture; (2) how the feedback will be received by the participants in the course; (3) how to introduce the 360-degree instruments in cultures that may not be ready for the experience in order to ensure utility; (4) how to coach managers in different cultures to be effective and successful based on the feedback they received; and (5) how to create on-the-job developmental experiences for managers to prepare them for foreign assignments.

6. In selecting a 360-degree instrument for use with a multicultural audience, look for (1) evidence to support a claim of comparability; (2) administration instructions that are in target languages to minimize variation across populations; (3) evidence that the choice of testing techniques such as answer formats for questions (for example, multiple-choice, forced-choice, essay), conventions and procedures in giving instructions (for example, language use in test rubric, layout, use of graphics), and presentation (for example, paper and pencil, PC-based software, computer scannable and scoreable sheets) are familiar to all intended populations. Appropriate statistical techniques[3] should be applied to establish the equivalence of different instrument versions and to identify aspects of instruments that may be inadequate in one or more of the intended populations; differences in instrument scores should not be taken at face value. When there is evidence that construct equivalence exists, mean and standard deviation comparisons can meaningfully be made.

Conclusion

Although there are many problems involved in applying the 360-degree feedback process across cultures, we believe that ultimately its multinational value will be realized. The ideas presented in this chapter should help people work toward this realization.

Notes

1. It is our position that *culture* refers to an orientation of a group of people who share common life experiences due to history, religion, geography, climate, social structure, values, and beliefs. Throughout this chapter we use the term *culture* to refer to regions of the world, to people of specific nations, and at times to organizations. Although we are addressing cultural influences relative to the 360-degree feedback process, many of the same issues apply locally.

2. This may be a valid concern outside the United States. The APA code of ethics (American Psychological Association, 1992) binds professionals to a norm of confidentiality. In other cultures there may be no equivalent that can supersede the power of government or organizational officials.

3. One of the most important statistical analyses in validating an instrument for use in two or more cultures is a differential item functioning study. The equivalence of an instrument for two or more populations

requires that there be evidence that when population members have equal ability, they should perform in an equivalent fashion on each item. Three other methodologies can be used to test measurement equivalence: (1) item-response-theory procedures (see, for example, Ellis, 1989), (2) the Mantel-Haenszel procedure (see, for example, Hambleton, Clauser, Mazor, and Jones, 1993; Holland and Thayer, 1988; Holland and Wainer, 1993), and (3) logistic regression procedures (Swaminathan and Rogers, 1990).

Chapter Nine

Using 360-Degree Surveys to Assess Change

Jennifer W. Martineau

This chapter differs from previous chapters in that it focuses on using 360-degree feedback surveys to measure what happens as a result of an intervention rather than using the data from 360-degree feedback to identify a needed development intervention. As such, it will discuss the methodological background that is necessary to explain the complex nature of measuring change. Before delving into the issues, though, let me provide a context for this chapter. The overall context is the evaluation of developmental human resources interventions when the goal of the intervention is to produce individual behavior change and, either directly or indirectly, group-level or organization-level change.

The interventions themselves can vary widely, from the use of 360-degree survey feedback,[1] to off-site development programs (courses, workshops), to developmental assignments (doing different work within the same job), to the use of developmental relationships (pairings of employees where at least three factors exist: motivation, learning opportunities, and support [McCauley and Douglas, 1998; McCauley and Young, 1993]).

Evaluation of these interventions can occur at several levels. I would like to differentiate between two in particular: *evaluation* and *impact*. As I will use these terms, *evaluation* encompasses the measurement of *impact*. Thus, evaluation describes a string of assessment activities such as determining (1) participants' reactions to the intervention, (2) whether the intervention is meeting its intended objectives, and (3) the effects of the intervention on individuals and their organizations. The latter activity will serve as this chapter's conceptualization of measuring impact and may be effectively assessed through the use of 360-degree surveys. Each of these activities serves to inform the overall evaluation of an intervention; results can be used to modify the intervention to meet its intended goals and outcomes.

Why Do We Measure Change?

Underlying the measurement of impact are two questions: (1) Will the intervention have a lasting impact? and (2) How do we know this? Many different parties need to understand the impact of an intervention, including (1) the participant, who wants to take responsibility for managing change through seeking feedback and monitoring progress; (2) the participant's manager, who can become a coach, as well as an agent for the change, with the impact data in hand; (3) the internal HR professional, who is functionally interested in or responsible for facilitating the process; (4) the organization, which usually pays for the intervention and is ultimately accountable for it; and (5) the external consultant or provider, who needs to ensure the quality of his or her services to the client.

We know that managers attending development programs at the Center for Creative Leadership gain self-awareness during their time there. Each program uses a carefully selected set of assessment tools, including, but not limited to, 360-degree instruments. Each tool provides feedback that helps managers understand their strengths and development needs, their personality as it relates to being an effective manager and interacting well with others, and the way their organizational complexities affect who they are and how they need to behave. (See, for example, Chapter Two of this book for a case example based on the experience of participants at CCL's Leadership Development Program). The combination of feedback is integrated to such an extent that participants understand the types of changes they need to make to their own behaviors and why they should make them. It is a powerful and moving experience to observe these managers learning about themselves and translating their learnings into action steps and goals.

However, it is one thing to know that an intervention such as this has "unfrozen" managers (one type of impact) and quite another to know whether they have made significant changes to their lives—

both at work and outside of work. This question of impact cannot be answered until managers are reintegrated into their lives and have faced the challenges of bringing new insight into an existing, and sometimes resistant, situation. At this stage, we are talking about individual-level impact—the changes that an individual manager has made to his or her own behaviors following a significant unfreezing experience. We certainly need to be able to appropriately and accurately assess this type of impact.

For many interventions, the goal is to make improvements at the individual level; the measurement of impact stops there. However, other interventions are implemented for the purpose of creating organizational change. Organization-level change raises additional issues of change measurement, over and above those at the individual level. Among these are (1) what it means to aggregate individual-level scores into a group score and (2) understanding the role of factors other than individual-level change in organization-level change.

This chapter will help readers understand how 360-degree surveys can be of help in the evaluation of HR interventions. It will also deal with using 360-degree surveys to assess both individual and organizational change, as well as why these surveys are of value in both cases. I will invariably use development as the exemplar of HR interventions, but the issues and potential solutions can be transferred to other types of interventions as well.

Some Basics About Measuring Change

At some point in their lives most people have been asked whether something has changed. Take, for example, clothing trends. You can randomly pick ten people off the street and ask them whether clothing styles have changed in the last ten years. Each will probably answer yes. This is a fairly objective question that simply requires each observer to imagine what people were wearing ten years ago and what they are wearing now.

Now ask the question a different way: How much have clothing styles *improved* over the last ten years? This time, you are likely to hear ten different responses. This question depends more heavily on *context* than does the first question. Depending on factors such as age, sense of style, socioeconomic status, and culture, each of those same ten people will have different opinions about the attractiveness of clothing styles at any given time. Improvement for one person may be decline for another. How, then, can you come to a conclusive answer about the state of clothing styles today, relative to those ten years ago?

Such is the dilemma posed by the question, "How much improvement has your intervention shown?" Definitions of a successful intervention may be as plentiful as the number of people defining it. Fortunately for evaluators of competency and skill development, more than two decades of research have been spent looking at this question. However, let me forewarn you—there is still no clear-cut, "best" solution.

Part of the reason for ambivalence lies in a methodological effect called *response-shift bias* (Howard, Ralph, Gulanick, Maxwell, Nance, and Gerber, 1979), which permeates the discussion of measuring change. The following situation illustrates this phenomenon:

A manager named Tony is preparing for a leadership development program and is completing the pre-program surveys. Tony considers himself to be a fairly good leader and gives himself a rating of 7 on a pretest that has a 10-point scale (10 being the best possible rating). During the program, he receives feedback from his boss, peers, direct reports, and others, who indicate he has some significant development needs to overcome before he can consider himself a good leader. In addition, he learns that leadership is a much broader concept and set of behaviors than he originally considered it to be. So, Tony sets some development goals and goes back to work. Both he and his colleagues notice a great improvement in his leadership abilities. When it is time to evaluate his leadership behavior again, he does so, this time in relation to what he has learned about himself and leadership in general. Therefore, he gives himself a rating of 6 on the same 10-point scale.

What happened? Tony has shown marked improvement that both he and his colleagues noticed. However, if an evaluator were to observe only the pre- and post-program ratings, the only possible conclusion would be that Tony's behaviors *worsened* as a result of the program. Although verbal testimony from Tony and his colleagues in this evaluation would have shown perceptions of positive change, evaluators are often challenged by clients to find hard data that prove the value of an intervention. Testimonials are perceived as subjective and, unfortunately, are not always valued as evaluation tools, so we resort to numeric ratings of behavior change.

What causes this response-shift bias, and how can it be overcome? Response-shift bias is usually observed with self-report data, and although not as much is known about such shifts in others' ratings, it is logical to assume that their expectations are also affected by the *knowledge* that a colleague has experienced an intervention. Therefore, this chapter will address both self- and others' ratings in the discussion of measuring change.

The processes behind response-shift bias have been labeled *beta change* and *gamma change* (Golembiewski, Billingsley, and Yeager, 1976; Golembiewski, 1989). True change is called *alpha change*. These terms are briefly defined here and depicted in Exhibit 9.1.

Alpha change is true change and is what we try to capture through evaluation techniques. If alpha change had been captured in our previous example, the improvements Tony made would have been reflected in his post-program ratings. Perhaps he would have given himself a rating of 8 or 9 on the 10-point scale, indicating noticeable positive change. Due to beta and gamma change, however, it is not always possible to capture alpha change.

The theory behind *beta change* is that the scale on which Tony is being rated has been recalibrated between the time the two ratings were made. Thus, the context of the performance itself has changed. Beta change occurs when a rater's (self or other) expectations for the target manager change. Continuing with the example, Tony's boss gives Tony a rating of 5 before the program, indicating a need for improvement. The boss then expects Tony to return from the program with an improved sense of leadership. This new set of related behaviors becomes the new baseline for the boss's evaluation. For example, Tony's boss now expects Tony to have an improved ability to make effective decisions because Tony was exposed to new decision-making techniques at this development program. Anything at the *new* baseline is acceptable (and is rated a 5, for example), but Tony must show dramatically improved leadership skills to be given a rating higher than 5. Behaviors that Tony's boss would have given a rating of 8 before the program receive a rating of 5 after the program. Tony *has* improved his behaviors but only to the point that they meet his boss's raised

Exhibit 9.1. Alpha, Beta, and Gamma Change.

Type of Change	Change in	Description	True Change	Measured Change
Alpha	True performance	The pretest and posttest ratings reflect the actual and true change that occurred.	Preintervention = 7.0 Postintervention = 9.0	Preintervention = 7.0 Postintervention = 9.0
Beta	Performance context	The pretest and post-test ratings reflect a combination of actual change and change in expectations for that behavior or capability.	Preintervention = 5.0 Postintervention = 8.0	Preintervention = 5.0 Postintervention = 5.0
Gamma	Performance definition	The pretest and post-test ratings reflect a combination of actual change and change in the scope of behaviors that are thought to define a particular behavior or capability.	Preintervention = 7.0 Postintervention = 8.0	Preintervention = 7.0 Postintervention = 6.0

expectations. Comparing the pre- and post-program ratings from the boss, it looks as if Tony has *not* changed.

Finally, *gamma change* occurs when the construct in question changes. This means that the scope of behaviors considered to be encompassed by the term *leadership* changes between the pre- and post-program ratings. This is easy to understand on the part of a manager like Tony, who actually experienced the leadership development program. He has now been exposed to new experiences, new models of leadership, and other leaders, all of which have helped him learn about the broader definition of leadership. For example, before the intervention, he may have thought that leadership encompassed six unique areas such as motivating others and having vision. After the intervention, he understands that leadership is very complex and is defined by (for example) twelve different dimensions to which he must attend. Tony thought he was pretty good in the six areas he first knew about and gave himself a rating of 7 before the program. Now, however, he realizes that he's doing well (and has even improved) on seven of the twelve areas but needs more work on the other five. Therefore, he gives himself a rating of 6.

Whether Tony's colleagues are affected by gamma change is less clear. It is possible that Tony shared his new learnings about leadership with his colleagues and that their conceptualization of leadership has also changed. However, because they did not experience the development program themselves, there is less likelihood that their concepts of leadership would change in the same way that Tony's would have. But because this possibility does exist, evaluators must be prepared for the shift.

So, what is an evaluator to do if there is a need to measure change? The method that seems most logical—testing for competencies before an intervention and then after the intervention—is not methodologically sound. The typical pretest-posttest designs are greatly affected by response-shift bias. Searching for other ways to measure change, the field of evaluation has created several alternatives. Some of these go by the names *retrospective pretests, change ratings,* and *ideal ratings*—each of which attempts to overcome the effects of response-shift bias. These will each be discussed next. A warning, however: there are criticisms of these types of measures as well as those related to pre-post measures. One of the best ways to assess change may be to use combinations of methods in 360-degree surveying.

Retrospective Pretests

One of the alternatives to traditional pretest-posttest methodologies in addressing the concerns of beta and gamma change is retrospective pretests. This methodology actually does not make use of true pretests at all. Rather, it requires two unique ratings at the same point several months *after* the intervention. The following example describes this type of evaluation process.

> Sharon is a manager whose organization has begun to use developmental relationships as a way of building the organization's leadership capacity as it looks into the next century. Sharon has been paired with a manager who is a few levels above her, and the pairing was by mutual agreement. The formal duration of the relationship will be six months. During this time, the relationship will motivate Sharon to want to learn and grow, expose her to learning opportunities, and provide her with support for her development (McCauley, Ruderman, Ohlott, and Morrow, 1994; Morrison, 1992).

> Because Sharon's organization is in the early stages of using developmental relationships, it has decided to evaluate the impact of this form of development. In addition, the organization believes that each aspect of the process should provide benefit to the participants, as well as provide information for the organization. Therefore, the decision is made to use a 360-degree survey, designed in a retrospective pretest-posttest format, to measure the effects of the program on the managers who participated.

> Four months into the relationship, Sharon receives a set of 360-degree surveys (see Exhibit 9.2 for a sample), which she distributes to her boss, some peers and subordinates, and some of the key clients with whom she works closely. The survey contains sixty-three behavioral statements and asks raters to give Sharon ratings for each of these on a 9-point scale, according to how well the statements describe Sharon's behavior. A rating of 1 would mean that Sharon is not able to perform the behavior; a rating of 9 would mean that she can perform it expertly.

> Because the purpose of the survey is to measure change, the raters are asked to give two ratings for each behavior. For the first, they are asked to reflect backward in time, giving a rating that describes Sharon's competence in each skill

Exhibit 9.2. Sample "Retrospective Pretest" Follow-Up Survey.

Not at All		To a Small Extent		To a Moderate Extent		To a Large Extent		To a Very Large Extent
1	2	3	4	5	6	7	8	9

Using the scale shown above, give the rating that appropriately describes the extent to which this person

	Before the Developmental Relationship	Now
1. Strives to be skilled at selling upward, influencing superiors	____	____
2. Considers the impact of his or her actions on the entire system	____	____
3. Appropriately involves others in the decision-making process	____	____

before she began the developmental relationship (a retrospective pretest rating). Second, they give a rating that describes her current level of competency for each skill (a posttest rating). Because both of these ratings are made at the same time, beta and gamma change are minimized.

The feedback that is provided to Sharon is rich. It tells her how much she is perceived to have changed as a result of the developmental relationship and also gives her a relative sense of her competency level by showing both sets of ratings on a 9-point Likert scale. Therefore, Sharon can focus on leadership competencies she's made significant improvements on (looking at the difference between the two ratings), as well as competencies to which she needs to give additional attention (by examining the value of the posttest ratings).

This description of the retrospective pretest methodology shows the power of the results for various uses. They give both the amount of change *and* the placement of the level of skill on a continuum; the receiver learns not only how much change is being perceived but also whether this is an area that still needs more attention or is sufficiently developed. Thus, retrospective pretests offer us what we don't get from one-time-only, 360-degree measures, that is, a picture of the change that has occurred. And from single-rating change measures, we don't see the relative performance levels of a particular skill or competency. To find out why this methodology is superior to the typical pre- and posttest measures, we need to go back into the research literature.

Retrospective Methodology in Research

In the late 1970s, a group of researchers theorized about the retrospective pretest methodology for measuring change. Several of their articles report that the use of retrospective pretests, as opposed to true pretests, was a more accurate representation of change (Howard and Dailey, 1979; Howard, Millham, Slaten, and O'Donnell, 1981; Howard and others, 1979). For example, the changes between participants' own retrospective pretest and posttest scores on interviewing skills were more in line with objective judges' behavioral incidence ratings of the first and last video-taped interviews than were changes between participants' pretest and posttest ratings of their interviewing capabilities (Howard and Dailey, 1979).

Even more remarkable is the result found with an additional self-report rating: "recall." After completing the retrospective pretest and posttest ratings, participants were asked to recall the ratings they'd given themselves for the true pretest. Note that this is different from recalling their interviewing skills before the program; it is simply a matter of trying to remember the ratings themselves. Four of the seven retrospective pretest ratings were significantly different from the recall (memory) ratings, whereas there was never any difference between the recall (memory) ratings and the true pretest ratings. Participants could remember the numbers they used to rate themselves before the program but gave themselves significantly different ratings of pretraining interviewing capability after they had experienced the intervention.

In the work we have done at CCL, we've seen how response-shift bias can obscure the true story of the impact of our programs, and we've learned that using retrospective pretests can be a powerful way to both learn about our programs and provide feedback to our participants (McCauley and Hughes-James, 1994; Palus and Rogolsky, 1997; Van Velsor, Ruderman, and Young, 1992).

In several program evaluation studies, we used the traditional pretest-posttest design to measure the impact of the program on managers. We also added open-ended questions that allowed respondents to comment more specifically on the managers' development. In many cases we found that comparing the pretest and posttest scores indicated that the managers who had participated in our programs had not shown significant changes in their at-work behaviors. However, the comments showed a very different picture. For example, one manager may have been given an overall rating of 6 for the pretest score and 4 for the posttest (on a 10-point rating scale where 10 is the best possible score). Comparing these scores would lead us to think that this person did not make significant, positive behavioral changes after participating in the program. However, the type of comment received for this type of situation was "I don't know what you did for this manager, but it has made all the difference in the world—a tremendous improvement—thanks!" Certainly, the comment was not consistent with the difference in the ratings.

Retrospective Methodology in Practice

We incorporated our learnings from our experience with pretest-posttest designs as we evaluated additional programs. As a result, our next foray into program evaluation used our first program-specific, research-based retrospective change tool (Young and Dixon, 1996). The content of the instrument was based around the content of the program for which it was used, LeaderLab, which is a six-month, two-part program that makes use of long-term contact with "process advisors" (Young and Dixon, 1996). The instrument was developed by first collecting open-ended data from program alumni and their raters that related to changes the participants made during the program. Through content analysis of the open-ended data, broad categories of impact were defined and items written for each of these categories. These items then became the basis of the retrospective change tool. The results showed us that positive change from the "before the program" to the "now" rating periods were positively related to effectiveness (Young and Dixon, 1996). This instrument helped us to learn about both the impact of this particular program and the use of a retrospective change tool.

We then used the LeaderLab evaluation experience, combined with the knowledge gained from many years of studying the impact of several other programs, to produce what is now known as REFLECTIONS—a research-based tool that also uses the retrospective pretest methodology and allows us to study change in relation to other topics of interest. For example, we can study individual change in relation to organizational impact, end-of-program evaluations, program design, personality data, and more. We would not be able to make these types of comparisons with confidence were we using a traditional pre-post design to measure change. I will present REFLECTIONS as a case study later in this chapter.

Change Ratings

Another suitable alternative to using the retrospective pretest for measuring change has been developed by David Peterson at Personnel Decisions, Inc. Calling his method a *retrospective degree of change* rating, Peterson (1993) used traditional pretests and posttests, along with a single rating of the degree of change made on a particular objective by a target manager as a result of an in-depth, year-long coaching relationship (see Exhibit 9.3). The manager, coach, and boss all gave ratings at multiple times. What this method has in common with retrospective pretests is that change is assessed directly, not inferred from the comparison of pre- and posttest scores. In Peterson's research, each respective group noted improvements in behaviors via the pretest and posttest ratings (contrary to many other findings), but the amount of change shown on the degree-of-change rating was more similar across rating perspectives (that is, coach, boss, participant) than was the amount of change shown with the pretest and posttest ratings. Peterson's conclusion was that the degree-of-change rating format was superior to the traditional pretest and posttest format because there is more common understanding among the various perspectives about the *meaning* of the degree-of-change ratings. That is, for all the reasons that people are not able to make consistent ratings before and after an intervention, the same is *not* true when someone is asked to give a single rating for the degree to which another person changed.

"Ideal" Ratings

Yet another alternative is to use a combination of pretest and posttest measurements, together with an "ideal" rating (Zmud and Armenakis, 1978; see Exhibit 9.4). That is, raters give the actual ratings for a manager's performance both before and after an intervention. At the same time, raters also provide a rating for how well an ideal manager would have performed the particular task or behavior being rated. This notion parallels the notion of competency models, where ideal managers should have certain standards of performance. In the Zmud and Armenakis study, comparisons between the actual and ideal ratings on both the pretest and the posttest, as well as comparisons of scores across the two testing phases, were made to determine whether the actual ratings are valid, therefore validating the evaluations of change. The authors were able to identify in which cases alpha, beta (or both), or no change had occurred. In practical terms, this method could be used to provide raters with a common metric upon which to base their ratings of a target manager, thereby reducing the "noise" that enters traditional pre-post ratings.

Exhibit 9.3. Sample "Change Ratings" Follow-Up Survey.

(Part A: Pretest Ratings)

Effectiveness:

Very Ineffective		Average Effectiveness			Very Effective
1	2	3	4	5	6	7

Using the scale shown above, rate this person's effectiveness in the following areas:

Current Effectiveness

1. Sells upward and influences superiors effectively ____

2. Considers the impact of his or her actions on the entire system ____

3. Appropriately involves others in the decision-making process ____

(Part B: Posttest Ratings)

Degree of Change:

No Change		Moderate Change		Great Change
1	2	3	4	5

Using the scale shown above (including the effectiveness scale shown under Part A), rate this person's effectiveness in the following areas:

Current Effectiveness   Degree of Change

1. Strives to be skilled at selling upward, influencing superiors ____ ____

2. Considers the impact of his or her actions on the entire system ____ ____

3. Appropriately involves others in the decision-making process ____ ____

Source: Based on Measuring Change: A Psychometric Approach to Evaluating Individual Training Outcomes by David B. Peterson, 1993.

Exhibit 9.4. Sample "Ideal Ratings" Follow-Up Survey.

(Part A: Pretest Ratings)

Not at All		To a Small Extent		To a Moderate Extent		To a Large Extent		To a Very Large Extent
1	2	3	4	5	6	7	8	9

First, using the scale shown above, give the rating that represents how the *ideal* manager would perform this behavior:
Second, using the scale shown above, give the rating that appropriately describes the extent to which the manager you are rating

	Ideal manager	Manager you are rating
1. Strives to be skilled at selling upward, influencing superiors	_____	_____
2. Considers the impact of his or her actions on the entire system	_____	_____
3. Appropriately involves others in the decision-making process	_____	_____

(Part B: Posttest Ratings)

First, using the scale shown above (in Part A), give the rating that represents how the *ideal* manager would perform this behavior.
Second, using the scale shown above (in Part A), give the rating that appropriately describes the extent to which the manager you are rating

	Ideal manager	Manager you are rating
1. Strives to be skilled at selling upward, influencing superiors	_____	_____
2. Considers the impact of his or her actions on the entire system	_____	_____
3. Appropriately involves others in the decision-making process	_____	_____

Source: Based on "Understanding the Measurement of Change," by R. W. Zmud and A. A. Armenakis. Copyright © 1978 by *Academy of Management Review.*

Designing 360-Degree Feedback Instruments to Measure Change

At CCL, we believe that a measure of change, if carefully designed and timed to fit with the objectives of the intervention, will accurately show which behaviors and skills have been affected by the intervention. In Chapter Four, Tornow points out that managerial effectiveness is a difficult concept to capture. So, too, is the measurement of change in managerial effectiveness. Change instruments should undergo the same evaluation for validity that other 360-degree instruments are subjected to (see Chapter Seven). They should be held to high standards of content and construct validity. However, problems with measuring change in participants should be considered more closely. Raters and a rating scale should be chosen carefully; the appropriate timing for measuring change in a particular skill or competency should be ensured; and the context within which the change is taking place should be taken into account. Each of these, as well as other issues, will be discussed next, and potential solutions will be offered.

Raters and Rating Scales

As with other types of 360-degree instruments, the rating scale and raters used should be selected according to the purpose of the measurement (see Chapter Seven for a comprehensive discussion of relevant guidelines). For example, the target manager should choose a set of raters who (1) knew the manager well enough before the intervention to recall the manager's behaviors at that point; (2) have been around the manager frequently enough to observe changes in his or her behavior since the intervention; and (3) understand the manager's job and work situation well enough to know the demands that are placed on his or her job and how this relates to both the intervention and the changes made. In addition, the raters should understand why they are rating the target manager (for example, for development purposes following an intervention).

The rating scale used for the ratings should fit with what the instrument is trying to measure. A frequency-type rating scale will show how frequently the manager displays specific skills or behaviors (for example, 1 = never, 3 = sometimes, 5 = always). Some 360-degree feedback instruments use frequency scales *and* include a way for raters to indicate that the target manager should "do more" or "do less" of the given behavior. Alternatively, a mastery-type or effectiveness scale will show how well the manager is able to perform those skills or behaviors. Because the types of interventions discussed in this chapter are usually implemented to improve the effectiveness of individual managers and entire organizations (or both), the latter type of scale will best provide the type of data needed to learn whether the intervention has been successful in promoting meaningful changes.

Timing of the Assessment

Another question we frequently hear about change instruments is whether the results will accurately reflect the types and areas of change or whether raters will generalize the change they *do* see to all behaviors being rated (even when there has not been change on every behavior). We know that it takes more time for certain types of change (for example, awareness, skills, behaviors) than for others (see Chapter Seven for more information about differential impact), so measurement of change in the various behaviors should show differential speeds with which the behaviors change.

One potential solution is to use control items in a change measure. In fact, the use of control items has demonstrated the validity of change measurement (Howard and others, 1981). The authors included some items that were unrelated to the treatment intervention, believing that no change should be noted on these items, whereas change would be indicated on the items that were relevant to the intervention. The results showed no change on the unrelated items and change on the relevant items, indicating that respondents were reporting changes brought about by the intervention itself rather than a general set of more favorable ratings. The fundamental question here is whether raters are able to discriminate between changes in certain areas versus those areas where there has not been notable change. The design of the instrument and the surveying process are critical to this discrimination.

Repetitive Measurement

Another issue in using 360-degree feedback instruments to measure individual development is that of repetitive measurement. That is, how many times can the same instrument be used for feedback?

Does the instrument or its content need to change as an individual's goals, development needs, and learning become more developed, more sophisticated, more specific, or more complex? Can a manager use the same 360-degree instrument many times and learn something new each time? The answers to these questions depend on the instrument itself—on its flexibility and complexity—and its ability to show managers different pictures of themselves at different times. Instruments that measure multiple dimensions and provide feedback in a variety of formats are more likely to be of value when used multiple times than are less complex and dynamic instruments that give a single presentation of the results.

However, it seems that there must be a saturation point for every instrument, and administrators should be aware of the limitations of any instrument they choose. The limitations are probably also linked to the purpose of the assessment. Using the same instrument several times to measure the impact of a single intervention may not be as useful as using the same instrument to look at the gradual development of competencies. The distinction, though slight, may be of critical importance.

Context

An area not yet discussed is the context within which change takes place. It is of critical importance that when any measure is used to evaluate change due to an intervention, the evaluators take into consideration the environment within which the individual resides. For that matter, the question of context should be addressed in the planning phases for the intervention. Let's look at this concept using two examples.

> Paul, a manager in a media services organization, has been supported in his development efforts by his boss. In Paul's organization, there is a common recognition of the value of development for both those experiencing development and for the organization itself. The human resources function of this organization, with the assistance of line managers from each of the separate functions, is able to create a development plan for managers in each function. For Paul, the plan includes periodic development meetings with his boss, a leadership development workshop, two content-oriented courses in his field, a long-term developmental relationship with a manager in the corporate func-

tion of the organization, specific plans that will allow Paul to spend time concentrating on development without letting the work for which he is responsible suffer, and a set of goals that spell out the long-term vision for his development.

Near the middle of Paul's development plan cycle, he requests a 360-degree assessment as a follow-up to his leadership development program. When he receives his feedback from this assessment, it shows several areas of performance that he has been able to strengthen and several others that demand some new attention. Overall, Paul was happy with the progress he had made and the way it was reflected in his feedback. It showed that others could also recognize the changes he had made and give him some new directions for development.

Steve is a manager in a manufacturing organization who participated in the same leadership development program. Steve's organization does not put the degree of importance on development that Paul's organization exhibits, but Steve has a very clear idea of where he wants to be in his career five years from now and what he needs to do to get there. However, Steve does not have the breadth of development opportunities available to him that are present for Paul. Although Steve's boss supported his attendance at the development program, it has been difficult for Steve to focus his energies on making the changes he had set out to make. His boss does not give Steve the support he needs to continue working on the new behaviors identified as development needs during his leadership development program. Steve finds himself becoming frustrated by his lack of ability to try out new behaviors and competencies on the job.

When Steve receives feedback from his 360-degree program follow-up assessment, he too finds several areas that are strengths and several that are development needs. However, Steve's feedback shows that he did not make as much progress as he had hoped to make by this time. The observations of others around him were not a surprise, because they also felt that his development was not occurring as smoothly and quickly as he had wanted it to. Instead of focusing on continuing to develop, Steve found himself disheartened with the feedback and not very motivated to continue working on his own personal development.

The differences in Paul's and Steve's situations may have very little to do with personal motivations and capabilities. They are both highly qualified managers who are motivated to develop themselves. Rather, the differences may be rooted in the way their respective organizations perceive the value of development. Paul's situation is an example of a development system that looks at development as an ongoing process, whereas Steve's represents a development event. The degree to which an organization is more like Paul's rather than Steve's will have a great deal to do with the impact of the development intervention. In a single organization, different bosses may give different amounts of support to their employees, creating differential impact of the same intervention within the same organization. Therefore, understanding the work situation will assist with the interpretation of 360-degree feedback results used to measure change from an intervention.

A development system is one in which development is set up as a process rather than as an event (see Chapter Three; Dalton and Hollenbeck, 1996). The process should have clear and specific catalysts for development; the program purpose and behaviors to be developed should be well defined and align with the business needs of the organization; the development process should begin with baseline behavioral feedback; managers of those who will experience the development process should be supportive of the entire process; and the process should be held accountable in terms of whether it is being run as intended, as well as whether participants are developing.

The combination of various factors has a strong and complex influence on whether a development event or process results in long-term positive outcomes for both the individual and the organization (Martineau, 1996; Mathieu, Tannenbaum, and Salas, 1992). For example, some components of a development system influence a manager's state of mind before going into a development experience, whereas other components hold more influence when the manager is attempting to create a new way of working as a result of the intervention.

The degree to which managers "live" within development systems speaks volumes about how much development will actually take place. Hence, using any type of instrumentation, 360-degree or not, to measure the success of development must be interpreted within the context of the system. If a development system does not exist, 360-degree feedback is not likely to show as much change as would a situation with a strong development system in place. Because it is desirable to measure change in many different circumstances, evaluators must be aware of the context within which an intervention has taken place and interpret the results of the 360-degree feedback (or whatever mode of measurement has taken place) within that context.

Applications of 360-Degree Feedback for Measuring Individual Development: One Road Map

Now that the technical aspects of using 360-degree instruments to measure change have been introduced, let's look at some of the situations in which this measurement might take place. The first of these is for measuring individual development.

One of the ways CCL is measuring individual development is through the use of a goal-setting and follow-up instrument mentioned earlier called REFLECTIONS. This instrument was designed as both a tool for use by our manager participants and as a means of collecting group-level data for the purposes of measuring impact. I will use it as an example for the points presented in this section. Briefly, REFLECTIONS works this way:

> During their time at CCL, participants are given a great deal of feedback regarding their leadership capabilities. Among the programs' strong points are that they are forward-looking and they assist participants in setting goals and creating action plans for use after they leave CCL and return to the workplace. REFLECTIONS is one of the tools we use for goal setting. Participants leave CCL having selected up to three career and personal goals from a set of twelve suggested goal areas. They share those goals with others, both at work and at home, and may continue to focus on their development indefinitely.

> Three months after leaving CCL, these managers receive a packet of surveys, including a survey for themselves and eight surveys for others. We recommend that participants select respondents who can make high-quality, well-informed evaluations of how the manager has changed over the course of time since attending the development program. These may include the manager's boss, other superiors, peers, direct reports, clients, or suppliers.

> At the follow-up stage, respondents make two ratings on the larger set of leadership behaviors from which participants had previously selected their target goal behaviors for development: (1) a retrospective pretest rating and (2) a

posttest rating. Ratings are given on the full set of behaviors rather than only on the subset that were selected as goals by the manager for two reasons: (1) to protect the confidentiality of the goals when sharing one's goals (that is, one's development needs) can put the manager's job at risk and (2) to provide broad-impact feedback. The feedback, therefore, presents all of the data while highlighting the participant's unique goals.

In using 360-degree feedback to measure change, the target manager is afforded a rich opportunity to learn about others' observations of the efforts he or she has made to develop. Therefore, the feedback itself should be provided in a flexible way that allows the target manager to learn about his or her development at different levels. In the example of REFLECTIONS, we give participants a great deal of feedback because we believe that this assessment is multifunctional. That is, the feedback these managers receive from others is not only helpful in showing their development progress thus far but also allows them to target other areas of potential development. This belief fits the notion that some skills and behaviors can be developed more quickly than others and that observers will be able to note significant change at different rates, depending on the amount of time spent and the level of their relationship with the target manager. Thus, managers will find that some goal behaviors have developed fully, others are developing but still need some attention, and some new behaviors are appearing as development needs. Why would new development needs appear that were not clear prior to and during the program? A participant's job may have changed during that time; the context within which the organization operates may have changed; or improvements in some of the participant's behaviors may have simply allowed observers to focus their attentions on new behaviors.

The concept of behaviors changing at different rates is a critical distinction that we believe presents a challenge to us as we prepare our participants for self-interpretation of their own feedback reports. We must provide feedback recipients with enough information that they can differentiate between behaviors they should expect to see change in and those where it is simply too soon for any changes to be observable.

The notion of factors external to (and sometimes beyond the control of) the target manager makes the job of evaluating impact much more complex. Those who are involved in the evaluation of impact must always interpret results in light of the context around the target manager. We must also be aware that impact can be bolstered by some of these factors, and we should strive to engage them whenever possible. For example, although the REFLECTIONS process is designed to be run by the manager him- or herself, taking responsibility for becoming a continuously developing person, we recognize that the process can benefit from the support of several additional factors. Examples of these are (1) individual motivation to learn, grow, and develop, (2) the support of one's boss, and (3) organizational support for development (Roullier and Goldstein, 1991; Tracey, Tannenbaum, and Kavanaugh, 1995). One of these deserves special mention here.

It is critical that the manager's boss stay linked up with the manager in the development process (Hazucha, Hezlett, and Schneider, 1993; Maurer and Tarulli, 1994). Just as the manager and his or her boss should work together to determine the manager's needs for, and the timing of, developmental activities, they should also work together during and after those activities to ensure a complete integration of development into the manager's work.

Thus, 360-degree feedback processes designed to measure change will benefit greatly from ongoing conversations between the manager and boss regarding the target goal behaviors, the feedback itself, and next steps. These conversations and the feedback cycle create an ongoing performance management process, including the sharing of feedback, making changes based on the feedback, measuring the change, and sharing the feedback again.

In sum, using 360-degree feedback processes to measure individual development provides a highly informative method of learning about one's progress in making changes. This method gives people the opportunity to seek feedback in a structured manner that may not be possible or likely using other methods. In today's business climate, it can be difficult to walk into a colleague's office and ask for personal feedback (especially in organizations without a developmental climate), be that person a boss, a peer, or a subordinate. In some situations, it can put incredible pressure on the person being asked to give feedback, which would mean that truly honest feedback will not be the result. So often, we are wary of hurting someone's feelings, not sure of the motivation behind such a request, or simply not prepared to answer the face-to-face question. The feedback that is delivered in such a spontaneous way is not as specific, targeted, and honest as feedback from 360-degree instruments can be. And although receiving this type of feedback is valuable for almost anyone, it is especially important for top levels of management, where such mechanisms are not common in performance appraisal.

Use of 360-Degree Feedback for Measuring Individual Alignment with Organizational Strategies

Typically used for individual-level feedback, the 360-degree feedback instrument has also had some attention as a means of looking at group-level data as part of organizational development. (See Chapter Four for an in-depth discussion.) In fact, because there is growing sentiment that this method is "the best way to produce an accurate picture of how people are perceived by the people with whom they work, be it their manager, coworkers, direct reports, clients, or customers" (Gebelein, 1996, p. 22), 360-degree feedback can help organizations focus development efforts, both at a group and individual level, in a world where "companies win only by continuous revolution" (Tichy, 1996, p. 47).

One of the forces behind this continuous revolution is organizational development, which focuses on change at the organization level, that is, trying to change the culture of an organizational system (Beer and Walton, 1990). The use of 360-degree feedback interventions to measure aggregate change in organizational development is a natural link because it recognizes that individual-level change is at the heart of organization-level change, and it reinforces the idea that the development of those individual-level behaviors and capabilities must be tied to business results. This section of the chapter will look at (1) the value of using 360-degree feedback instruments to measure individual alignment relative to organizational strategies and (2) aggregation of individual-level feedback data, where 360-degree feedback falls short in measuring organizational change.

Value of 360-Degree Feedback to the Executive as an Indicator of Organizational Change

Probably the most immediately recognized reason for using 360-degree feedback in this way is to measure change in multiple individuals, then aggregating the data to make conclusions about group- or organization-level change. Because organizational change and the strategies by which it is accomplished ultimately depend on the individuals within the organization, it is critical that attention be paid to the individual skills, behaviors, and competencies needed to achieve the change goals (Gebelein, 1996). Measuring change in those individuals will first help each person to know specifically how he or she is doing in relation to the change efforts. Upon aggregation, the champions of the change effort can look at groups of people (for example, departments, regional offices) to determine which are in need of additional attention and which are moving in the intended direction of the change. The amount of change shown in the 360-degree ratings, along with the relative magnitude of the ratings, will provide this indicator. For example, a group that has moved from an overall rating of 2 to 5 on a 9-point rating scale (9 indicating the best possible score) should be applauded in its efforts to make change but is still not finished with its work to make improvements in this area.

The organizational executive has a special interest in the use of 360-degree feedback to indicate organizational change. As one of the drivers of the change, the executive needs to be well informed on the progress being made toward implementing organizational strategy. No longer can it be assumed that employees can, and will, do what the organization's executives feel is best for the organization. Even if they want to move into alignment with the executives' efforts toward change, many forces produce tension in any such effort.

Organizations are influenced by external pressures. As such, the changes they must continuously undergo to remain successful and competitive are both linear (gradual and incremental, based on stable conditions, with predictable outcomes) and nonlinear (discontinuous, with multidirectional interactions, based on conditions in constant flux, with unpredictable and delayed outcomes [Uhlfelder, 1996]). To accomplish business goals, people within organizations must also be able to adapt their skills, competencies, and behaviors in line with the organizational change (Gebelein, 1996). Under these conditions, executives must facilitate change, build competencies, and be model communicators, diagnosticians, leaders, and "process advisors" (Uhlfelder, 1996). The presence of a continuous learning culture, where "organizational members share perceptions and expectations that learning is an important part of everyday life" (Tracey and others, 1995), is a primary means of enabling managers to fulfill these roles. (Chapter Six discusses continuous learning cultures in more depth.)

Given these demands, one of the key pieces of information that executives can have at their disposal is 360-degree feedback. The data from these instruments can help executives understand the way in which development is unfolding in an aggregate sense, comparing key skills and competencies of work groups relative to where they need to be.

Why should 360-degree instruments be used to measure change within organizations? Because change is never finished. Change must always continue, even when initial goals are achieved; ongoing assessment will help to direct attention in the appropriate directions (Gebelein, 1996). There are many reasons that 360-degree feedback instruments can be used to measure organizational change relative to organizational strategies. First, they can be used to communicate key skill sets required for the change. Second, 360-degree feedback can indicate areas of performance that may still be problematic and can be addressed through additional development efforts. Third, developmental planning efforts can be assessed and evaluated. Fourth, the results may help to delineate various groups in the organization that have, or have not, responded appropriately to the organizational intervention. Finally, the data may also be broken down by organizational levels to show which may be in need of additional attention. Each of these will be discussed.

Successful Communication of Key Skill Sets

A primary benefit of using 360-degree instruments to measure individual and group change is to communicate to employees consistently that a new skill or behavior set is being developed in an effort to effectively implement a new business strategy or direction. It has been widely confirmed that 360-degree feedback interventions are rarely successful unless they are tied to a business strategy or a business need (see Chapter Three). If implemented properly, using 360-degree feedback to measure change will promote greater continuous alignment between the goals of the organization, relative to its business strategy, and the goals of individuals needed to support the strategy (see Chapter Four). In Chapter Three, the author recognizes that some organizations use 360-degree feedback as a strategy to communicate to employees that a new skill set will be needed for an anticipated organizational or culture change in work methods, work content, work flow, or work demand. Just as 360-degree feedback may be used to communicate a key skill set, organizational strategy, or a business need, so may the monitoring of change using 360-degree feedback maintain the focus of the organization's members on where they stand relative to those goals, and on the very fact that the organization is making these changes. Showing employees a personal side to the organizational change strategies will make for a more powerful motivator for individual change than simply telling them about the change. Therefore, knowing (1) what changes are needed in the organization and (2) how individual change will support the organizational change are necessary before implementing 360-degree feedback to demonstrate how people (individually and in the aggregate) are moving in the desired direction.

Identifying Performance Problems

As a performance management technique, 360-degree feedback can be of value for measuring change by continuously making performance expectations clear and salient to individuals. It can communicate changes over time in the valued performance dimensions in line with changing organizational goals and can emphasize the strategies that are of importance to the organization.

By receiving the data from change versions of 360-degree feedback tools (for example, using retrospective pretest ratings, change ratings, or ideal ratings), employees will be involved in the organizational change efforts and will become partners for that change. Thus, the areas of performance that are highlighted as needing additional attention (for example, they are important to the change effort but have not shown adequate improvement) help to bring individual goals and development plans in line with those of the organization. The end result is a stronger linkage of individual and organizational goals that continue to be measured and realigned together (see Chapter Four).

Measuring the Success of Developmental Planning

A third reason for using 360-degree feedback interventions to measure aggregated individual change is to continuously evaluate and revise the development plans that were put in place by a prior intervention. Although we would like to believe that development plans maintain a focal point in a manager's daily life, all readers of this book surely have experienced the tension between continuous development and getting one's work accomplished. Properly designed in a development systems framework, development plans would be integrated into the work itself, and the development of intended behaviors would be rewarded by the organization (see Chapter Three). Using 360-degree feedback to periodically assess progress made in line with the development plan would help to keep appropriate focus on development. Taken to the organization level, the leaders of an organization would be able to respond more rapidly to newly arising issues in the face of organizational change, directing attention to new interventions that become necessary. Leaders would know when the organization has reached a critical mass of change in a certain area and could keep a finger on the pulse of the organization.

Delineating Group Change

In addition to looking at organizationwide data, executives can also break apart the organization-level data in several ways. One of these is by functional group. For example, a review of 360-degree feedback aggregated across the entire organization will enable the executive to get a sense of the progress being made toward individual change strategies by the entire organization but will not differentiate between groups that are succeeding quite well in the change initiative versus those that are not. Breaking the data apart by functional groups can be an informative way of determining which groups may be in need of additional attention and (possibly) interventions, which groups are progressing well, or which groups are progressing so well that they may be used as learning sites, possibly using their change efforts as an example for other groups. The executive will be able to integrate the organization's multiple parts, aligning their goals using a common metric, and can identify areas where additional work is needed to bring the goals of separate groups closer together (see Chapter Four).

Delineating Change Within and Between Organization Levels

Similarly, there will be times when the organizational change strategies are not communicated well across various levels of the organization, are received better by some levels than by others, or are simply working against the culture of a certain level.

The executive can use 360-degree feedback to identify the areas where some levels have been able to change but others have not. Working with a set of dimensions that is smaller than the whole, the executive can devote more effort to determining why change is not occurring and make the appropriate adjustments to either the change strategy or the interventions used to work toward the future goal.

Issues to Consider in Using Aggregate 360-Degree Feedback to Measure Alignment with Organizational Change Strategies

Several issues must be considered when using 360-degree feedback to measure alignment with organizational change strategies. Beginning with the notion of individual-level 360-degree feedback for these purposes, I will discuss aggregation issues. Next, I'll offer some alternatives to individual-level 360-degree feedback instruments: group- or team-level 360 instruments and non-360-degree measures.

Measuring Individual Change in the Aggregate

Measuring organizational change using 360-degree feedback instruments is different from measuring individual change with them. If individuals select their respondents carefully, as discussed earlier, valid and reliable 360-degree feedback instruments will give them a good picture of themselves, as seen by others. The group of raters is thinking about, and rating, a single individual, and the ratings will reflect various dimensions of that person.

Measuring alignment with organizational change by aggregating individual-level 360-degree feedback data, however, is not as simple as averaging all the ratings together. The only way it would be this simple is if every individual in the entire organization were rated and given feedback. However, many organizations do not choose to survey the entire organization. In these cases, those in charge of the effort will select a subsample of the organization (where all of the organization's members have been a part of the change effort) and make inferences based on that group's scores.

If the organization were to select a stratified random sample, so that each unique group within the organization was represented by a random set of its members, it would be feasible to infer organizational change from the aggregate change for the individuals.

Individual-level change data are part of the whole, but inferring organizational change is not as simple as adding the pieces together. There are interactions involved that make it more than an additive process. An example follows.

> The XYZ Corporation is in the second of five years targeted for an organizational change strategy that is designed to bring the company into the twenty-first century as a major competitor in the consumer products industry. The vice president for human resources has the task of implementing 360-degree feedback for the purpose of checking the progress of the change effort. The implementation of the feedback initiative has been designed so that each group participates every eight months. During the most recent phase of surveying, the data showed that one group is not developing and changing as intended. Obviously, this group is in need of some additional intervention to bring it in line with the organizational change strategies. Unfortunately, though, the solution is not as simple as this. Due to the highly interdependent nature of the various groups within this organization, the slow progress of change in one group will affect other groups. Therefore, the vice president called a meeting with the CEO and the directors of this group, as well as others who were involved in the design of the change efforts, so they could examine all of the various groups and factors necessary in determining how to redirect the situation.

This example illustrates the notion that individual change, or even aggregated individual change, is not always indicative of organizational change. Unless the proper perspective is taken when examining change data, the use of aggregated 360-degree feedback does not make sense.

One of the best ways to measure alignment toward organizational change using 360-degree feedback is to select an instrument that addresses the objectives of the organizational change strategy, which is consistent with the need to link individual development to the organization's business and strategic goals (Hall, 1995). For example, if the organization were attempting to move from having customer service be a small part of the business to having it become a focal goal for improvement, a 360-degree tool that addresses customer service behaviors would be recommended. If one of the business needs was to become more flexible in offering products to clients, particularly by being able to customize certain products without reinventing the products each time, a 360-degree tool that measured flexibility and the ability to innovate would be advised.

Another method for ensuring the relevance and accuracy of aggregated 360-degree feedback data is to survey a relatively stable group of employees. Similar to selecting a stable group of raters for individual-level feedback, it is desirable to include in the assessment, to the extent possible, only employees who have had relatively little change in their jobs (other than through the intervention itself) since the intervention began. The most informative data available regarding the impact of the intervention will come from employees for whom the intervention could have had maximum impact—those for whom the intervention was the only source of significant change. At the very least, only employees who were in the organization (or group) at the time preceding the intervention should be included.

Alternative Ways of Measuring Alignment with Organizational Change Strategies

Certainly, 360-degree feedback is not the only way to measure alignment with organizational change strategies. Climate surveys and analysis of change in business results are two examples of alternatives. Each of these gives a different picture of change than do 360-degree instruments: climate surveys can address changes in attitudes and perceptions toward the organization's change interventions; analysis of business results can indicate whether the intervention was successful at changing individual and group behaviors and capabilities to the extent that the organization is able to meet or approach its business goals.

In addition, it is also possible to use group-level 360-degree feedback instruments (Hallam, 1996) to obtain ratings of groups rather than ratings of sets of individuals. The difference is a consensus agreement regarding the performance of the group as a whole versus ratings of each individual within the group. This method appropriately looks at the construct of group performance rather than assuming that aggregate individual change is the same as group change.

Overall, the value of 360-degree feedback as a measure of organizational change is to maintain a specific, focused, ongoing knowledge of how groups of individuals within the organization react to and grow with organizational change. Armed with this knowledge and the ability to make adjustments to organizational change strategies as needed, the executive will better be able to move the organization into the twenty-first century as a successful, competitive entity.

Conclusion

This chapter has shown the value of 360-degree feedback in the assessment of both individual-level and aggregate-level change. I have presented examples of each, issues that accompany them, and potential solutions. This chapter has cross-referenced several other chapters of this book, as well as other resources, due to the complexity of issues surrounding measurement of change using 360-degree surveys. Readers are urged to investigate the purpose of a human resources intervention, its intended outcomes, and the level at which those outcomes can be best assessed before deciding on any single method of measuring change. The solution can be unique to the particular situation and may well involve multiple methods of measurement; 360-degree feedback may be only one of those.

Note

1. This chapter will not specifically address the issue of using 360-degree survey feedback to create change. For research on this topic, readers are referred to the work of Atwater, Roush, and Fischthal (1995); Reilly, Smither, and Vasilopoulos (1996); Smither, London, and Vasilopoulos (1995).

Challenges and Implications for Maximizing 360-Degree Feedback

Walter W. Tornow
Manuel London

We have, in the preceding pages, taken a close look at how the process of 360-degree feedback can contribute to individual and organizational development. Key themes have been that 360-degree feedback should be a core part of development, that it fits the realities of the new workplace, and that it is multifaceted in purpose and value. Its use, however, involves many challenges for the individual and the organization, and there are important issues and implications related to the process that must be considered.

Challenges

There are several important challenges we need to be aware of from the perspective of the individual and the organization. The first is the increased information-processing complexity that comes with the richness inherent in 360-degree feedback. The second is the person's readiness to accept the feedback. A third is costs—direct and indirect as well as short- and long-term. A fourth challenge deals with how we manage expectations. And a final challenge revolves around the purpose of the 360-degree feedback process: development versus appraisal and other administrative decision making.

249

Information Complexity

The use of 360-degree feedback requires much more from managers and other recipients of such feedback than if they were dealing only with feedback from their immediate supervisors. First of all, there is a great deal more information to interpret. Then, the ratings may be inconsistent, not because they are unreliable but because the manager has different roles and relationships with different constituencies. Also, the ratings are averaged by source (except for the supervisor), so the manager will have a picture of what subordinates or peers think on the average. There may be information about the variation of ratings within the source (for instance, the lowest and highest rating), which further complicates the feedback. The feedback report may also present normative information—the average of how other managers were rated by their subordinates, peers, customers, and supervisor. Moreover, there may be information indicating changes in results from the last survey. The recipient of this 360-degree feedback is supposed to interpret all this information and glean ideas for development—areas of performance excellence that need to be maintained and enhanced, and performance gaps that need to be closed.

Clearly, this is no small task. It requires a good deal of cognitive complexity, in addition to affective acknowledgment of the validity and legitimacy of the feedback. It also requires balancing multiple and perhaps conflicting perspectives, as well as balancing a sense of self with the larger context and role requirements. Therefore, the importance of training cannot be overemphasized. Such training should include raters and ratees. Further, the supervisor's role needs to be seen as key when it comes to facilitating the 360-degree feedback process and ensuring the necessary organizational support, not just for assessment and feedback but also for action planning and follow-up.

Readiness to Accept Feedback

Although self-assessment can motivate development, fear of knowing more can also prevent development (Whetten and Cameron, 1991, p. 53). However, feedback results that are verifiable, predictable, and controllable are difficult to deny (London and Smither, 1995). What is important is that there be the maturational readiness for feedback, that is, an ability and a willingness to accept the feedback and to do something with it that will result in change. Then, 360-degree feedback can become a powerful motivator for facilitating such change.

This suggests that employees must have confidence in the 360-degree feedback process for it to work. They must understand the purpose of the 360-degree instrument, recognize the importance of knowing that others' evaluations of their performance on the items is valuable, and trust that the results will be used as promised (for instance, used for development only and the results not given to supervisors or integrated with other information to make administrative decisions about salary or promotion).

Costs

Organizations pay directly and indirectly for 360-degree feedback (London and Smither, 1995); time and money must be spent for preparation and implementation. For instance, the purpose of the program must be communicated clearly to employees and managers. Also, managers should be trained on how to use the feedback. The use of 360-degree feedback adds complexity to the appraisal administration, which requires the distribution of forms to the right individuals. It also requires analyzing the data, possibly with the use of sophisticated computer programming and outside help. The raters may believe that the process imposes potential risks that their ratings won't be anonymous. Ratees may fear that their results won't be confidential.

Building trust in the process requires paying careful attention to details, consistency, and time. Value and trust in the process should grow with its continued use if perceptions of the process and how it actually works match its intended and communicated goals. Thus, initial implementation costs need to be supplemented with important types of follow-up activities and costs. These are associated not only with the ongoing administration of the feedback program but also with the kind of evaluation follow-up activities necessary to determine its impact on individuals and the organization.

Expectations

Finally, 360-degree feedback establishes expectations that behavior will change. This can set up potential role conflicts for the target managers in that it may highlight the need to be different things to different people in different contexts. It provides a lot of information to integrate, and this increases the likelihood of selective perception and information distortion among the managers' many different constituencies. Therefore, care needs to be taken that these challenges are addressed in the communication and training plans when implementing 360-degree feedback processes.

Expectations need to be managed carefully for both raters and ratees to ensure that their respective frameworks are taken into consideration and matched against what's realistic. Expecting too much, too soon may be a common enough mistake; so would the opposite, that is, expecting too little, too late. It's the supervisor's job to work with the individual as part of the 360-degree feedback process and ensure that realistic action plans are developed. That is, they should incorporate development goals that are a stretch for the individual but also attainable.

Purpose

As mentioned in the Introduction to this book, there is a great debate about whether 360-degree feedback should be used for development only or for appraisal and other administrative decision making. Many of the chapter authors fall on the side of development-only because the conditions typically associated with appraisal and evaluation are believed to run counter to those needed to promote personal growth. However, a reframing of the debate might lend itself to forward movement here. Instead of considering this an either-or situation, the challenge for practitioners is to determine under what conditions *both* purposes can exist. Then, we can design 360-degree feedback systems and create the kinds of conditions in our organizations that are conducive to development, while also integrating 360-degree feedback with other human resources management processes, such as reward systems, for purposes of accountability and alignment.

Doing so will take skill in (1) clear communication of purpose and expectations, (2) phased-in implementation, starting with development-only for system orientation and adaptation, (3) training of raters and ratees, and (4) ongoing monitoring for feedback and corrective action-taking to ensure that the program's effects match its intents. Care also should be taken to avoid the pitfalls that have traditionally plagued performance appraisal systems—for example, to disentangle in time and place the conversations focused on development from those targeting administrative actions. This will make it possible for managers not to have to play the roles of coach and judge at the same time. Finally, both individuals and the organization need to adopt a learning frame when looking at the 360-degree feedback process. Only then can 360-degree feedback become recognized and therefore fully used for its value—to the individual and the organization—as a learning tool and facilitator of continuous improvement.

Issues and Implications

Five important issues should be considered with respect to the use of 360-degree feedback: (1) linking individual with organizational change, (2) mapping the impact of 360-degree feedback, (3) looking at development as a system, (4) managing connectivity inherent in the relationships that define the work that organizations need to get done, and (5) looking at 360-degree feedback both as a means and as an end. These issues can have significant implications for both the practice and research we do with 360-degree feedback.

Linking Individual with Organizational Change

If change is the name of the game—the raison d'être for 360-degree feedback—then we need to understand more fully how to link individual-level change with organization-level change. That is, how does organizational change get implemented at the individual level? And how does individual-level change affect organization-level change? To the practitioner, for example, this is a question of how organizational strategy and core values can be translated into individual-level behavioral feedback that informs the individual manager on whether he or she is perceived as an exemplar of the organization's espoused values. To the researcher, this may mean better understanding what role the instrument, the administration process, and management practices play in aligning organizational with individual development goals. And then, how do we effectively bridge back individual development planning, resulting from 360-degree feedback, with organizational needs and goals? The latter suggests a more integrated approach to development and business planning; using the 360-degree feedback process is a vehicle to achieve such integration.

Mapping the Impact of 360-Degree Feedback

We need to recognize that both individual and organizational development are processes, not events. They take time, and they span time. Therefore, our practices need to facilitate this process of growth and change by taking more of a longitudinal perspective. For the practitioner, this means that development activities are designed to be part of an overall process of development that build on one another, rather than separate activities or events that may have little perceived relationship to each other. For the researcher, the implication is that more longitudinal, multiyear follow-up research should be done that will allow us to map more fully the outcomes of 360-degree feedback on the individual and the organization.

Care should be taken to specify just what the 360-degree feedback intervention actually encompasses. For example, is it simply providing participants with their feedback reports? Or is the 360-degree feedback facilitated and part of a training program? Or is it integrated with a follow-up coaching relationship as part of an organizational change effort? Obviously, the nature and quality of the 360-degree feedback intervention—at the time it is delivered as well as during the follow-up to ensure appropriate transfer of learning—can make a big difference in whether the individual and the organization benefit. Any impact research should help us understand what the individual and organizational factors are that act as facilitators or inhibitors to long-term change. These would include both readiness to change on the part of the individual and the organization and transfer of feedback-related learnings into action plans back on the job.

Looking at Development as a System

We need to look at the larger context of the organization and its overall processes of development as a *development system* and then see how well integrated the 360-degree feedback process is. That is, what are the different policies, practices, and tools that the organization is already using for purposes of development? For example, competency models, succession planning, management development programs, performance management tools, and coaching may already be part of an organization's development strategy. Then, we need to ask how well they play together in an integrated way and how linked they are to the organization's business goals and strategies.

When looked at from a systems perspective, we can then examine how a 360-degree feedback process fits, or doesn't, into the organization's existing development system. Obviously, how integrated the organization's development system is as a system, and how integrated it is with its business goals and strategies, are two important precursors that tend to moderate any impact research that can demonstrate the effects of the 360-degree feedback processes.

Managing Connectivity

As noted in the Introduction, one way of picturing organization and work is through the many work relationships that are established—a form of connectivity. Individuals are connected in that they derive meaning with and through other people about what is expected of them and how well they're doing. Both are critically important forms of work-oriented communication. The 360-degree feedback process allows people to become connected, and, in so doing, it facilitates the building of effective working relationships around work-oriented communication. It then becomes an important performance-management tool—a tool that assumes its value through the quality of work-oriented communication it promotes and the cooperative relationships it allows people to build and maintain.

This realization that 360-degree feedback can be a tool to manage connectivity is very much in line with the changing nature of the workplace and the relationships employees have with their employers. This includes taking greater responsibility for self-management and participating more in the leadership processes of the organization in how work gets done. This kind of employee empowerment is enabled by 360-degree feedback processes.

360-Degree Feedback: A Means or an End?

Finally, we need to recognize that practitioners and researchers may bring multiple perspectives themselves to this subject (Tornow, 1993). That is, one can picture 360-degree feedback either as an end in itself—focusing on the measurement aspects of the tool and how to do it right—or as a means toward an end—emphasizing the tool's usefulness for achieving desired outcomes such as individual and organizational change. Although the polarities mentioned next between researchers and practitioners are purposefully exaggerated and are in reality not of an either-or nature, they are described in their extremes for illustration purposes.

For the researcher, 360-degree feedback frequently is treated more as an end in itself. The focus tends to be on the instrument, its reliability and validity, or how well it measures what it is supposed to measure. Concern is for accuracy of measurement and reducing error variance among raters. Frequently, the underlying operating assumption behind the statistical analysis of the ratings is that there is something like a "true score," and the trick is to approximate it through strict rater instructions and training. A good deal of attention is placed on what we need to do in creating forms and processes that eliminate as much so-called rater bias and variation among ratings as possible.

For the practitioner, in contrast, 360-degree feedback is seen more as a means, not an end itself. Here, the purpose of measurement is more important, and any concern with measurement lies more with its usefulness to have impact. Utility becomes the driving question, in addition to issues of validity and reliability. The practitioner also recognizes that variation among ratings comes from the different rater perspectives, which, after all, represent multiple realities. These differences in perspectives are not seen as errors of measurement to be reduced but as legitimate differences to be aware of and understood. Information about ranges, norms, and changes over time therefore can be very helpful as well for their added interpretive value. Obviously, the instrument still needs to be reliable and valid so that any particular rating means what it says. Moreover, like a hammer in search of things to pound, its application needs to fit the situation and the intended goals.

360-Degree Feedback: A Fad or a Fit?

In sum, when 360-degree feedback is treated as a one-time event, the likelihood that it will survive and work effectively in the eyes of employees and management is slim. If, however, the organization has a clear purpose in mind that links the 360-degree feedback process to its business goals, and the organization integrates it with its other human resources management tools and processes, then the likelihood that it will take root and be successful is vastly increased.

If the purpose for having 360-degree feedback is not clear, if it's not integrated with the other systems, and if there is a history of mistrust because of abuse or poor communication, it will come across more like a fad—and go the way fads usually go.

Also, the mechanics of administration need to be kept efficient. What the organization wants to avoid is overwhelming multiple raters with repeated requests for ratings on multiple target individuals— all at the same time and all on forms that seem long and complex to fill out. Ideally, there should be a computer-assisted system that allows a coordinator to maximize the complementary value of multiple raters for any target individual, while minimizing the demand for ratings on any selected rater.

One thing is clear: 360-degree feedback processes are here to stay if they become part of an organization's development system. That means the organization looks at development holistically, as a process, and from a systems point of view. This will ensure that all the different components of the development system are identified, along with any missing pieces, and 360-degree feedback is clearly anchored in this development system for maximum value.

Similarly, individuals can assume a parallel mind-set and look at their development holistically, as a process, and from a systems point of view. This way, individuals will not look at 360-degree feedback simply as an event but as part of an ongoing process of giving and receiving feedback and continuous development—as part of their side of the equation when it comes to performance management and career development.

A final point refers to how the use of 360-degree feedback may change over time as organizations gain experience with it. We may picture its use as a dynamic and evolutionary process in organizations. As employees get used to the process and continuous learning becomes part of the corporate culture, the organization can experiment with new approaches. Different performance dimensions or items can be added to keep the process fresh and reflect changing business goals and strategies. New techniques and approaches may be tried, such as computer-based administration and feedback. In addition to individuals, groups may use 360-degree feedback to obtain information about how they are viewed by other groups.

Also, 360-degree feedback processes may encourage an organizational climate where people feel free to ask, give, and receive feedback in person as part of the normal day-to-day course of doing business rather than waiting for formal ratings. Then, the periodic 360-degree ratings can serve to reinforce this feedback-rich climate by more systematically maintaining attention to different views about performance and the value that is placed on monitoring whether others' performance expectations are being met.

In conclusion, organizations can maximize the value of 360-degree feedback as a process that will create successful individual and organizational development. This can be done by being intentional and systemic when designing and implementing a 360-degree feedback program such that it fits with the intended purpose, is aligned with the business goals and strategies, and is integrated with the other HR systems.

References

American Psychological Association. (1992). Ethical principles of psychologists and code of conduct. *American Psychologist, 47*(12), 1597–1611.

Antonioni, D. (1994). The effects of feedback accountability on upward appraisal ratings. *Personnel Psychology, 47,* 349–356.

Antonioni, D. (1996, Autumn). Designing an effective 360-degree appraisal feedback process. *Organizational Dynamics, 25*(2), 24–38.

Atwater, L., Roush, P., & Fischthal, A. (1995). The influence of upward feedback on self- and follower ratings of leadership. *Personnel Psychology, 48,* 35–49.

Austin, J., & Villanova, P. (1992). The criterion problem: 1917–1992. *Journal of Applied Psychology, 77,* 836–874.

Bales, R. (1991). SYMLOG. San Diego: SYMLOG Consulting Group.

Beer, M., & Walton, R. E. (1990). Developing the competitive organization: Interventions and strategies. *American Psychologist, 45,* 154–161.

Bernardin, H. J., & Beatty, R. W. (1987). Can subordinate appraisals enhance managerial productivity? *Sloan Management Review, 28*(4), 63–73.

Bernardin, H. J., Dahmus, S. A., & Redmon, G. (1993). Attitudes of first-line supervisors toward subordinate appraisals. *Human Resource Management, 32,* 315–324.

Bigoness, W. J., & Blakely, G. L. (1996). A cross-national study of managerial values. *Journal of International Business Studies, 27*(4), 739–752.

Borman, W. C. (1974). The rating of individuals in organizations: An alternate approach. *Organizational Behavior and Human Performance, 12,* 105–124.

Borman, W. C. (1991). Job behavior, performance, and effectiveness. In M. Dunnette & L. Hough (Eds.), *Handbook of industrial and organizational psychology* (2nd ed., Vol. 2, pp. 105–124). Palo Alto, CA: Consulting Psychologists Press.

Bracken, D. W., Dalton, M. A., Jako, R., McCauley, C. D., & Pollman, V. A. (1997). *Should 360-degree feedback be used only for developmental purposes?* Greensboro, NC: Center for Creative Leadership.

Bridges, W. (1996, April). *De-jobbing*. Paper presented at the annual conference of the Human Resource Planning Society, San Diego.

Brockner, J. (1995). Self processes in leading downsized and other changed organizations. In D. Noer & K. Bunker (Eds.), *Best practices in leading downsized organizations: Conference proceedings*. Greensboro, NC: Center for Creative Leadership.

Brutus, S., Fleenor, J. W., & McCauley, C. D. (1996, April). *Self-other rating discrepancy in 360-degree feedback: An investigation of demographic and personality predictors*. Paper presented at the meeting of the Society for Industrial and Organizational Psychology, San Diego.

Bunker, K. A., & Webb, A. D. (1992). *Learning how to learn from experience: Impact of stress and coping*. Greensboro, NC: Center for Creative Leadership.

Burd, K. A., & Ryan, A. M. (1993). *Reactions to developmental feedback in an assessment center*. Paper presented at the eighth annual meeting of the Society for Industrial and Organizational Psychology, San Francisco.

Campbell, D. (1991). Campbell Leadership Index. Minneapolis, MN: National Computer Systems.

Campbell, D., & Hallam, G. L. (1994). Campbell-Hallam Team Development Survey. Minneapolis, MN: National Computer Systems.

Carver, C. S., & Scheier, M. F. (1982). Control theory: A useful conceptual framework for personality, social, clinical, and health psychology. *Psychological Bulletin, 92*, 111–135.

Chappelow, C. (1998). 360-degree feedback in individual development. In C. D. McCauley, R. Moxley, & E. Van Velsor (Eds.), *The Center for Creative Leadership's handbook of leadership development*. San Francisco: Jossey-Bass.

Chen, C., Lee, S., & Stevenson, H. W. (1995). Response style and cross-cultural comparisons of rating scales among East Asian and North American students. *American Psychological Society, 6*(3), 170–175.

Couch, A., & Keniston, K. (1960). Yeasayers and naysayers: Agreeing response set as a personality variable. *Journal of Abnormal Psychology, 60*, 151–174.

Dalton, M. A. (1992). An unsuspected impact of 360-degree-feedback instruments. *Issues & Observations, 12*(1), 7–8.

Dalton, M. A. (1995). *Ethical and psychometric issues to be addressed in exporting multi-rater feedback instruments*. Paper presented at the seventh annual meeting of the Society for Industrial and Organizational Psychology, Orlando, FL.

Dalton, M. A. (1996). Multirater feedback and conditions for change. *Consulting Psychology Journal, 48*(1), 12–16.

Dalton, M. A., & Hollenbeck, G. P. (1996). *How to design an effective system for developing managers and executives.* Greensboro, NC: Center for Creative Leadership.

Dalton, M. A., Lombardo, M. M., McCauley, C. D., Moxley, R., & Wachholz, J. (1996). *Benchmarks developmental reference points: A manual and trainer's guide.* Greensboro, NC: Center for Creative Leadership.

Daudelin, M. W. (1996). Learning from experience through reflection. *Organizational Dynamics, 24,* 36–48.

De Meuse, K. P., & Tornow, W. W. (1990). The tie that binds has become very, very frayed! *Human Resource Planning, 13*(3), 203–214.

Dixon, N. (1994). *The organizational learning cycle: How we learn collectively.* London: McGraw-Hill.

Doron, R., & Parot, F. (1991). *Dictionnaire de psychologie.* Paris: Presses Universitaires de France.

Drath, W. H., & Palus, C. J. (1994). *Making common sense: Leadership as meaning-making in a community of practice.* Greensboro, NC: Center for Creative Leadership.

Eagly, A. H., Karau, S. J., & Makhijani, M. G. (1995). Gender and the effectiveness of leaders: A meta-analysis. *Psychological Bulletin, 117,* 125–145.

Eastman, L. J. (1995). *Succession planning: An annotated bibliography and summary of commonly reported organizational practices.* Greensboro, NC: Center for Creative Leadership.

Edwards, M. R., & Ewen, A. J. (1996). *360-degree feedback.* New York: American Management Association.

Eggers, J. H., Leahy, K. T., & Churchill, N. C. (1997). *CEO self-perception accuracy and entrepreneurial organizational performance.* Paper presented at the 1997 Kauffman Foundation/Babson College Entrepreneurship Research Conference, Boston.

Ellis, B. B. (1989). Differential item functioning: Implications for test translations. *Journal of Applied Psychology, 74*(6), 912–921.

Farh, J. L., Cannella, A. A., & Bedeian, A. G. (1991). Peer ratings: The impact of purpose on rating quality and user acceptance. *Group and Organizational Studies, 16*(4), 367–386.

Farh, J. L., Dobbins, G. H., & Cheng, B. S. (1991). Cultural relativity in action: A comparison of self-ratings made by Chinese and U.S. workers. *Personnel Psychology, 44,* 129–147.

Farh, J. L., & Werbel, J. D. (1986). Effects of purpose of the appraisal and expectation of validation on self-appraisal leniency. *Journal of Applied Psychology, 71,* 527–529.

Fleenor, J. W., McCauley, C. D., & Brutus, S. (1996). Self-other rating agreement and leader effectiveness. *Leadership Quarterly, 7*(4), 487–506.

Fox, S., Ben-Nahum, Z., & Yinon, Y. (1989). Perceived similarity and accuracy of peer ratings. *Journal of Applied Psychology, 74,* 781–786.

Gebelein, S. H. (1996). "To see ourselves as others see us": The value of multi-rater feedback in achieving organizational change. *Manage, 48,* 22–23.

Golembiewski, R. T. (1989). The alpha, beta, gamma change typology: Perspectives on acceptance as well as resistance. *Group and Organization Studies, 14,* 150–154.

Golembiewski, R. T., Billingsley, K., & Yeager, S. (1976). Measuring change and persistence in human affairs: Types of change generated by OD designs. *Journal of Applied Behavioral Science, 12,* 133–157.

Gryskiewicz, N. (1995). *An international study on the role of multi-rater feedback instruments in management development.* Proceedings. Innovation, technology and information management for global development and competitiveness, Fourth World Business Congress of International Management Development Association, pp. 572–578.

Hackman, J. R., & Oldham, G. R. (1980). *Work redesign.* Reading, MA: Addison-Wesley.

Hall, D. T. (1995). Executive careers and learning: Aligning selection, strategy, and development. *Human Resource Planning, 18*(2), 14–23.

Hall, E. T. (1966). *The hidden dimension.* New York: Doubleday.

Hall, E. T. (1976). *Beyond culture.* New York: Doubleday.

Hallam, G. L. (1996). *The adventures of Team Fantastic: A practical guide for team leaders and members.* Greensboro, NC: Center for Creative Leadership.

Hallam, G. L., & Campbell, D. P. (1994). *Manual for the Campbell-Hallam Team Development Survey.* Minneapolis, MN: National Computer Systems.

Hambleton, R. K. (1993). Guidelines for adapting educational and psychological tests: A progress report. *Bulletin of the International Test Commission,* pp. 229–234.

Hambleton, R. K., Clauser, B. E., Mazor, K. M., & Jones, R. W. (1993). Advances in the detection of differentially functioning test items. *European Journal of Psychological Assessment, 9,* 1–18.

Hampden-Turner, C., & Trompenaars, A. (1993). *The seven cultures of capitalism: Value systems for creating wealth in the United States, Japan, Germany, France, Britain, Sweden, and the Netherlands.* New York: Currency.

Harris, M., & Schaubroeck, J. (1988). A meta-analysis of self-supervisor, self-peer, and peer-supervisor ratings. *Personnel Psychology, 41,* 43–61.

Hazucha, J. F., Hezlett, S. A., & Schneider, R. J. (1993). The impact of 360-degree feedback on management skills development. *Human Resource Management, 32,* 325–351.

Hazucha, J. F., Szymanski, C., & Birkeland, S. (1992). *Will my boss see my ratings? Effect of confidentiality on self-boss rating congruence.* Paper presented at the 100th annual meeting of the American Psychological Association, Washington, D.C.

Heckler, V. J. (1997). *Using peers to enhance learning: Evolving techniques.* Paper presented at the Tools/Benchmarks Users Conference. Greensboro, NC: Center for Creative Leadership.

Heilman, M. E., Block, C. J., Martell, R. F., & Simon, M. C. (1989). Has anything changed? Current characterizations of men, women, and managers. *Journal of Applied Psychology, 74,* 935–942.

Hofstede, G. (1976, March). The construct validity of attitude survey questions dealing with work goal. (Working Paper #76–8). Brussels: European Institute for Advanced Studies in Management.

Hofstede, G. (1980). *Culture's consequences: International differences in work-related values.* Beverly Hills, CA: Sage.

Hofstede, G. (1991). *Culture and organizations: Software of the mind.* London: McGraw-Hill.

Holland, P. W., & Thayer, D. T. (1988). Differential item performance and the Mantel-Haenszel procedure. In H. Wainer & H. I. Braun (Eds.), *Test validity* (pp. 129–145). Hillsdale, NJ: Erlbaum.

Holland, P. W., & Wainer, H. (Eds.). (1993). *Differential item functioning.* Hillsdale, NJ: Erlbaum.

Hoppe, M. H. (1990). *A comparative study of country elites: International differences in work-related values and learning and their implications for management development and training.* Unpublished doctoral dissertation, The University of North Carolina at Chapel Hill.

Howard, A., Byham, W., & Hauenstein, P. (1994). *Multirater assessment and feedback: Applications, implementation, and implications.* Pittsburgh, PA: DDI.

Howard, G. S., & Dailey, P. R. (1979). Response shift bias: A source of contamination of self-report measures. *Journal of Applied Psychology, 64,* 144–150.

Howard, G. S., Millham, J., Slaten, S., & O'Donnell, L. (1981). Influence of subject response style effects on retrospective measures. *Applied Psychological Measurement, 5,* 89–100.

Howard, G. S., Ralph, K. M., Gulanick, N. A., Maxwell, S. E., Nance, D. W., & Gerber, S. R. (1979). Internal invalidity in pretest-posttest self-report evaluations and a re-evaluation of retrospective pretests. *Applied Psychological Measurement, 3,* 1–23.

Hui, C. H., & Triandis, H. C. (1989). Effects of culture and response format on extreme response style. *Journal of Cross-cultural Psychology, 20*(3), 296–309.

Isaacs, W. N. (1993). Taking flight: Dialogue, collective thinking, and organizational learning. *Organizational Dynamics, 22*(2), 24–39.

Kabagarama, D. (1993). *Breaking the ice: A guide to understanding people from other cultures.* Boston: Allyn & Bacon.

Kaplan, R. E. (1997). SkillScope. Greensboro, NC: Center for Creative Leadership.

Kaplan, R. E., Drath, W. H., & Kofodimos, J. R. (1987). High hurdles: The challenge of executive self-development. *Academy of Management Executive, 1,* 195–205.

Kaplan, R. S., & Norton, D. P. (1996). Using the balanced scorecard as a strategic management system. *Harvard Business Review, 74*(1), 75–85.

Kerr, S. (1995). 0n the folly of rewarding A, while hoping for B. *Academy of Management Executive, 9*(1), 7–14.

Kim, U. (1994). *Individualism and collectivism: Theory, method and application.* Thousand Oaks, CA: Sage.

Kluckhohn, F. R., & Strodtbeck, F. L. (1961). *Variations in value orientations.* Westport, CT: Greenwood Press.

Kluger, A. N., & DeNisi, A. (1996). The effects of feedback interventions on performance: A historical review, a meta-analysis, and a preliminary feedback theory. *Psychological Bulletin, 119,* 254–284.

Kurtzman, J. (1997, February 17). Is your company off course? Now you can find out why. *Fortune,* 128–130.

Landy, F. L., & Farr, J. L. (1983). *The measurement of work performance.* San Diego: Academic Press.

Lawler, E. (1986). *High involvement management.* San Francisco: Jossey-Bass.

Lepsinger, R., & Lucia, A. (1997). *The art & science of 360º feedback.* San Francisco: Pfeiffer.

Leslie, J. B., & Fleenor, J. W. (1998). *Feedback to managers* (3rd ed.). Greensboro, NC: Center for Creative Leadership.

Levinson, H., Price, C. R., Munden, K. J., & Solley, C. M. (1962). *Man, management and mental health.* Cambridge, MA: Harvard University Press.

Liden, R. C., & Mitchell, T. P. (1983). The effects of group interdependence on supervisor performance. *Personnel Psychology, 36*(2), 289–299.

Locke, E. A. (1968). Toward a theory of task motivation and incentives. *Organizational Behavior and Human Performance, 3,* 157–189.

Lombardo, M. M., & Eichinger, R. W. (1996). *Learning Agility: The Learning II Architect*. Greensboro, NC: Lominger Limited.

Lombardo, M. M., & Eichinger, R. W. (in press). High potentials as learners. *Human Resource Management Journal*.

Lombardo, M. M., & McCauley, C. D. (1994). *Benchmarks: A manual and trainer's guide*. Greensboro, NC: Center for Creative Leadership.

London, M. (1994). Interpersonal insight in organizations: Cognitive models for human resource development. *Human Resource Management Review, 4,* 311–332.

London, M. (1995). *Self and interpersonal insight: How people learn about themselves and others in organizations*. New York: Oxford University Press.

London, M. (1997). *Job feedback: Giving, seeking, and using feedback for performance improvement*. Mahwah, NJ: Erlbaum.

London, M., & Beatty, R. W. (1993). 360-degree feedback as a competitive advantage. *Human Resource Management, 32*(2&3), 353–373.

London, M., & Mone, E. (1994). Managing marginal performance in an organization: Striving for excellence. In A. Korman (Ed.), *Human dilemmas in work organizations*. New York: Guilford Press.

London, M., & Smither, J. W. (1995). Can multi-source feedback change self-evaluations, skill development, and performance? Theory-based applications and directions for research. *Personnel Psychology, 48,* 803–839.

London, M., Smither, J. W., & Adsit, D. J. (1997). Accountability: The Achilles heel of multisource feedback. *Group and Organization Management, 22*(2), 162–184.

London, M., & Wohlers, A. J. (1991). Agreement between subordinate and self-ratings in upward feedback. *Personnel Psychology, 44,* 375–390.

London, M., Wohlers, A. J., & Gallagher, P. (1990). 360-degree feedback surveys: A source of feedback to guide management development. *Journal of Management Development, 9,* 17–31.

Mabe, P. A., & West, S. G. (1982). Validity of self-evaluation of ability: A review and meta-analysis. *Journal of Applied Psychology, 67,* 280–296.

MacLachlan, M., Mapundi, J., Zimba, C. G., & Carr, S. C. (1995). The acceptability of Western psychometric instruments in a non-Western society. *The Journal of Social Psychology, 135*(5), 645–648.

Marin, G., Gamba, R. J., & Marin, G. V. (1992). Extreme response style and acquiescence among Hispanics. *Journal of Cross-Cultural Psychology, 23,* 498–509.

Martineau, J. W. (1996). *A contextual examination of the effectiveness of a supervisory skills training program.* Unpublished doctoral dissertation, The Pennsylvania State University, State College.

Mathieu, J. E., Tannenbaum, S. I., & Salas, E. (1992). Influences of individual and situational characteristics on measures of training effectiveness. *Academy of Management Journal, 35,* 828–847.

Maurer, T. J., & Tarulli, B. A. (1994). Investigation of perceived environment, perceived outcome, and person variable in relationship to voluntary development activity by employees. *Journal of Applied Psychology, 79,* 3–14.

McCall, M. W., & Spreitzer, G. M. (1993). Identifying Leadership Potential in Future International Executives. Presentation to the eighth annual conference of the Society of Industrial and Organizational Psychology. San Francisco.

McCall, M. W., Spreitzer, G. M., & Mahoney, J. (1996). *Prospector: Discovering the ability to learn and lead.* Greensboro, NC: Center for Creative Leadership.

McCauley, C. D., & Douglas, C. (1998). Developmental relationships. In C. D. McCauley, R. Moxley, & E. Van Velsor (Eds.), *The Center for Creative Leadership's handbook of leadership development.* San Francisco: Jossey-Bass.

McCauley, C. D., & Hughes-James, M. (1994). *An evaluation of the outcomes of a leadership development program.* Greensboro, NC: Center for Creative Leadership.

McCauley, C. D., Moxley, R., & Van Velsor, E. (Eds.). (1998). *The Center for Creative Leadership's handbook of leadership development.* San Francisco: Jossey-Bass.

McCauley, C. D., Ruderman, M., Ohlott, P., & Morrow, J. (1994). Assessing the developmental components of managerial jobs. *Journal of Applied Psychology, 79*(4), 544–560.

McCauley, C. D., & Young, D. P. (1993). Creating developmental relationships: Roles and strategies. *Human Resource Management Review, 3,* 219–230.

McGregor, D. (1957). An uneasy look at performance appraisal. *Harvard Business Review, 35*(3), 89–94.

McIntyre, R. M., Smith, D. E., & Hassett, C. E. (1984). Accuracy of performance ratings as affected by rater training and perceived purpose of rating. *Journal of Applied Psychology, 69*(1), 147–156.

Meyer, H. H. (1980). Self-appraisal of job performance. *Personnel Psychology, 33,* 291–295.

Meyer, H. H., Kay, E., and French, J. (1965). Split roles in performance appraisal. *Harvard Business Review, 43,* 123–129.

Mintzberg, H. (1989). *Mintzberg on management: Inside our strange world of organizations*. New York: Free Press.

Morrison, A. M. (1992). *The new leaders: Guidelines on leadership diversity in America*. San Francisco: Jossey-Bass.

Murphy, K. R., & Cleveland, J. N. (1995). *Understanding performance appraisal: Social, organizational, and goal-based perspectives*. Thousand Oaks, CA: Sage.

Nadler, D. A. (1977). *Feedback and organization development: Using data based methods*. Reading, MA: Addison-Wesley.

Nelson, T. D. (1993). The hierarchical organization of behavior: A useful feedback model of self-regulation. *Current Directions in Psychological Science, 2*, 121–126.

Newman, K. L., & Nollen, S. D. (1996). Culture and congruence: The fit between management practices and national culture. *Journal of International Business Studies, 27*(4), 753–779.

Nilsen, D., & Campbell, D. (1993). Self-observer rating discrepancies: Once an overrater, always an overrater? *Human Resource Management, 32*, 265–281.

Noer, D. M. (1993). *Healing the wounds: Overcoming the trauma of layoffs and revitalizing downsized organizations*. San Francisco: Jossey-Bass.

Noer, D. M. (1996). *Breaking free: A prescription for personal and organizational change*. San Francisco: Jossey-Bass.

Nonaka, I. (1994). A dynamic theory of organizational knowledge creation. *Organization Science, 5*(1), 14–37.

Palus, C. J., & Rogolsky, S. R. (1996). *Development of, and development within, a global, feedback-intensive organization*. Unpublished manuscript, Center for Creative Leadership.

Palus, C. J., & Rogolsky, S. R. (1997). *Wilhelmsen Lines research summary*. Unpublished report, Center for Creative Leadership.

Peterson, D. B. (1992, August). *Personality predictors of correspondence between self-report and observer ratings*. Paper presented at the meeting of the American Psychological Association, Washington, DC.

Peterson, D. B. (1993). *Measuring change: A psychometric approach to evaluating individual training outcomes*. Paper presented at the eighth annual conference of the Society for Industrial and Organizational Psychology, San Francisco.

Porter, M. E. (1980). *Competitive strategy*. New York: Free Press.

Porter, M. E. (1996). What is strategy? *Harvard Business Review, 74*(6), 61–78.

Raabe, M., & Palus, C. J. (1997). Creating a feedback-rich leadership development system. In *The Global Leadership Development Conference: Conference Proceedings* (pp. 137–177). Lexington, MA: Linkage Incorporated.

Randlesome, C., Brierley, W., Burton, K., Gordon, C., & King, P. (1993). *Business cultures in Europe*. London: Butterworth-Heinemann.

Reilly, R. R., & Chao, G. T. (1982). Validity and fairness of some alternative employee selection procedures. *Personnel Psychology, 35,* 1–62.

Reilly, R. R., Smither, J. W., & Vasilopoulous, N. L. (1996). A longitudinal study of upward feedback. *Personnel Psychology, 49,* 599–612.

Rogolsky, S. R., & Drath, W. H. (1997). *Organizational self study: Ideas on the process.* Unpublished manuscript, Center for Creative Leadership.

Roullier, J. Z., & Goldstein, I. L. (1991). *Determinants of the climate for transfer of training.* Paper presented at the sixth annual conference of the Society for Industrial and Organizational Psychology, St. Louis.

Saavedra, R., & Kwun, S. K. (1993). Peer evaluation in self-managing groups. *Journal of Applied Psychology, 78,* 450–462.

Schein, E. H. (1993). On dialogue, culture, and organizational learning. *Organizational Dynamics, 22*(2), 40–51.

Schneier, C. E., Shaw, D., & Beatty, R. W. (1991). Performance measurement and management. *Human Resource Management, 30,* 279–301.

Seibert, K., Hall, D. T., & Kram, K. (1995). Strengthening the weak link in strategic executive development: Integrating individual development and global business strategy. *Human Resource Management, 34,* 529–547.

Senge, P. M. (1990). *The fifth discipline: The art and practice of the learning organization.* New York: Doubleday.

Senge, P. M. (1996). The ecology of leadership. *Leader to Leader, 2,* 18–23.

Smither, J. W., London, M., & Vasilopoulos, N. L. (1995). An examination of the effects of an upward feedback program over time. *Personnel Psychology, 48,* 1–34.

Spreitzer, G. M., McCall, M. W., & Mahoney, J. D. (1997). Early identification of international executive potential. *Journal of Applied Psychology, 82,* 6–29.

Swaminathan, H., & Rogers, H. J. (1990). Detecting differential item functioning using logistic regression procedures. *Journal of Educational Measurement, 27,* 361–370.

Thompson, A. A., & Strickland, A. J. (1995). *Strategic management.* Chicago: Erwin.

Thornton, G. C. (1980). Psychometric properties of self-appraisals of job performance. *Personnel Psychology, 33,* 263–271.

Tichy, N. (1996). Simultaneous transformation and CEO succession: Key to global competitiveness. *Organizational Dynamics, 25,* 45–59.

Timmreck, C. W., & Bracken, D. W. (1997). Multisource feedback: A study of its use in decision making. *Employment Relations Today, 24*(1), 21–27.

Tornow, W. W. (Ed.). (1993). Special Issue on Service Quality and Organizational Effectiveness. *Human Resource Planning, 14*(2), 86–169.

Tornow, W. W. (1993). Perceptions or reality: Is multi-perspective measurement a means or an end? *Human Resource Management, 32*(2&3), 221–230.

Tornow, W. W. (Ed.). (1993). Special Issue on 360-Degree Feedback. *Human Resource Management, 32*(2&3), 209–408.

Tornow, W. W., & De Meuse, K. D. (1994). New paradigm approaches in strategic human resource management: A commentary. *Group & Organizational Management, 19*(2), 165–170.

Tracey, J. B., Tannenbaum, S. I., & Kavanagh, M. J. (1995). Applying trained skills on the job: The importance of the work environment. *Journal of Applied Psychology, 80*, 239–252.

Triandis, H. C. (1986). *Individualism and collectivism.* Boulder, CO: Westview.

Uhlfelder, H. F. (1996). It's a new world out there. *Journal for Quality and Participation, 19*, 26–35.

Ulrich, D. (1997). *Human resource champions: The next agenda for adding value and delivering results.* Cambridge, MA: Harvard Business School Press.

Ulrich, D., & Lake, D. (1990). *Organizational capability.* New York: Wiley.

Van Velsor, E., & Leslie, J. B. (1991). *Feedback to managers, Volume II: A review and comparison of sixteen multi-rater feedback instruments.* Greensboro, NC: Center for Creative Leadership.

Van Velsor, E., Leslie, J. B., & Fleenor, J. W. (1997). *Choosing 360: A guide to evaluating multi-rater feedback instruments for management development.* Greensboro, NC: Center for Creative Leadership.

Van Velsor, E., Ruderman, M., & Young, D. (1992, August). The impact of feedback on self-assessment and performance in three domains of managerial behavior. Paper presented at the annual meeting of the American Psychological Association, Washington, DC.

Wallace, A., Sawheny, N., & Gardjito, W. (1995). Leader characteristics that incline people to willingly follow in Japan, India, Indonesia, and the United States. In G. Tower (Ed.), *Asian Pacific international business: Regional integration and global competitiveness.* Perth, Australia: Murdoch University.

Whetten, D. A., & Cameron, K. S. (1991). *Developing management skills* (2nd ed.). New York: HarperCollins.

Wilson, C., & O'Hare, D. (1989). Survey of Leadership Practices (SLP). Silver Spring, MD: C. Wilson.

Wilson, M. S., Hoppe, M. H., & Sayles, R. S. (1996). *Managing across cultures: A learning framework.* Greensboro, NC: Center for Creative Leadership.

Young, D. P., & Dixon, N. M. (1996). *Helping leaders take effective action: A program evaluation.* Greensboro, NC: Center for Creative Leadership.

Yu, J., & Murphy, K. R. (1993). Modesty bias in self-ratings of performance: A test of the cultural relativity hypothesis. *Personnel Psychology, 46,* 357–363.

Yukl, G. (1995). Compass. Stamford, CT: Manus.

Yukl, G., & Van Fleet, D. D. (1992). Theory and research on leadership in organizations. In M. Dunnette & L. Hough (Eds.), *Handbook of industrial and organizational psychology* (2nd ed.). Palo Alto, CA: Consulting Psychologists Press.

Zax, M., & Takahashi, S. (1967). Cultural influences on response style: Comparisons of Japanese and American college students. *Journal of Social Psychology, 71,* 3–10.

Zedeck, S., & Cascio, W. F. (1982). Performance appraisal decisions as a function of rater training and purpose of the appraisal. *Journal of Applied Psychology, 67*(6), 752–758.

Zeithaml, V. A., Berry, L. L., & Parasuraman, A. (1996). The behavioral consequences of service quality. *Journal of Marketing, 60*(2), 31–46.

Zmud, R. W., & Armenakis, A. A. (1978). Understanding the measurement of change. *Academy of Management Review, 3,* 661–669.

About the Center
for Creative Leadership

The Center for Creative Leadership is an international, nonprofit educational institution whose mission is to advance the understanding, practice, and development of leadership for the benefit of society worldwide. Founded in Greensboro, North Carolina, in 1970 by the Smith Richardson Foundation, the Center is today one of the largest institutions in the world focusing on leadership. In addition to our locations in Greensboro; Colorado Springs, Colorado; San Diego, California; and Brussels, Belgium, we have an office in New York City and maintain relationships with more than 28 Network Associates and other partners in the U.S. and abroad.

We conduct research, produce publications, and provide a variety of educational programs and products to leaders and organizations in the public, corporate, educational, and nonprofit sectors. Each year through our programs we reach more than 27,000 leaders and several thousand organizations worldwide. The Center also serves as a clearinghouse for ideas on leadership and creativity. We regularly convene conferences and colloquia by scholars and practitioners, and our staff members are frequent presenters at conferences around the world.

We derive our funding primarily from tuition, sales of products and publications, royalties, and fees for service. The Center seeks grants and donations from corporations, foundations, and individuals in support of its educational mission.

For more information on the Center and its work, call Client Services at 336-545-2810, send an e-mail to info@leaders.ccl.org, or visit our World Wide Web Home Page at http://www.ccl.org

Products, Publications, and Programs

The Center offers a variety of assessment tools, simulations, publications, and programs that help individuals, teams, and organizations learn about themselves.

Instruments

Benchmarks® is a comprehensive 360-degree leadership tool for middle- to upper-level managers. Assessing strengths and development needs, it provides indications of promotability to future leadership positions (as well as the potential of derailment), a strategy for change that links development needs with specific suggestions that the manager can use to effect change, and valid, reliable, comparative data that individuals can use to compare themselves to other managers in similar positions.

Prospector™ is the product of extensive research and has demonstrated both validity and reliability, ensuring that all feedback is pertinent to effective leadership. It was developed primarily under a grant from the International Consortium for Executive Development Research (ICEDR). Additional support was received from the Center for Effective Organizations (CEO), the International Business Education and Research program (IBEAR), and the Leadership Institute at the University of Southern California School of Business. Research for Prospector was conducted by Morgan McCall, Gretchen Spreitzer, and Joan Mahoney, faculty members at the University of Southern California School of Business.

SkillScope® is a straightforward, effective, 360-degree feedback tool that assesses managerial strengths and development needs. It creates a channel through which managers and supervisors can get feedback from peers, direct reports, superiors, and bosses.

Publications

Choosing 360: A Guide to Evaluating Multi-rater Feedback Instruments for Management Development presents a step-by-step process that takes the reader through such issues as instrument development, validity and reliability, feedback display, scoring strategies, and cost. The guide includes a checklist and glossary.

Feedback to Managers (3rd ed.) presents an in-depth evaluation of twenty-five of the leading 360-degree-feedback instruments. For each instrument, such issues as target audience, reliability and validity, types of feedback display, scoring process, and cost are considered.

Programs

Leadership Development for Human Resource Managers is a six-day program that provides participants with the opportunity to become more effective and productive, and, as leaders, to help others achieve these same goals. This model-driven program is about process, awareness, change, and growth.

Tools for Developing Successful Executives is a three- or four-day program for human resources executives, line managers, and career development professionals. It provides participants with the opportunity to learn and apply some of the Center's best research-based practices and instruments in the field of executive development.

CENTER FOR CREATIVE LEADERSHIP

LEADERSHIP.
LEARNING.
LIFE.

GREENSBORO
BRUSSELS
COLORADO SPRINGS
SAN DIEGO

Index

A

Accountability: for learning, 126, 141–142; and tracking of change, 92–94

Accuracy of feedback: for performance appraisal, 70–71, 97–98, 150–151; and sense of safety, 51. *See also* Rater bias; Reliability; Validity

Adaptability, 124, 241–242. *See also* Continuous learning; Learning culture

Administrative process: for clarification of purpose, 150–152; for communication about confidentiality and anonymity, 152–154; for customer input, 155–156; guidelines for, 150–157; importance of, 149; for rater selection, 154–155; for support for development, 156–157

Adsit, D. J., 93

Age, and rating discrepancies, 23–24

Aggregate feedback data, 93–95, 108; for change measurement, 240–248; for measuring alignment, 240, 245–247

Alignment: change measurement of, 240, 242–248; customer feedback and, 103–105, 116, 117–118; 360-degree feedback for, 94–96, 240, 242–247; top-to-bottom, 117–118

Alpha change (true change), 221, 222

American Psychological Association (APA): code of ethics, 215n.2; Guidelines, 195n.1

Anonymity: and breakout of rater data, 174, 176; communication about, 152–154; cultural differences and, 203–205; in customer ratings, 109; defined, 152; in downward ratings, 16; impact of, on ratings, 153–154; in upward ratings, 17, 153–154, 174, 176; and verbatim comments, 190, 192. *See also* Confidentiality; Safety

Antonioni, D., 96

Armenakis, A. A., 229

Asian countries, response scales and, 210

Atwater, L., 248n.1

Austin, J., 14

B

Back-translation, 211–212

Balanced scorecard approach, 110–112, 116

Bales, R., 159, 182

Bank credit-card division, 360-degree feedback in, 136–137

Bar graphs, examples of, 180, 181

Beatty, R. W., 2, 20, 95, 96, 105, 108

Bedeian, A. G., 70, 205

Beer, M., 240

Behaviors versus traits, 159–160

Benchmarks instrument, 13–14, 153–154, 169

Ben-Nahum, Z., 17

Bernardin, J. H., 2, 16

Berry, L. L., 107

Beta change, 221, 222, 223

Bigoness, W. J., 198

Billingsley, K., 221
Birkeland, S., 70
Blakely, G. L., 198
Block, C. J., 24
Borman, W. C., 15, 18
Bracken, D. W., 72, 69, 70, 71–72, 97, 98
"Bravo Data Corporation (BDC)" case example, 78–100; introduction of, 78–81
Breakout of rater data, 172, 174–177; example of, 175
Bridges, W., 85
Brierley, W., 199
Brockner, J., 84
Brutus, S., 11, 23–24, 210
Building Effective Teams exercise 37–39
Bunker, K. A., 124
Burd, K. A., 203
Burton, K., 199
Business-driven rationale, 76, 77, 242
Byham, W., 16

C

Cameron, K. S., 250
Campbell, D. P., 23, 86, 136
Campbell Leadership Index (NCS), 179, 180
Campbell-Hallam Team Development Survey (TDS), 86, 87, 136
Cannella, A. A., 70, 205
Career development, do-it-yourself 360-degree feedback for, 63–68
Carr, S. C., 202–203
Carver, C. S., 26
Cascio, W. F., 205
Center for Creative Leadership (CCL), 271–273; assessment for development at, 4, 7; Benchmarks instrument of, 13–14, 153–154; change measurement research of, 218, 227–228, 232, 237–238; importance ratings research of, 189; leadership defining of, 88; Leadership Development Program (LDP) of, 28–29; organizational development at, 134–135; use of 360-degree feedback at, 4. *See also* Leadership Development Program

Change: challenges of, 6; differential impact and, 233, 238; individual commitment to, 44–50; individual recognition of need for, 35–36; learning and, 124, 241–242; practice in, 39–41; types of, 221–223. *See also* Learning culture; Organizational culture change; Performance improvement

Change measurement: ambivalence in, 219–223; basics of, 219–228; change ratings methodology for, 228–229, 230; context of development and, 234–237, 239; designing instruments for, 232–237; for development planning, 243–244; example of, for individual development, 237–240; of group change, 244; ideal ratings method of, 229, 231; of individual alignment with organizational strategies, 240, 245–247; intervention evaluation and, 217–218; methodologies for, 224–231; for organizational development, 240–245; of organizational levels, 244–245; pretest-posttest designs for, 220–223; rater selection for, 232; rating scales for, 232–233; rationales for, 218–219; repetitive measurement and, 233–234; response scales for, 165–166; response-shift bias in, 220–223, 227; retrospective pretest methodology for, 224–228; and support for development, 193–194;

360-degree feedback for, 92–94, 131–132, 157, 171, 217–247, 248; timing of, 233, 238; value of, to executives, 240–245

Change ratings method, 228–229; example of, 230

Chao, G. T., 17

Chappelow, C., 152

Chen, C., 210

Cheng, B. S., 210–211

China, self-rating in, 210–211

Churchill, N. C., 164

Clauser, B. E., 216n.3

Cleveland, J. N., 16, 17, 18, 24, 150–151

Climate surveys, 247

Collective learning: characteristics of, 125–126; organizational development linked to, 140–142, 144; organizational readiness for, 144; sharing of individual feedback for, 132–135; 360-degree feedback on, 136–140. See also Learning culture; Organizational development

Collectivistic cultures, 200; response scales and, 209–210

Comfort zones, 124

Comments, 190, 192

Commitment: employee, versus management control, 86, 88–89; to individual development, 44–50; and new psychological contract, 84–86

Communication, in low-context versus high-context cultures, 204–205

Comparability, of scores across cultures, 212–213, 214, 216n.3

Comparison to an ideal, 179, 182; example of, 183

Comparison to norms, 177–179; cultural influences on, 208; examples of, 178, 180, 181; graphic displays of, 172, 177, 178; percentile rankings for, 179, 181; standard scores for, 179, 180

Compass, Manus, Inc., 190, 191

Competitive advantage, of customer involvement, 101–102. See also Customer involvement

Competitive environment: and learning cultures, 123; and outside-in orientation, 81–83

Confidentiality: communication about, 152–154; cultural differences and, 203–205; defined, 152; in downward ratings, 16; in high-potential development feedback, 62; and rater candor, 174; and sense of safety, 51; in 360-degree feedback for appraisal, 69; in upward ratings, 17, See also Anonymity; Safety

Conflict avoidance, 203

Conjoint analysis, 113, 114

Connectivity, 4–5, 255–256

Conservative, use of word, in questionnaire items, 160

Consulting company, 360-degree feedback for performance appraisal in, 70–71

Consumer products company, collective feedback in, 133–134

Context, and change measurement, 234–237, 239

Continuous learning, 360-degree feedback for, 89–92, 241–242. See also Learning culture

Control items, 233

Core values, alignment around, 94–95

Costs, of 360-degree feedback, 251

Couch, A., 209

Counseling, and do-it-yourself programs, 64

Cross-cultural 360-degree feedback, 196–216; best-case scenario of, 207; case studies of, 196–197, 206–207; comparability of scores and, 212–213, 214, 216n.3; cultural assumptions and, 198–207; cultural influences on, 208–213;

Cross-cultural 360-degree feedback
    (*continued*)
    implementation guidelines for,
    213–215; worst-case scenario of,
    206. *See also* Cultural differences
Cultural differences: in anonym-
    ity, 203–205; in confidentiality,
    203–205; in constructs measured,
    201–203; in feedback accep-
    tance, 203; in feedback interpre-
    tation, 207–213; in language,
    211–213; in management/
    leadership models, 201–203; in
    manager development, 199–201,
    206, 207; normative comparisons
    and, 280; in popularity of psycho-
    metric instruments, 205–206; in
    power distance, 200–201; and re-
    sponse scales, 209–210; in self-
    rating, 210–211; in source of
    identity, 200; and 360-degree
    feedback for development,
    198–207; of values, 200–201
Culture, defined, 215
Culture change. *See* Learning
    culture; Organizational culture
    change
Customer focus: in First Union case
    study, 109–117; and involvement
    in 360-degree feedback, 101–
    106; and outside-in orientation,
    81–83; and strategic manage-
    ment, 111–118
Customer involvement, 101–119;
    administrative process and,
    155–156; case study of, 109–117;
    caveats of, 108–109; competitive
    advantage of, 101–102; feedback
    criteria and, 117; investment in,
    118; mechanisms of, 106; for
    strategic alignment, 103–106,
    108, 109, 117–118; top-to-bottom
    focus and, 117–118; types of feed-
    back from, 106–108; value of,
    103–106

Customer Loyalty Index, 116
Customer ratings/feedback: benefits
    of, 101, 103–106; in case study,
    113–115; customer orientation
    and, 101–106; for individual
    development, 18, 19, 101; for
    organizational development,
    101–1198; outcome, 107–108;
    performance dimensions ob-
    served by, 18, 19; process and
    behavioral, 106–108; types of,
    106–108
Customer satisfaction & retention
    information (CSRI), 109–118;
    key drivers of, 114–115, 117;
    long-term, 107–108; process-re-
    lated factors in, 107
Customers: defining of, 102; exter-
    nal, 102; internal, 102
Customer-supplier model, 102

D
Dahmus, S. A., 16
Dailey, P. R., 226–227
Dalton, M. A., 5, 7, 59, 61, 63, 69, 70,
    97, 196, 198, 201, 203, 236
Daudelin, M. W., 21
De Meuse, K. P., 84, 85
Decisiveness, cultural differences in,
    201
Defense mechanisms, 70
DeNisi, A., 25, 26
Design. *See* 360-degree feedback
    design
Developability, of qualities assessed,
    170–171
Development: context of, and
    change measurement, 234–237,
    239; cultural assumptions
    underlying, 198–207; evaluation
    of, 217–218; interventions for,
    217–218; as system, 255; 360-
    degree feedback for, versus
    appraisal, 7–8, 96–98, 150–152,
    252–253. *See also* Change

measurement; Individual development; Organizational development; Self development; 360-degree feedback for individual development; 360-degree feedback for organizations

Development materials, 193

Development planning: administrative process for, 150; change measurement and, 243–244; for high-potential development, 61–62; for individual development, 26, 44–51; and new psychological contract, 85; support for, 192–194

Development program, individual: challenges of, 52; change measurement of, 234–240; commitments to change in, 44–50, 53–54; components of, 43–54, 56; context of, and change measurement, 234–237, 239; distraction-free environment for, 53; feedback reception in, 29–39; follow-up to, 53–54; goal setting in, 50–51; impact of, 218; practice of new behaviors in, 39–41; recognition of need for change in, 35–36; relevance in, 43–44; safety in, 51–52; 360-degree feedback in context of, 28–56. *See also* Individual development; 360-degree feedback for individual development

Developmental workshops, 193

Dixon, N. M., 125, 228

"Do more/do less" information, 189–190; example of, 191

Dobbins, G. H., 210–211

Do-it-yourself 360-degree feedback programs, 63–68; for on-demand feedback, 131–132

Doron, R., 205

Downward ratings. *See* Supervisory ratings

Drath, W. H., 25, 88, 110, 139

E

Eagly, A. H., 24

Eastman, L. J., 60, 62

Edwards, M. R., 105

Egalitarian company, do-it-yourself 360-degree feedback program of, 66–67

Eggars, J. H., 164

Eichinger, R. W., 124, 129

Ellis, B. B., 216*n*.3

Employee attitude surveys, 2, 75, 80–81

Employee commitment, versus management control, 86, 88–89

Employment contract, new, 63, 84–86

Environment: distraction-free, for development program, 53; and 360-degree feedback for culture change, 74–75, 78–81. *See also* Organizational trends

Environmental trends. *See* Organizational trends

Evaluation, defined, 217–218. *See also* Change measurement; Performance appraisal

Ewen, A. J., 105

Executive Leadership Survey, 185; example of, 186–187

Executives, 360-degree feedback's value to, 240–245

Expectations, management of, 252

F

Face validity, 161

Facilitation: and do-it-yourself programs, 64–65; and verbatim comments, 192

Factor analysis, 168

Farh, J. L., 17, 70, 205, 210–211

Feedback: changing organizational norms of, 75; on learning competencies, 127–131; on-demand, 131–132; open sharing of, 132–135, 144; relevance of, 43–44, 76;

Feedback *(continued)*
on self as learner, 127–131, 144; self-management model of, 33–35, 36, 54–55. *See also* Feedback reports; Rating sources; *360-degree feedback headings*
Feedback acceptance, 250–251; factors in individual, 21–23; safety and, 51–52, 70, 71
Feedback data. *See* Feedback reports
Feedback displays, 171–172
Feedback interpretation. *See* Feedback reports
Feedback presentation: collective, 132–135; factors in effective, 20–21, 27, 15–52; safety in, 51–52, 153. *See also* Feedback reports
Feedback recipient: blindsiding of, 51–52, 64; commitment of, 44–50, 53–54; feedback reception skill training for, 37–39, 250; individual characteristics of, 23–25; information processing of, 20–25; initial reactions of, in case study, 29–33; involvement of, 54–55, 91–92, 98–99; openness of, to feedback, 21–23; peer feedback and, 36–39; practice for, 39–41; readiness of, for feedback, 250–251; recognition of need to change of, 35–36; relevance of feedback to, 43–44; self-management model for, 33–35, 36, 54–55
Feedback reports: breakout of rater responses in, 172, 174–177; comments in, 190, 192; comparison to an ideal in, 179, 182, 183; comparison to norms in, 177–179, 208; cultural influences on, 207–213; design alternatives for, 171–192; display types for, 171–172; "do more/do less" information in, 189–190; feedback scales for, 167–170; graphic, 171–172; highlighting in, 184–188; importance data in, 188–

189; item-level feedback in, 182, 184; narrative, 171–172. *See also* Feedback presentation
Feedback scales: for change measurement, 232–233; construction of, 167–170; cultural differences and, 209–210; reliability of, 167–169; validity of, 169–170. *See also* Response scales
Feedback surveys, 75
Financial services company, collective feedback in, 135
First Union Corporation, Model, 110–118; balanced scorecard approach and, 110–112; customer involvement and, 109–117; development of, 113–115; implementation of, 115–117; learning points from, 117–118; overview of, 109–110; strategic management process of, 112–113
Fischthal, A., 248*n*.1
Fleenor, J. W., 11, 23–24, 157, 177, 194, 209, 210
Follow-up, to 360-degree feedback individual development program, 53–54. *See also* Change measurement; Support
Food producer, high-potential development program of, 62–63
Fox, S., 17
France: manager recruitment in, 199, 205–206; peer feedback in, 203; psychometric instruments in, 205–206
French, J., 97
Frequency response scales, 164–165; for change measurement, 232–233; "do more/do less" information and, 189–190, 191

G

Gallagher, P., 2, 16
Gamba, R. J., 210
Gamma change, 221, 222, 223
Gardjito, W., 201–202

Gebelein, S. H., 240, 241, 242
Gender, and rating discrepancies, 23–24
Gerber, S. R., 220
Goal reports, in case study, 45–58
Goal setting: for individual development, 26–27, 44–51; support for, 192–194; theory of, 26
Goldstein, I. L., 239
Golembiewski, R. T., 221
Gordon, C., 199
Grandes Écoles, 199
Graphic displays, 171–172, 173, 180, 181
Graphology, 205–206
Group learning. See Collective learning
Groups: change measurement and, 240, 244; collective learning in, 125–126, 132–135; organizational development and, 140–142; 360-degree feedback on, 136–140. See also Collective learning; Organizational development; Organizations
Gryskiewicz, N. D., 196, 206
Gulanick, N. A., 220

H

Hackman, J. R., 88
Hall, D. T., 61, 95, 246
Hall, E. T., 204–205
Hallam, G. L., 86, 136, 247
Hambleton, R. K., 212, 213, 216n.3
Hampden-Turner, C., 200
Hands-off 360-degree feedback programs, 63–68; for on-demand feedback, 131–132
Harris, M., 18, 19, 210
Hassett, C. E., 205
Hauenstein, P., 16
Hazucha, J. F., 25–26, 67, 70, 239
Heckler, V. J., 135
Heilman, M. E., 24
Hezlett, S. A., 25–26, 67, 239
Hierarchy effect, 145

High tech company, do-it-yourself 360-degree feedback program of, 65–66
High-context cultures, 204–205
Highlighting: benefits and downsides to, 185, 188; example of, 186–187; high/low items, 184; high/low scales, 184; self/rater discrepancies, 185, 186–187
High-potential development programs, 60–63; cross-cultural, 207
Hispanics, response scales and, 208, 210
Hofstede, G., 200, 204, 209
Holland, P. W., 216n.3
Hollenbeck, G., 5, 61, 63, 203, 236
Hollow Square exercise, 43–44
Hoppe, M. H., 200
Howard, A., 16, 18
Howard, G. S., 220, 226–227, 233
Hughes-James, M., 67, 156, 227
Hui, C. H., 208, 210
Human resource (HR) systems, integration and alignment of, 95–96

I

Ideal ratings method, 229; example of, 231
Impact: of interventions, change measurement and, 217–219; of 360-degree feedback, mapping of, 254. See also Change measurement
Implementation: cross-cultural, 213–215; effective, 96–99; in low-trust cultures, 99. See also 360-degree feedback design
Importance data, 188–189
India, leader effectiveness in, 202
Individual characteristics, and 360-degree feedback, 23–25
Individual development, 2–3; career development and, 63–68; change measurement and, 247–240, 245–247; development plan for, 26, 44–51, 243–244; goal-setting

Individual development *(continued)* for, 26–27, 44–51; for high-potential individuals, 60–63; impact of feedback on, 25–27; in leadership development case study, 28–56; learning competencies and, 127–131; learning cultures and, 120–122, 124–125, 127–131; new psychological contract and, 84–86; organizational development linkage to, 140–142, 144, 240, 245–247, 253–254; organizational value of, 59; support process for, 27, 76, 142, 156–157, 192–194; 360-degree feedback for, 2–3, 11–27, 28–56. *See also* Development; Development planning; Development program, individual; Learning culture; 360-degree feedback for individual development

Individual learning: characteristics of, 124–125; organizational development linked to, 140–142, 144, 240, 245–247, 253–254; organizational readiness and, 144; 360-degree feedback on, 127–132. *See also* Individual development; Learning culture

Individualistic cultures, 200; response scales and, 209–210

Information sharing: for collective learning, 132–135, 144; organizational readiness for, 144

Input. *See* 360-degree feedback instruments

Instructions, 157–158

Instruments. *See* 360-degree feedback instruments

Integration, 360-degree feedback for, 94–96. *See also* Alignment

Interdependencies, work, 83, 85–86; and employee leadership, 88; and rater selection, 91

Internal consistency, 167–169

International company, collective feedback in, 134–135. *See also*

Cross-cultural 360-degree feedback; Multinational organizations

Interpersonal insight, 22

Intervention(s): change measurement and, 218–219, 234–237; context of, 234–237, 239; evaluation of, 217–219. *See also* Change measurement

Involvement: administrative process and, 157; continuous learning and, 91–92; customer, 103–106; for effective implementation, 98–99; need for active, 54–55. *See also* Customer involvement; Customer ratings/feedback

Isaacs, W. N., 125

Italy, trait philosophy of leadership in, 200

Item-level feedback, 182, 184; examples of, 175, 191

Item-response-theory procedures, 216n. 3

Items. *See* Questionnaire items

J

Jako, R., 7, 69, 97

Japan: feedback acceptance in, 203; leader effectiveness in, 202; management development in, 206

Job enrichment, 88

Jones, R. W., 216n.3

K

Kabagarama, D., 205

Kaplan, R. E., 25, 110, 158

Karau, S. J., 24

Kavanagh, M. J., 122, 239

Kay, E., 97

Kealey, T., n.1

Kelly-Radford, L., 120

Keniston, K., 209

Kerr, S., 95

Kim, U., 200

King, P., 199

Kluckhohn, F. R., 200

Kluger, A. N., 25, 26

Kofodimos, J. R., 25, 110
Kram, K., 61
Kurtzman, J.; 110
Kwun, S. K., 17

L

Lake, D., 102
Landy, F. L., 17
Language differences, 211–213
Latin American countries, feedback
    acceptance in, 203
Lauter, B., 109, 112–113
Lawler, E., 86
LeaderLab, 228
Leadership: changing role of, 86,
    88–89; cultural differences in
    201–203; trait theories of,
    199–200
Leadership behaviors, customer
    feedback on, 107, 108
Leadership development: cross-
    cultural differences in, 199–201,
    206, 207; program for, in case
    study, 28–56; 360-degree feed-
    back for, 4, 7. *See also* Develop-
    ment program, individual;
    360-degree feedback for in-
    dividual development
Leadership Development Program
    (LDP), 28–29; case study of,
    28–56; impact of, 218; overview
    of, 28–29. *See also* Center for
    Creative Leadership
Leadership Practices Inventory, 181
Leahy, K. L., 164
Learning Agility instrument, 129
Learning competencies: versus end-
    state competencies, 127, 128;
    hierarchy effect on, 145;
    360-feedback on, 127–132
Learning culture(s): accountability
    in, 126, 141–142; challenges of,
    143, 145; collective learning in,
    125–126, 132–138; defined, 123;
    group development in, 140–142;
    individual development and,

120–122, 140–142; individual
    learning in, 124–125, 127–132;
    mind-set of, 123; on-demand
    feedback in, 131–132; organiza-
    tional development in, 140–142,
    241–242; organizational practices
    in, 126–127; signs of, 123–124;
    360-degree feedback in, 120–122,
    127–146; 360-degree feedback
    in, implementation issues of,
    142–146; 360-degree feedback
    for groups and organizations in,
    136–142. *See also* Organizational
    culture change
Learning journal, 50
Learning mode, 124
Lee, S., 210
Leniency effect, 153–154. *See also*
    Rater bias
Lepsinger, R., 157
Leslie, J. B., 16, 157, 177, 194, 196,
    209
Levinson, H., 84
Liden, R. C., 17
Line graph, example of, 172
Locke, E. A., 26
Logistic regression procedures,
    216n. 3
Lombardo, M. M., 13, 124, 129, 169,
    201
London, M., 1, 2, 6, 11, 13, 15, 16,
    18, 20, 22, 24, 25, 27, 70, 93, 96,
    105, 248n.1, 249, 251
Low-context cultures, 204–205
Lucia, A., 157

M

Mabe, P. A., 18, 24
MacLachlan, M., 202–203, 214
Mahoney, J. D., 124, 129
Makhijani, M. G., 24
Management: changing roles of, 86,
    88–89; cultural differences in
    201–203
Management behaviors, customer
    feedback on, 107, 108

Management processes, cultural differences and, 198

Manager recruitment/development, cultural differences in, 199–201, 206–207

Managerial Behavior Inventory, "BDC," 79

Managerial effectiveness: change measurement and, 232; cultural assumptions and, 201–203; impact of feedback on, 25–26

Managers: development program for, in case study, 28–56; genderized standards for, 24; performance dimensions for, 13, 18–19; self-reflection of, 21; 360-degree feedback for, 13–27, 28–56

Mantel-Haenszel procedure, 216n. 3

Manufacturing organization, 360-degree feedback for culture change in, 73–74

Mapundi, J., 202–203

Marin, G., 210

Marin, G. V., 210

Market research, 104, 108. See also Customer ratings/feedback

Martell, R. F., 24

Martineau, J. W., 217, 236

Mastery response scales, 164, 189, 233

Mathieu, J. E., 236

Maurer, T. J., 239

Maxwell, S. E., 220

Mazor, K. M., 216n.3

McCall, M. W., 68, 124, 129

McCauley, C. D., 7, 13, 23–24, 61, 67, 69, 97, 120, 157, 169, 192, 201, 210, 217, 224, 227

McGregor, D., 97

McIntyre, R. M., 205

Meyer, H. H., 97, 210

Miller, R., 116–117

Millham, J., 226

Mintzberg, H., 21

Mitchell, T. P., 17

Mone, E., 13

Morrison, A. M., 224

Morrow, J., 61, 224

Moxley, R., 157, 201

Multinational organizations: case study of, 196–197; 360-degree feedback in, 196–216. See also Cross-cultural 360-degree feedback; Cultural differences

Multiple constituencies/perspectives: on groups and organizations, 136–138, 144; outside-in orientation and, 82–83; 360-degree feedback and, 15–16, 18–19. See also Rating sources; 360-degree feedback headings

Munden, K. J., 84

Murphy, K. R., 16, 17, 18, 24, 150–151, 211

N

Nadler, D. A., 2

Nance, D. W., 220

Narrative reports, 171–172; highlighting self/rater discrepancies in, 185

Nelson, T. D., 26

Newman, K. L., 198

Nilsen, D., 23

Noer, D. M., 84, 124

Nollen, S. D., 198

Nonaka, I., 2

Normative comparison. See Comparison to norms

Norton, D. P., 110

O

Observability: of questionnaire items, 161–162; and response scale design, 164

O'Connor Wilson, P., 120

O'Donnell, L., 226

O'Hare, D., 185

Ohlott, P., 61, 224

Oldham, G. R., 88

On-demand feedback, 131–132; organizational readiness for, 144

One-on-one feedback sessions, 41–42; verbatim comments in, 192

Organization, use of word, in questionnaire items, 160

Organizational culture change: alignment and, 94–96, 242–243; in case study, 78–81; change measurement and, 242–243; 360-degree feedback for, 73–75, 94–96. *See also* Learning culture

Organizational development: alignment and, 94–96, 240, 242–248; change measurement for, 92–94, 240–248; continuous learning and, 89–92, 241–242; external aspects of, 101–109; individual and group development linked to, 140–142, 144, 240, 245–247, 253–254; integration and, 94–96; internal aspects of, 78–100; learning cultures and, 120, 140–142; performance management and, 89–94, 243; 360-degree feedback for, 89–99, 136–142; 360-degree feedback implementation and, 96–99. *See also* 360-degree feedback for organizations

Organizational practices, in learning cultures, 126–127

Organizational readiness, assessment of, 143, 144

Organizational self-study, 139

Organizational trends, 81–89; in "BDC" case study, 78–81; of management and leadership roles, 86, 88–89; 360-degree feedback and, 78–100; of transformation to outside-in orientation, 81–83; of transformation of work, 84–86

Organizations: 360-degree feedback on, 136–142; value of 360-degree feedback in, 59–77, 89–99. *See also* 360-degree feedback for organizations

Other-orientation mind-set, 81–83

Outcomes: of do-it-yourself 360-degree feedback programs, 68; of 360-degree feedback for individuals, 25–27; of 360-degree feedback for organizations, causes of poor, 59–60, 76–77. *See also* Change measurement

Outdoor activities, 39–41

Output. *See* Feedback reports

Outside-in orientation, 81–83

Outward Bound, 39, 40

Ownership of feedback, 6, 98–99; administrative process and, 157; feedback formatting and, 184; rater selection process and, 155

P

Palus, C. J., 88, 227

Paradise-Tornow, C. A., 18–19, 101

Parasuraman, A., 107

Parot, F., 205

Paternalism, 84

Peer feedback sessions, 36–39, 40–41

Peer ratings: cultural differences and, 203; for individual development, 17, 18, 19; performance dimensions observed by, 18, 19; receiving feedback of, 36–39

Percentile rankings, 179; example of, 181

Performance appraisal, 360-degree feedback for, 2, 7–8, 68–73, 96–98, 150–151; guidelines for, 72–73; rater candor and, 70–71, 97–98, 150–151; survey of, 71–72. *See also* Individual development; 360-degree feedback for individual development

Performance dimensions, 13–14; multiple rating perspectives on, 18–19

Performance improvement, individual: individual tracking of, 131–132; 360-degree feedback impact on, 25–27. *See also* Change measurement; Individual

Performance improvement, individual *(continued)* development; 360-degree feedback for individual development

Performance information: multiple perspectives in, value of, 15–16; presentation of, 20–21; rating sources for, 16–20; from 360-degree feedback, 14–20. *See also* Feedback reports

Performance management: Customer Satisfaction & Retention Information (CSRI), example of, 110–118; change measurement and, 92–94, 243; continuous learning and, 89–92; customer feedback and, 101, 103–106; 360-degree feedback for, 89–94, 243

Performance standards, 89–90; communication of, with 360-degree feedback, 13–14, 21

Personality, and rating discrepancies, 23–24

Personnel Decisions, Inc., 228–229

Peterson, D. B., 24, 228–229

Pharmaceutical company, 360-degree feedback in, 138–140

Pilot tests, 163

Pollman, V., 7, 69, 97

Porter, M. E., 102

Postassessment data, 193–194. *See also* Change measurement

Power distance: and confidentiality, 204; defined, 204; and power distribution, 200

Power distribution, cultural differences in, 200–201

Practice, of new behaviors, 39–41

Pretest-posttest designs: alternatives to, 223–231; response-shift bias in, 220–223, 227

Price, C. R., 84

Process feedback, from customers, 106–108

Prospector instrument, 129

Psychological contract, new, 84–86

Punishment, 360-degree feedback tied to, 69, 96–98. *See also* Human resource systems; Performance appraisal

Q

Qualifiers, 162

Questionnaire guidelines, 157–167. *See also* 360-degree feedback instruments

Questionnaire items: content of, 159–160; control, 233; design of, 158–163; face validity of, 161; observability of, 161–162; test-retest reliability of, 162–163; translation of, to other languages, 211–213; unidimensionality of, 160–161; unnecessary qualifiers in, 162; wording of, 160. *See also* 360-degree feedback instruments

R

Race, and rating discrepancies, 23–24

Ralph, K. M., 220

Randlesome, C., 199, 200

Rater anonymity. *See* Anonymity

Rater bias: anonymity and, 153–154, 174; cultural differences in, 210–211; and purpose of feedback, 70–71, 97–98, 150–151

Rater selection: based on work interdependencies, 91; for change measurement, 232; guidelines for, 155; by target manager, 154–155, 232

Rating discrepancies: demographic factors in, 23–24; highlighting of, 185, 186–187; personality and, 23–24; self/other, 23–25, 70, 185, 186–187

Rating scales. *See* Feedback scales; Response scales

Rating sources: breakout of responses by, 172, 174–177; cultural differences and, 203, 208, 210–211; customer, 18–19, 101–118; discrepancies in, 23–25,

70, 185, 186–187, 208–209, 210–211; discrepancies in, factors in, 23–25; for groups and organizations, 136; for individual feedback, 16–20; making use of multiple, 18–19; peer, 17, 18, 19, 36–39; performance dimensions and, 18–19; questionnaire item selection based on, 161–162; self, 19–20; subordinate, 16–17, 18, 19; supervisory, 16, 18, 19; value of multiple, 15–16. *See also* Anonymity; Customer ratings/feedback; Self-ratings; Subordinate ratings; Supervisory ratings

Readiness: assessment of organizational, 143, 144; of individuals to accept feedback, 250–251

Recall ratings, 227

Redmon, G., 16

REFLECTIONS, 228, 237–240

Reilly, R. R., 17, 21, 26

Relevance, 43–44, 76

Reliability, 76; of feedback scales, 167–169; internal consistency, 167–169; of questionnaire items, 162–163; test-retest, 162–163, 168, 194. *See also* Accuracy of feedback

Repetitive measurement, 233–234

Response scales: for change measurement, 165–166, 232–233; cultural differences and, 208, 209–210; design of, 163–167; frequency, 164–165, 189, 232–233; mastery, 164, 189, 233; "not applicable" options in, 161–162, 166–167; number of points on, 165–166. *See also* Feedback scales

Response-shift bias, 220–223, 227; designs for overcoming, 223–231; in pretest-posttest designs, 223; types of change and, 221–223

Retribution, fear of 17, 152

Retrospective pretest methodology, 224–226; example of, 224–225; in practice, 228; in research, 226–227

Retrospective-degree-of-change-rating method, 228–229; example of, 230

Return on quality, assessment of, 113

Rewards: for learning, 126; 360-degree feedback tied to, 69, 96–98. *See also* Human resource systems; Performance appraisal

Rogers, H. J., 216n.3

Rogolsky, S. R., 139, 227

Roullier, J. Z., 239

Roush, P., 248n.1

Ruderman, M., 61, 224, 227

Ryan, A. M., 203

S

Saavedra, R., 17

Safety: provisions for, 51–52, 152–154; and 360-degree feedback for performance appraisal, 70, 71, 98. *See also* Anonymity; Confidentiality

Salas, E., 236

Sawheny, N., 201–202

Sayles, R. S., 200

Schaubroeck, J., 18, 19, 210

Scheier, M. F., 26

Schein, E. H., 125

Schneider, R. J., 25–26, 67, 239

Schneier, C. E., 108

Seibert, K., 61

Self-determination, administrative process and, 157

Self-development, 360-degree feedback as core of, 4–5. *See also* Individual development; 360-degree feedback for individual development

Self-management, and organizational trends, 84–89

Self-management model of feedback, 33–35, 36, 54–55

Self-perception: individual characteristics and, 23–25; openness to

Self-perception *(continued)* feedback and, 21–23; rating discrepancies and, 23–25, 70

Self-ratings, 19–20; cultural effects on, 210–211; discrepancies between, and other, 23–25, 70, 185, 186–187, 208–209, 210–211; response-shift bias in, 221

Self-reflection, 21

Senge, P. M., 123, 125, 145

Shaw, D., 108

Simon, M. C., 24

SkillScope, 158

Slaten, S., 226

Smith, D. E., 205

Smither, J. W., 2, 15, 16, 18, 20, 21, 25, 27, 70, 93, 248n.1, 251

Social class, 199

Social information processing, 21–23

Solley, C. M., 84

Spreitzer, G. M., 68, 124, 127, 129

Standard scores, 179; example of, 180

Sternbergh, W. W., 28

Stevenson, H. W., 210

Strategic alignment: change measurement and, 240, 242–248; customer feedback and, 103–106, 108, 116, 117–118. *See also* Alignment

Strategic management process, customer feedback in, 112–118

Strickland, A. J., 104

Strodtbeck, F. L., 200

Subordinate ratings (upward ratings): anonymity in, 153–154; for individual development, 16–17, 18, 19; performance dimensions observed by, 18, 19

Success criteria, 110–112; key drivers for, 110–112, 114, 115, 116, 117

Succession planning, 60–63

Supervisor communication, in change measurement, 239

Supervisory ratings (downward ratings): anonymity of, 17, 153–154, 174, 176; breakout of, 174, 176; for individual development, 16;

performance dimensions observed by, 18, 19

Support: administrative process and, 156–157; for individual development, 27, 76, 142, 156–157, 192–194; in learning cultures, 126–127, 142

Survey of Leadership Practices, 173

Swaminathan, H., 216n.3

SYMLOG, 159, 160, 182; example of, 183

Systems perspective, 96, 255, 257–258

Szymanski, C., 70

T

Taiwan, self-rating in, 210, 211

Takahashi, S., 209–210

Tannenbaum, S. I., 122, 236, 239

Tarulli, B. A., 239

Team-based organizations: learning cultures in, 121–122, 141; 360-degree feedback for performance appraisal in, 69–70, 71; 360-degree feedback for relationship building in, 85–86

Team-building exercises, 85–86; in individual development program, 37–41, 43–44. *See also* 360-degree feedback instruments

Team-building survey instrument, 86, 87, 136

Teams: sharing of individual feedback with, 132–135; 360-degree feedback on, 136–138. *See also* Collective learning; Groups

Test-retest reliability: of feedback scales, 168; and postassessment data, 194; of questionnaire items, 162–163. *See also* Change measurement

Thayer, D. T., 216n.3

Thompson, A. A., 104

Thornton, G. C., 210

360-degree feedback: challenges of, 249–253; for change measurement, 92–94, 131–132, 157, 171, 217–247, 248; as core of self-development, 4–5; costs of, 251; cross-cultural, 196–216; do-it-yourself programs of, 63–68; as end versus means, 256–257; expectations of, 252; issues and implications of, 253–256; as multifaceted challenge, 6; as ongoing process, 1, 92, 256–258; origins of, 1–2; popularity of, 2–4, 59; purposes of, developmental versus appraisal, 7–8, 96–98, 150–152, 252–253; uses of, today, 2–4; and the new workplace, 5, 85–86, 88–89. *See also* Change measurement; Cross-cultural 360-degree feedback; Cultural differences

360-degree feedback design, 149–195; administrative process guidelines for, 150–157; cultural differences and, 196–216; essential elements of, 194–195; feedback report guidelines for, 167–192; questionnaire guidelines for, 157–167; support for development and, 192–194. *See also* Cross-cultural 360-degree feedback

360-degree feedback for individual development, 11–27, 28–56, 237–240; in development program case study, 28–56; elements of, 11–27; feedback recipient response to, 20–25, 29–39; feedback relevance in, 43–44; follow-up to, 53–54; goal setting based on, 44–51; on learning competencies, 127–131; learning cultures and, 120–122, 127–131; outcomes of, 25–27; performance dimensions for, 13–14; performance information from, 14–20; performance standards communicated through, 13–14, 21; practice in, 39–41; recognition of need for change and, 35–36;

safety in, 51–52; self-management model of, 33–35, 36, 54–55. *See also* Development program, individual; Individual development; Learning culture

360-degree feedback for organizations, 59–77, 78–100, 101–119, 240–245; best practices for, 75–77; for changing of feedback norms, 75; clarity of purpose for, 96–98; for continuous learning, 89–92, 241–242; for culture change, 73–75, 78–81, 242–243; customer involvement in, 101–119; for development, 96–98; for employee career development, 63–68; for establishment of learning cultures, 120–146; evolutionary nature of, 143; forces affecting, 81–89; for high-potential development programs, 60–63; implementation of, 96–99; individual development and, 59; for integration and alignment, 94–96; organizational readiness for, 143, 144; outcomes of, causes of poor, 59–60, 76–77; for performance appraisal, 68–73, 96–98; for performance management, 89–92, 243; rationales for, 59–77; for tracking of change, 92–94; value added by, 89–99, 240–245. *See also* Customer involvement; Learning culture; Organizational development

360-degree feedback instruments, 157–167; administrative process for, 150–157; in "BDC" case study, 79; for change measurement, 232–237; computerized, 64, 66, 131–132; cross-cultural comparability of, 212–213, 214, 215, 216n.3; cultural assumptions underlying, 198–207; for customer input, 155–156; customization of, 105–106, 131–132, 149;

360-degree feedback instruments *(continued)* developability of qualities assessed in, 170–171; development materials and, 193; development planning and, 192–194; do-it-yourself, 64–68, 131–132; feedback reports from, 167–192; feedback scales for, 167–170, 232–233; guidelines for, 157–167; for individual development, 33–34, 51, 56, 129–131; instructions for, 157–158; item construction for, 158–163; off-the-shelf versus tailored, 105–106, 131–132; performance dimensions in, 13–14; pilot tests of, 163; rater selection for, 91, 154–155, 232; repetitive use of, 233–234; response scales for, 163–167, 232–237; for self as learner, 129–131; support for development and, 192–194; for teams, 86, 87; translation of, into different languages, 211–213. *See also* Administrative process; Change measurement; Cross-cultural 360-degree feedback; Cultural differences; Feedback reports; Feedback scales; Questionnaire items; Response scales; Team-building exercises

Tichy, N., 240

Timmreck, C. W., 71–72, 98

Tornow, W. W., 1, 78, 84, 85, 232, 249, 256

Total quality management (TQM), 102, 110

Tracey, J. B., 122, 239, 241

Trait theories of leadership, 199–200

Traits versus behaviors, 159–160

Transition, adaptability to, 124, 241–242. *See also* Continuous learning; Learning culture

Translation, 211–213

Trends. *See* Organizational trends

Triandis, H. C., 200, 208, 210

Trompenaars, A., 200

True change. *See* Alpha change

Trust, 152–154, 194, 251. *See also* Safety

U

Uhlfelder, H. F., 241

Ulrich, D., 95, 102

Unidimensionality, 160–161

United States: cultural assumptions of, 198–207; leader effectiveness in, 202; standardized instruments in, 197

Upward Feedback Forum, 71–73, 98

Upward ratings. *See* Subordinate ratings

V

Validity, 76; in change measurement, 233; construct, 167–168; of cross-cultural use of instruments, 212–213, 214, 216*n*.3; and developability, 170–171; face, 161; of feedback scales, 167–168; of importance data, 189; of questionnaire items, 161. *See also* Accuracy

Values, cultural differences in, 200–201

Van Fleet, D. D., 15, 199

Van Velsor, E., 16, 149, 157, 194, 209, 227

Vasilopoulous, N. L., 21, 248*n*.1

Verbatim comments, 190, 192

Villanova, P., 14

W

Wachholz, 261, 201

Wainer, H., 216*n*.3

Wallace, A., 201–202

Walton, R. E., 240

Webb, A. D., 124

Werbel, J. D., 210

West, S. G., 18, 24
Whetten, D. A., 250
Wilson, C., 185
Wilson, M. S., 200, 203
Wohlers, A. J., 2, 16, 24
Work: changing nature of, 84–86; finding meaning in, 88
Work contract, new, 63, 84–86
Work relationships, 360-degree feedback for, 90–91
Workplace, new, 360-degree feedback and, 5, 85–86, 88–89
Write-in comments, 190, 192

Y

Yeager, S., 221
Yinon, Y., 17
Young, D. P., 217, 227, 228
Yu, J., 211
Yukl, G., 15, 199

Z

Zax, M., 209–210
Zedeck, S., 205
Zeithaml, V. A., 107
Zimba, C. C., 202–203
Zmud, R. W., 229